IMAGES
of America

ASHE COUNTY

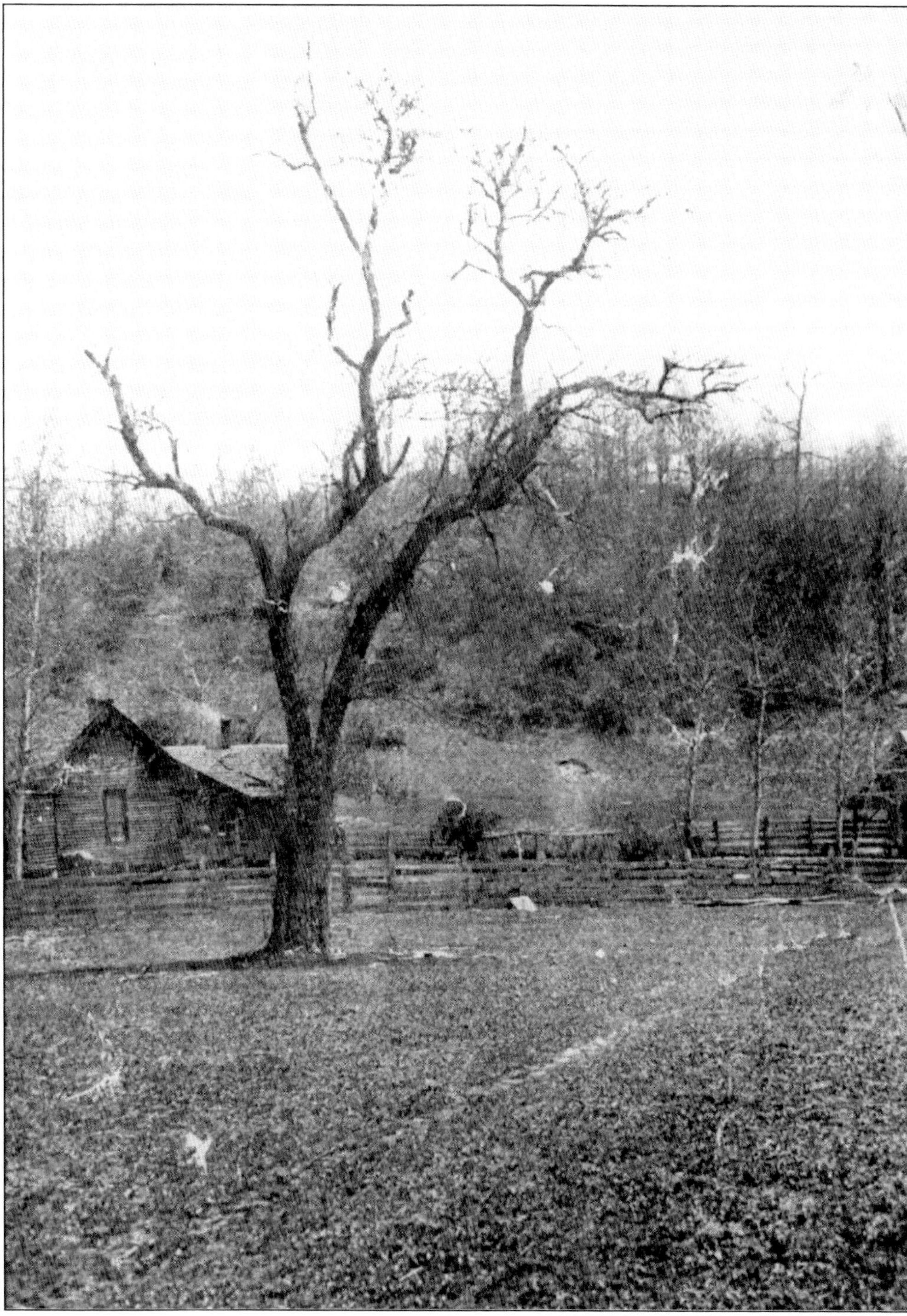

THE OLD PERKINS PLACE. On this site, Tory soldiers led by Captain William Riddle captured Ben Cleveland, a Revolutionary War colonel, in 1781.

IMAGES
of America

ASHE COUNTY

John Houck, Clarice Weaver, and Carol Williams
Ashe County Historical Society

ARCADIA
PUBLISHING

ISBN 978-0-7385-0615-9

Published by Arcadia Publishing
Charleston, South Carolina

Printed in the United States of America

Library of Congress Catalog Card Number: 00-106086

For all general information contact Arcadia Publishing at:
Telephone 843-853-2070
Fax 843-853-0044
E-Mail sales@arcadiapublishing.com
For customer service and orders:
Toll-Free 1-888-313-2665

Visit us on the Internet at www.arcadiapublishing.com

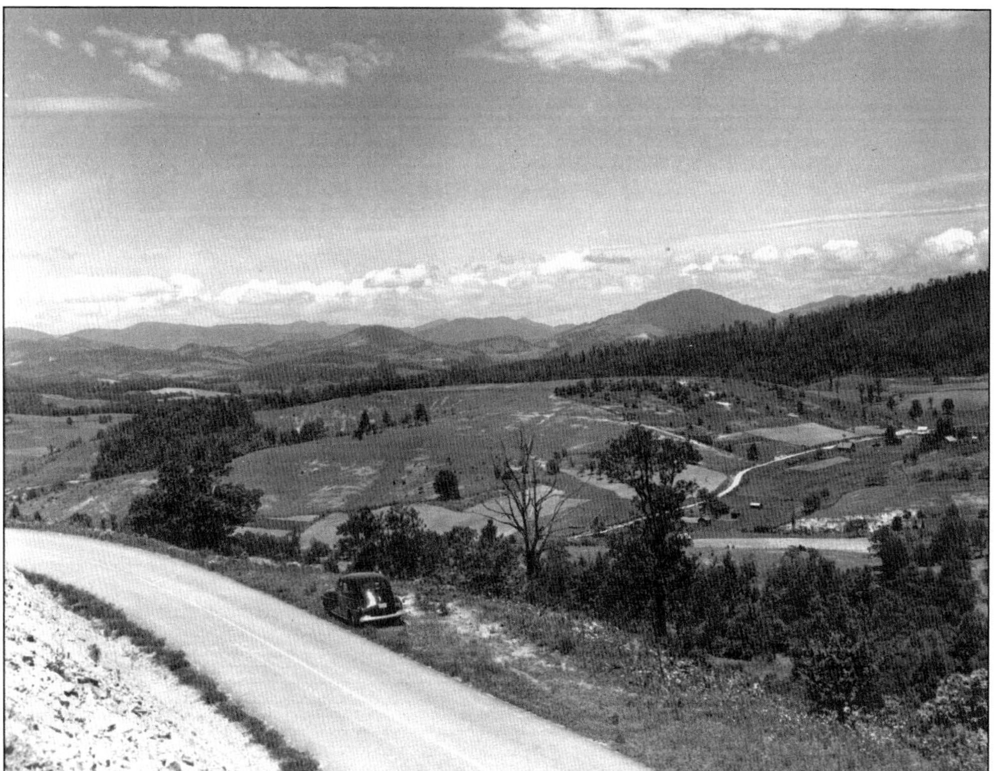

VIEW OF ASHE COUNTY, MID-1940S. This picture was taken from the Blue Ridge Parkway with Mount Jefferson visible in the background.

Contents

ACKNOWLEDGMENTS

In this volume the Ashe County Historical Society presents a pictorial record of the people and places that formed the past, and are molding the present and future of this corner of the High Country. To spend time in the pages of this book is to feel the presence of the forces that have brought Ashe County into the 21st century. In no way should this be considered a formal history of Ashe County.

The Ashe County Historical Society is grateful for the use of the collections of Ed Reed, Tom Worth, and the archives of the Ashe County Library. Ed Reed's fascination with his native county has led him eagerly to pursue pictures from every source for his collection. He has long had a dream of a book of pictures that he said should be entitled *So I've Been Told*, a phrase he has heard many times from people telling stories that explain the pictures they are sharing with him.

The Worth family is part of the fabric of Ashe County. The Worth family's picture collection is important to appreciating Creston, one of the earliest settled areas of the county, as well as Jefferson, one of the largest townships.

The library also opened its archives to the authors. A major portion of the archives included pictures from the morgue of the *Skyland Post*, a local newspaper for more than 75 years. Jo Greene, head librarian, and her staff were supportive and helped the committee with meetings, research materials, and documentation.

Equally important are pictures from the many individuals who heeded our request for old family pictures and scenes of Ashe County: Leet Vannoy, Mabel Coleman, Kathy Hentschel, Shirley Baldwin, Geneva Greer, Ruth Craven, Martha Kincaid, Bill Butcher, Shirley Killen, Calvin Miller, Pat Mills, C.E. Miller, Frank Colvard, the Chessie Church family, and Jack Weaver.

Even picture books rely on words and the committee has been ably and happily aided by some superior wordsmiths. Thank you Frank Colvard, Sam Shumate, Sherry Winebarger-Houck, Burl Fowler, Lonnie Jones, and Anne Howell Winebarger.

The expertise and helpfulness of Mark Berry of Arcadia Publishing has been central to the successful completion of this project.

The royalties from this book will go to the Ashe County Historical Society to further the programs of historical preservation and restoration, which continue to give the public a perspective on the past and a prism through which to view the future.

INTRODUCTION

Picture no houses, roads, people, cars, stores, businesses—nothing but nature growing prolifically around your home. That scene portrays Ashe County 300 years ago. Our ancestors saw our mountains as a wilderness when they first came up the rugged paths to see what was over the next ridge. They were looking for game, wealth, land, escape, fewer neighbors, freedom from taxes, or a way to leave debt and poverty behind.

The Native Americans did not live here. However, the area was a hunting ground that many tribes fought over. Various tribes came through hunting game and taking food from the land. For years they did this, leaving little trace of their activities on the land or of their use of the natural resources of the mountains. The ecology of the mountains was not disturbed during the many years the tribes fought over and hunted in the area.

The first white men came seeking game, furs, and ways to make a profit from the land, and they found what they were looking for. The rivers and streams teemed with fish, the deer ran in herds, and turkey and squirrel were everywhere. These white men were hunters and trappers from Virginia and eastern North Carolina and were attracted by the vast amounts of game and the fact that most others in their trade had not been here. As visitors do now, they fell in love with the beauty of the area. Some returned as early as the 1740s and 1750s to bring their families and build homes. They settled first in the Helton Creek, Grassy Creek, and Old Fields areas of the county.

Rugged beauty has always been a main feature and attraction in the Ashe County area and the people grew to match their mountains. These new frontiersmen were rugged individualists—quiet, proud, reserved, filled with a beauty of soul, at peace with the land, with man, and with a strong faith in God. The early settlers came from many countries: 71% were from the British Isles and another 17% were from Germany. The remaining 12% were from other European countries. There were a few American Indians and a few African Americans. The population of slaves and free blacks in the area was limited by a geography that prevented large farms and plantations from existing. Still there were slaves and freed blacks living in the region, and many descendants of those initial families remain in the area today.

Ashe County was formed in 1799 from Wilkes County. At the time it included parts of what are now Ashe, Allegheny, Watauga, Avery, and Burke Counties. Immediately following the Revolutionary War the region became part of the State of Franklin, an area formed in western North Carolina and Eastern Tennessee, with the intention of keeping the mountain area together in one political unit. The individualism that had led many to remain loyal to the

King during the American Revolution made the creation of the State of Franklin a sensible idea. In the ensuing years the people also opposed the secessionist movement before the Civil War and remained Unionist during that war. In fact, over the years residents of the area have been so removed from the mainstream that the region was called the "Lost Province." This spirit remains intact today, as many are slow to leave old ways, accept new things or people, and welcome change in the county.

Imagine a life where everything you had came from the few acres you controlled or owned. Whether 10, 20, or 100 in number, the land had to give you food, shelter, clothing, heat, and money. In fact, if it was not obtainable from the land, you most likely did not have it. Not ever! If it was available, something from the land had to be traded for it. Social life nearly always involved family or church. Each day included working for the next day's livelihood. As you look at the faces in these pictures, you will see their pride, strength, resolve, faith, and contentment.

From these people and the mountain land came the place we now call Ashe County. Caught in the pictures of this book, you will see glimpses into a by-gone era, one we often look to with envy and say we miss, but one requiring a hardier way of life than we have ever known or can imagine.

The land was peaceful and rugged and it created a rugged people who loved peace. The land was great in natural beauty, supporting animal and plant life in abundance. It created a people filled with a great love for the mountains, land, plants, animals, family, and friends, a people whose inner strength and beauty is still evident today in their descendants and the place they built.

Possibly, the "Lost Province" exists no longer. But, although the area has been discovered as a tourist and vacation mecca, the spirit of individualism remains strong.

—Lonnie Jones, president of the Ashe County Historical Society

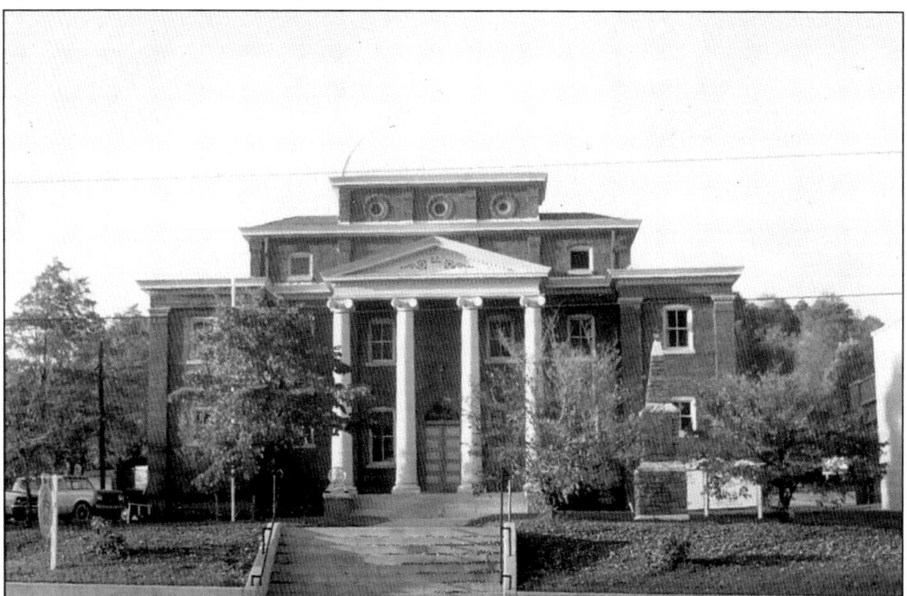

ASHE COUNTY 1904 COURTHOUSE. The courthouse, a combination of Greek and Renaissance architectural styles, was an imposing structure when constructed in 1904.

One

Scenes and Buildings

The typical home in early Ashe County was a log cabin or a one-room house, often with a lean-to along one side. Meals were prepared on open fireplaces and hearths. Some early houses were shanties, which were early stick-constructed houses of crude sawn lumber. Foundations were merely stacks of large stones that were leveled to hold joists. Roofs were made of wood shingles. The mid-1800s brought water-powered sawmills that provided carpenters with uniform lumber from virgin forests.

After the coming of trains in the early 1900s, larger homes were constructed. Also, glass and decorative materials could be mail ordered. Many local silversmiths, blacksmiths, and tinsmiths contributed to the building of Ashe County's stately colonial homes, which are still in use and enhance the scenic landscape.

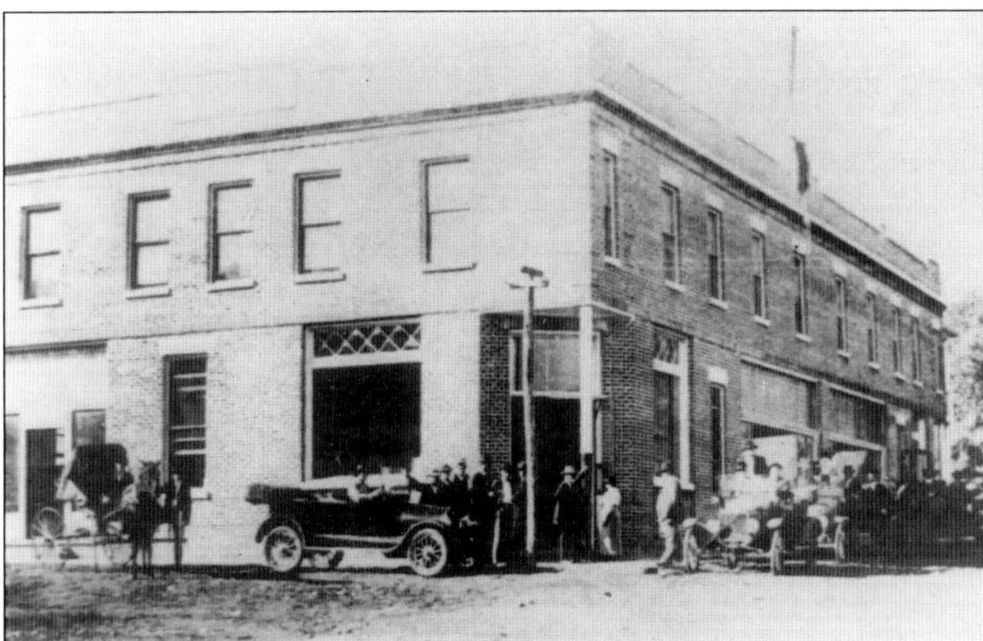

Old Hotel in West Jefferson. This brick structure was built on the corner of Jefferson Avenue and Main Street in 1917 to replace the original wooden hotel that had burned earlier the same year. The photograph was taken in the early 1920s.

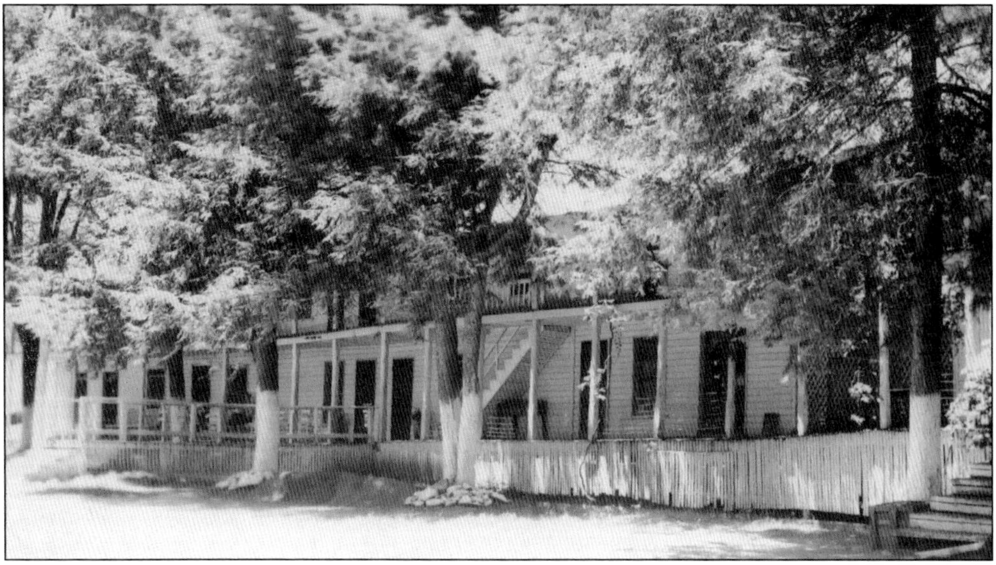

HEALING SPRINGS HOTEL. Originally built in 1888, it was a very popular social gathering place for people living in Ashe and the surrounding counties. It burned in 1912.

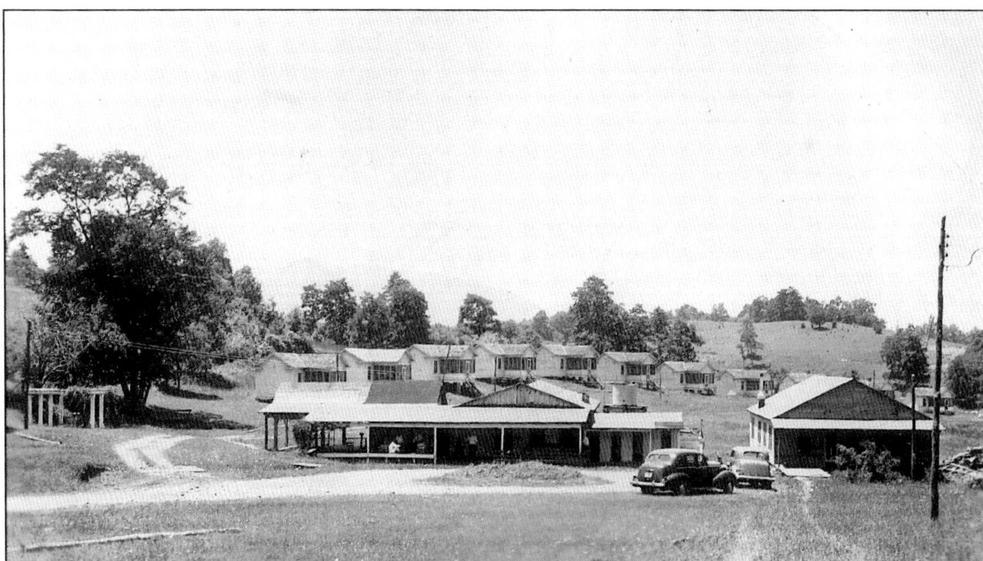

SHATLEY SPRINGS IN THE 1940S. These healing springs were discovered by Martin Shatley in 1890. The Shatley Springs restaurant is known throughout the southern United States.

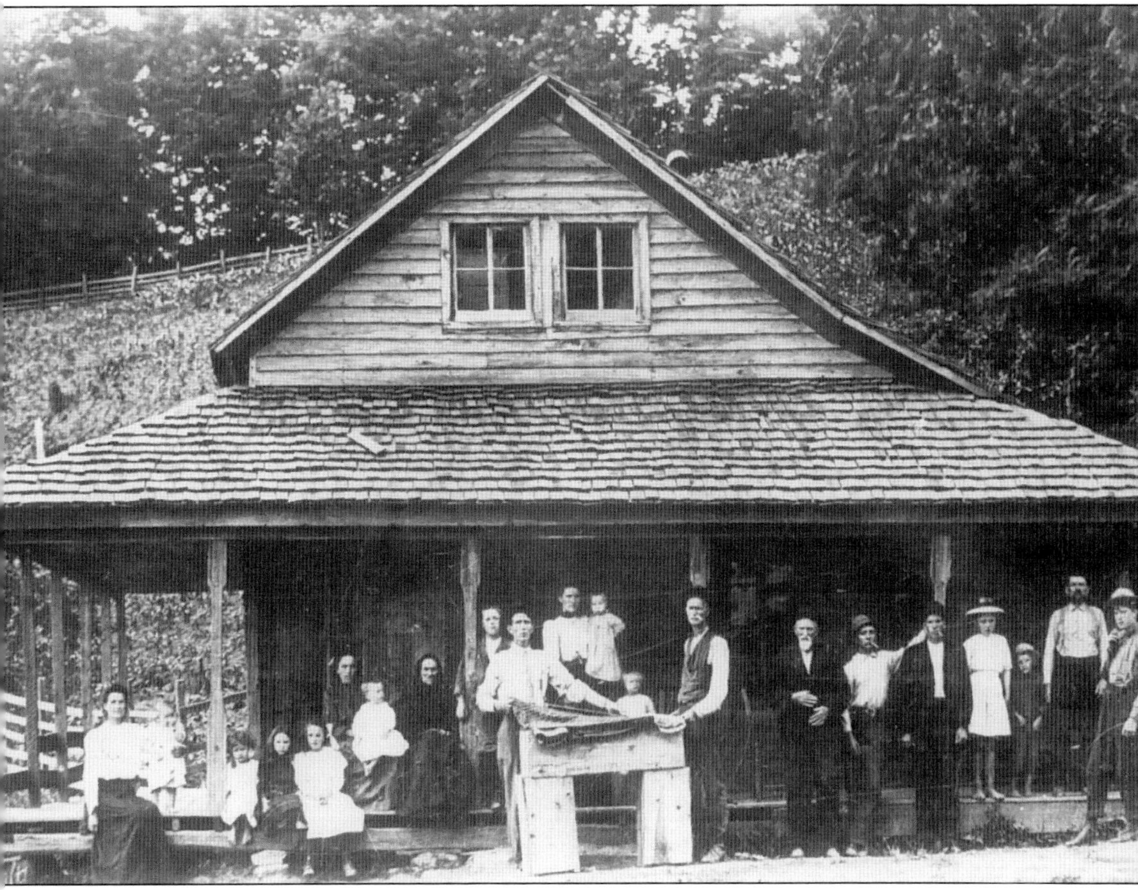

FAIRVIEW STORE NEAR GRASSY CREEK. This photograph dating from the 1800s pictures two veterans of the Civil War on the far right.

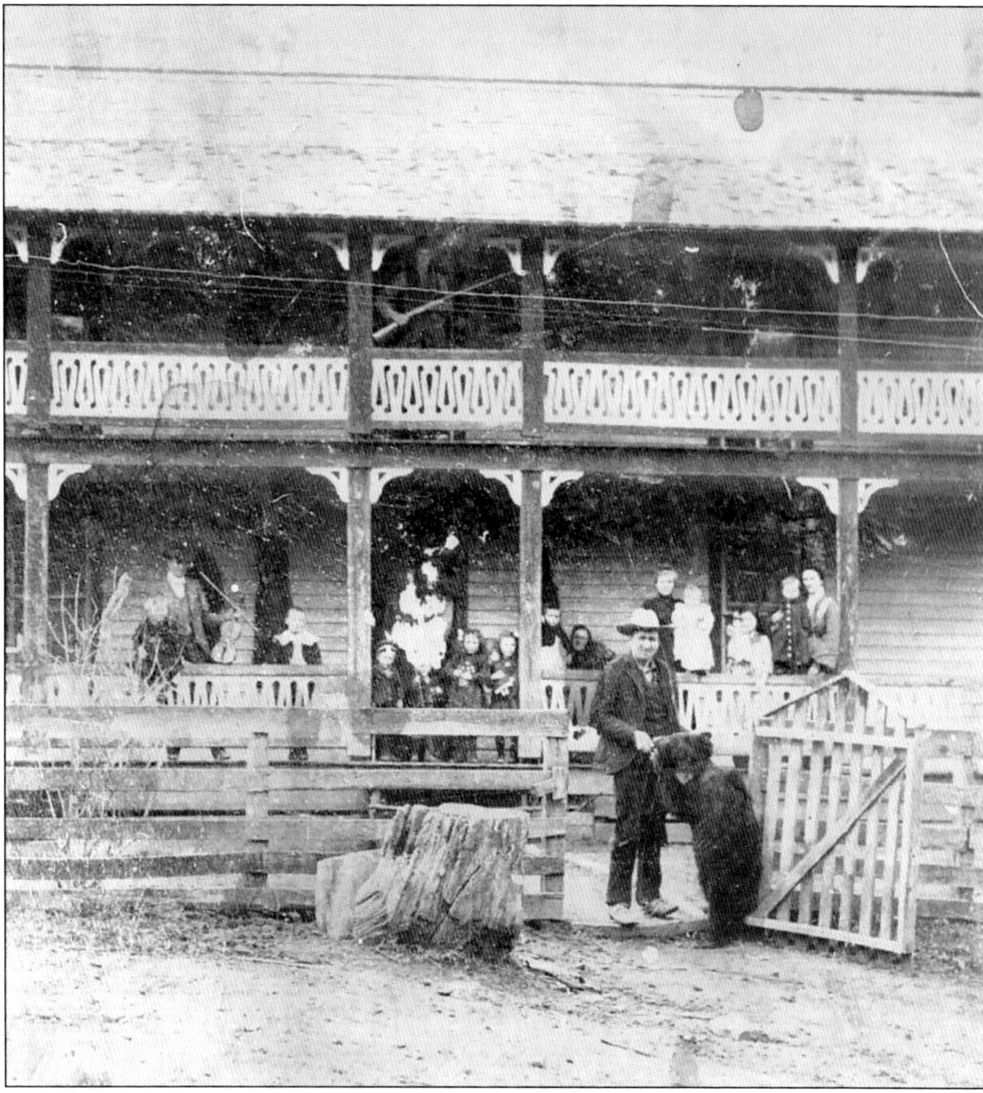

A Scene from Grassy Creek (c. 1902). Irwin Young and his pet bear are pictured in the foreground. The tree stumps provided an aid for women to mount their horses.

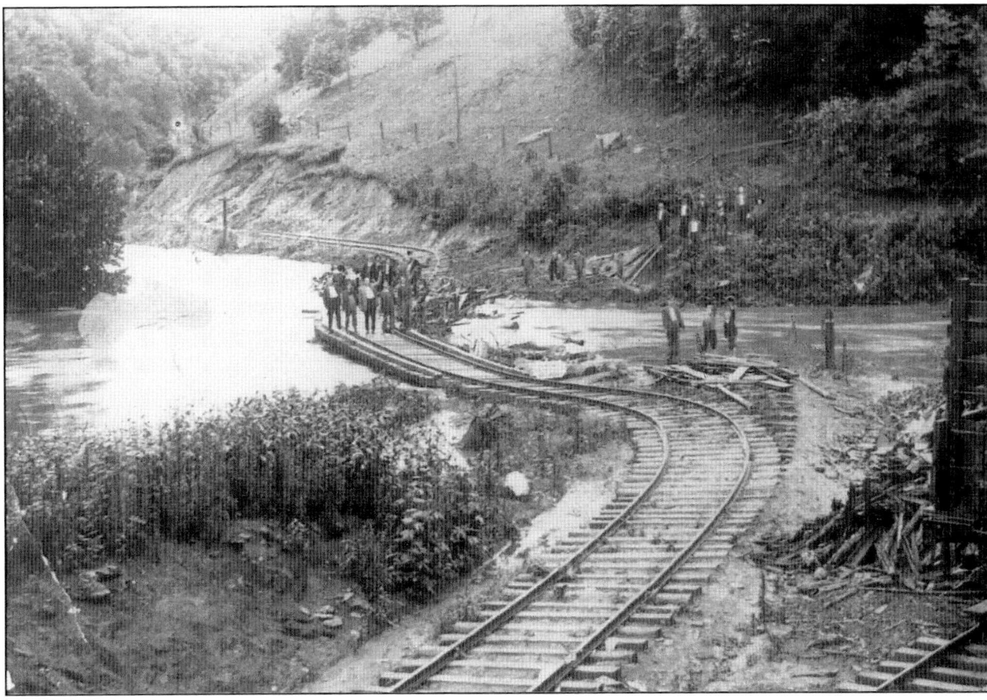

LANSING FOLLOWING THE 1940 FLOOD. Located above Lansing, this site is where Little Horse Creek flows into Big Horse Creek.

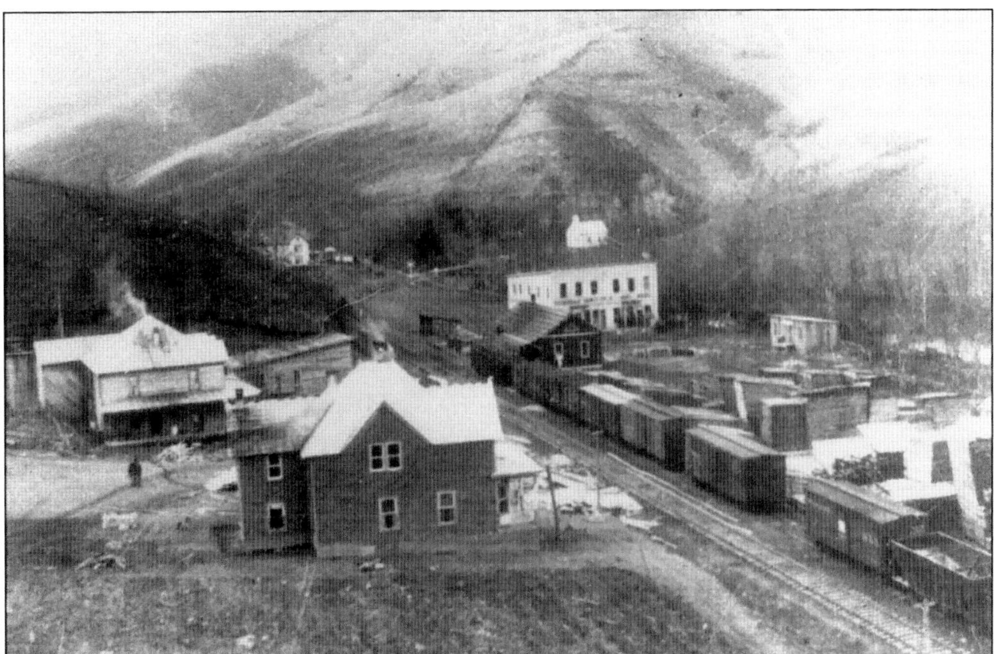

TUCKERDALE. Hotels and boardinghouses cluster around the Tuckerdale depot. Note the stacks of lumber ready for shipment.

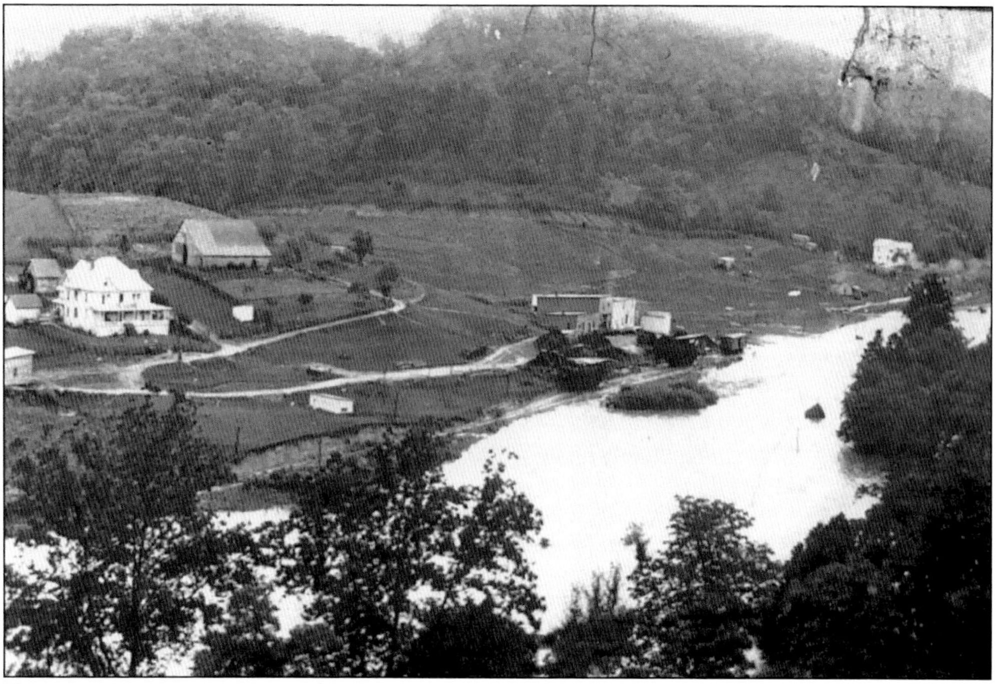

The 1916 Flood. Horse Creek's rising waters are seen here in Lansing. The large white house on the left is known as the Henry Gentry house, and the white house on the extreme right is known as the Cicero Faw house.

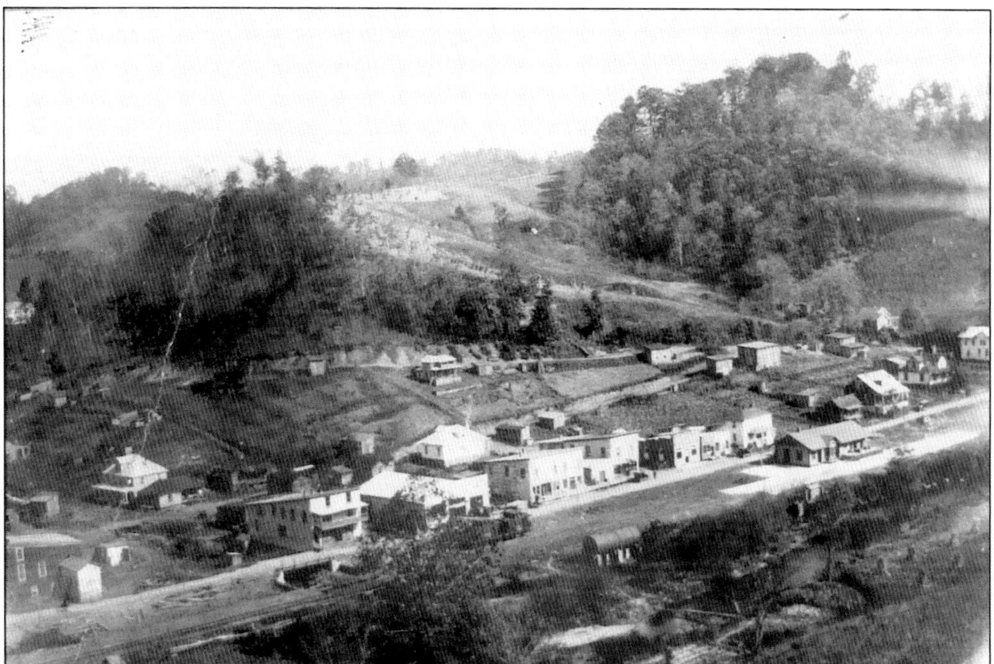

The Lansing Community Before 1928. Lansing, incorporated in 1928, included a cheese plant, clothing store, coffin shop, doctor's office, hardware store, bank, and restaurant.

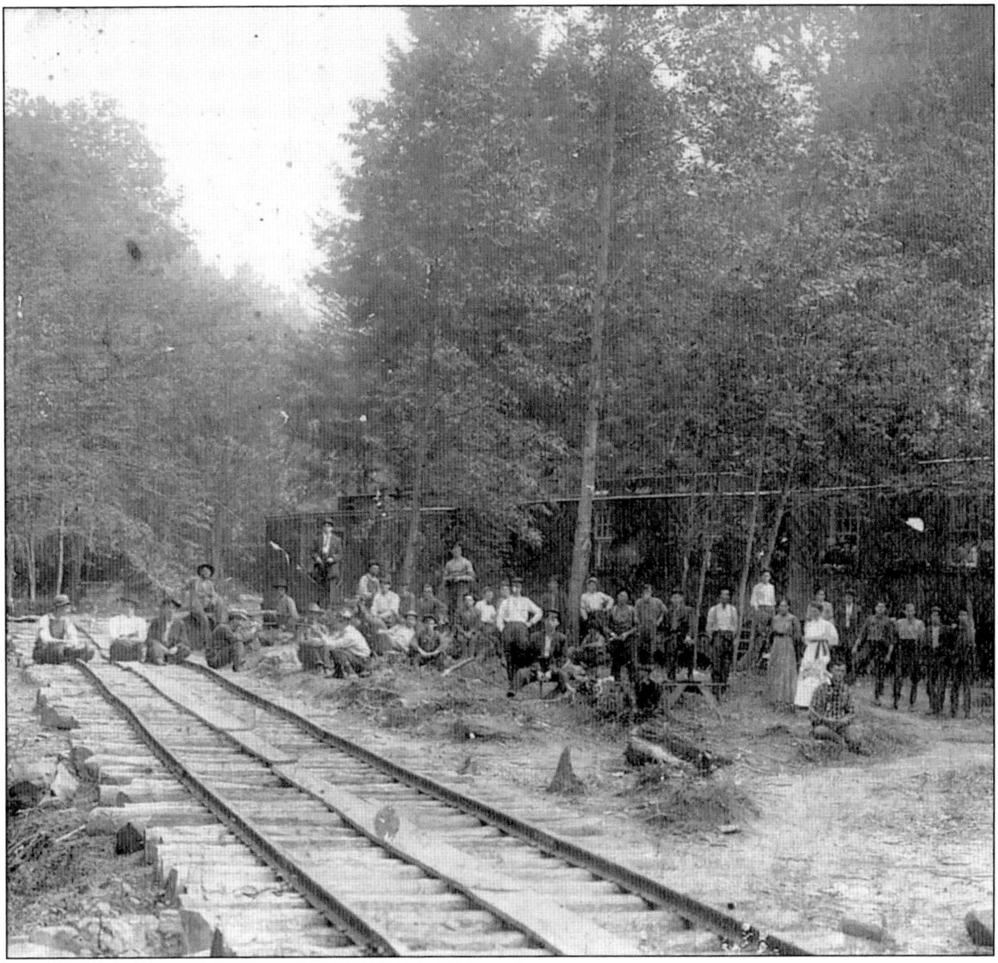

MELLICOO. This lumbering spur was one of the largest in the county. The camp provided many jobs for local men, cutting virgin timber to be transported to Abingdon, Virginia.

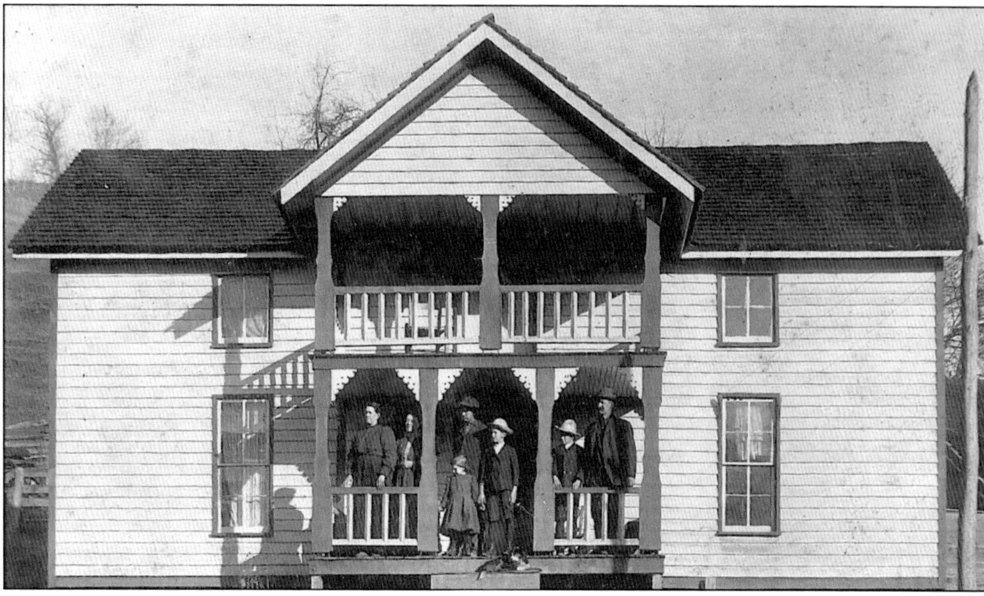

PRIVATE HOME IN LITTLE HORSE CREEK (C. 1903). This house was occupied by Nelson Ham's family until he left for Kentucky around 1918. Pictured here, from left to right, are Luvenie Perry Ham, Ollie Cordilia Ham, Solomon Lillard Ham, Nelson Elzie Ham, Ellis Edward Ham, Nelson Ham, and Nettie Elizabeth Ham.

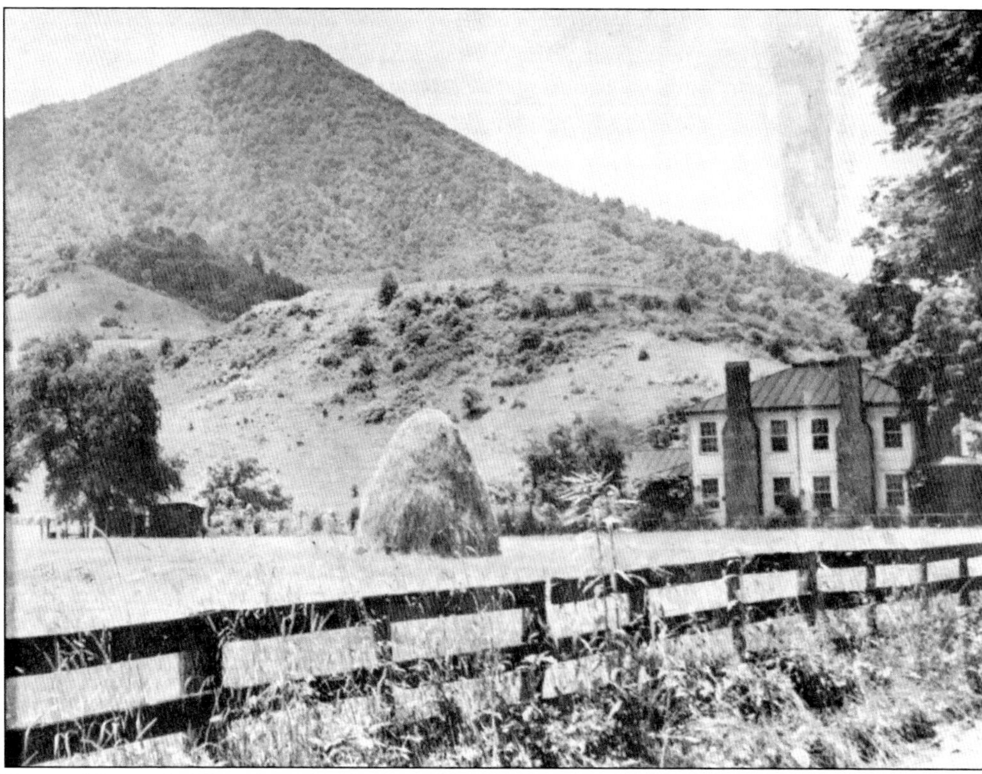

DAVID WORTH'S HOME IN CRESTON. This photograph, with The Peak in the background, appeared on the cover of *Our State* magazine in the early 1900s.

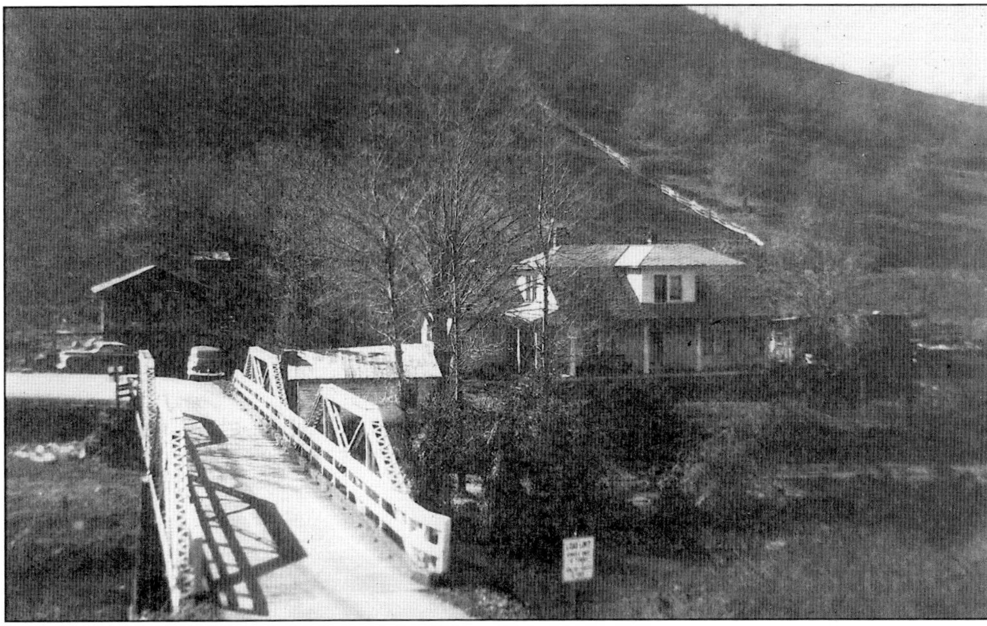

Warrensville Before the Bypass. Pictured here are the Shoaf house and the second bridge over Buffalo Creek (c. 1950).

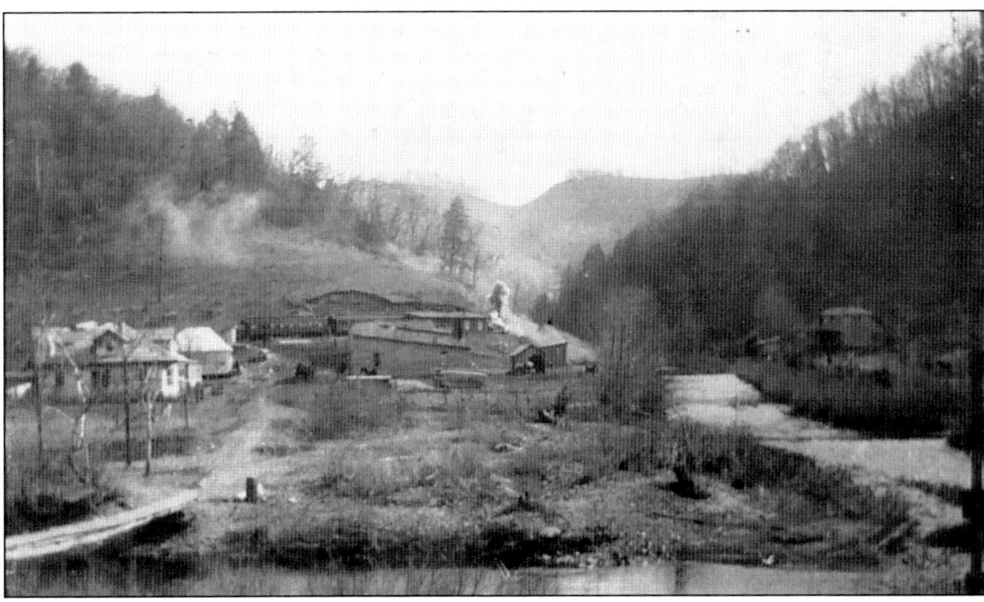

The Train Pulling out of Warrensville (c. 1916). The Shoaf home is across the bridge.

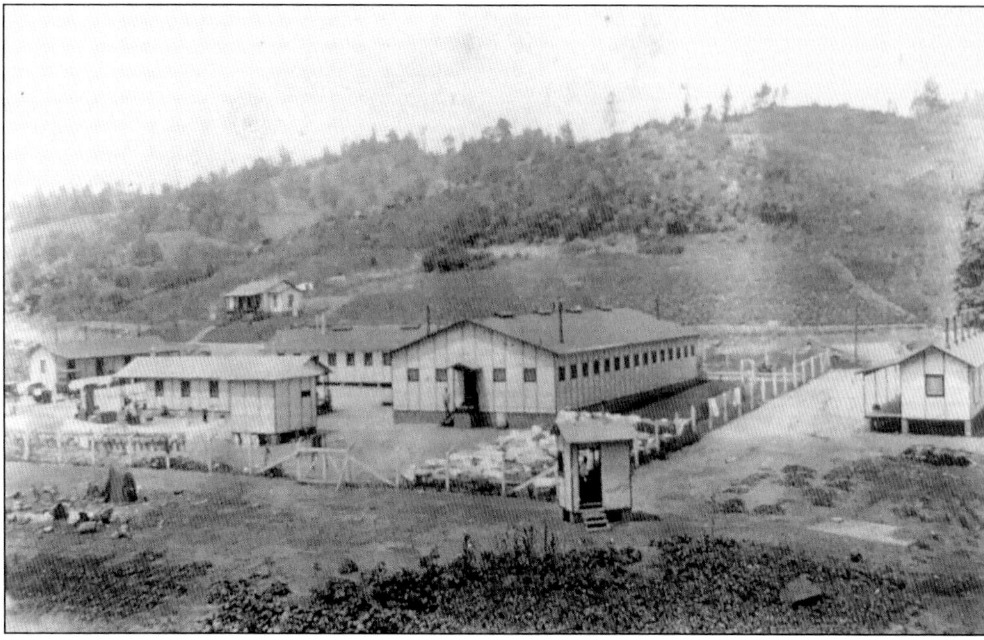

STATE PRISON CAMP. In the early 1930s, the state ran a minimum-security prison in Warrensville. This photograph was taken from the railroad tracks looking toward the Jake Faw house in the background.

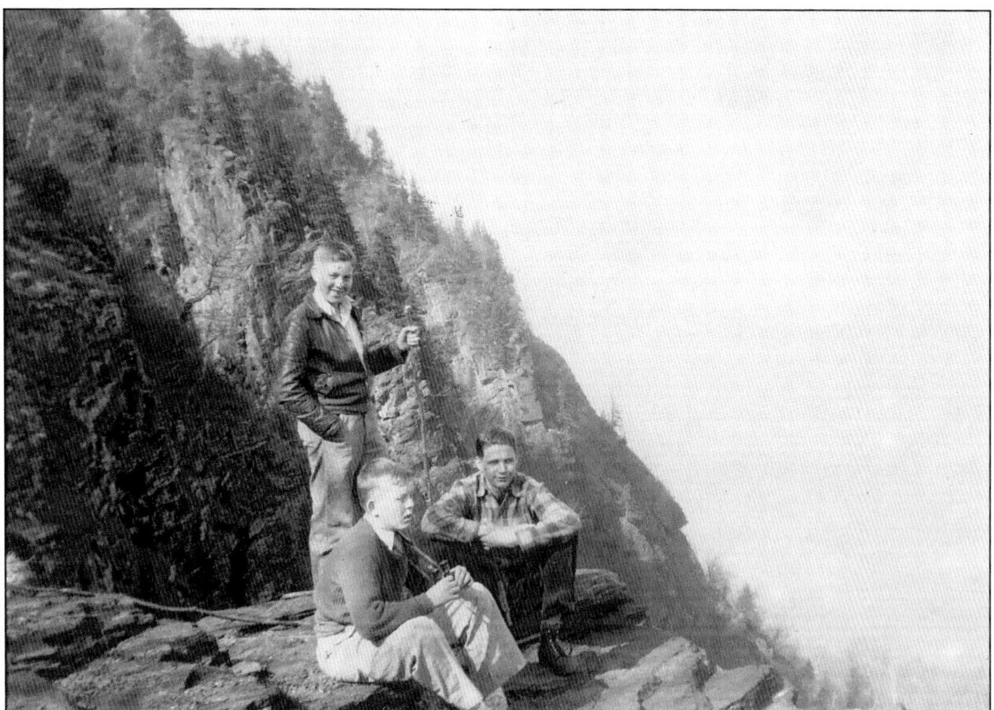

ON TOP OF BLUFF MOUNTAIN IN 1941. The Nature Conservancy now owns the land and preserves the unique flora that grows atop this mountain. Pictured here, from left to right, are Harold Dollar, Basil Duke Barr Jr., and Carl Jackson.

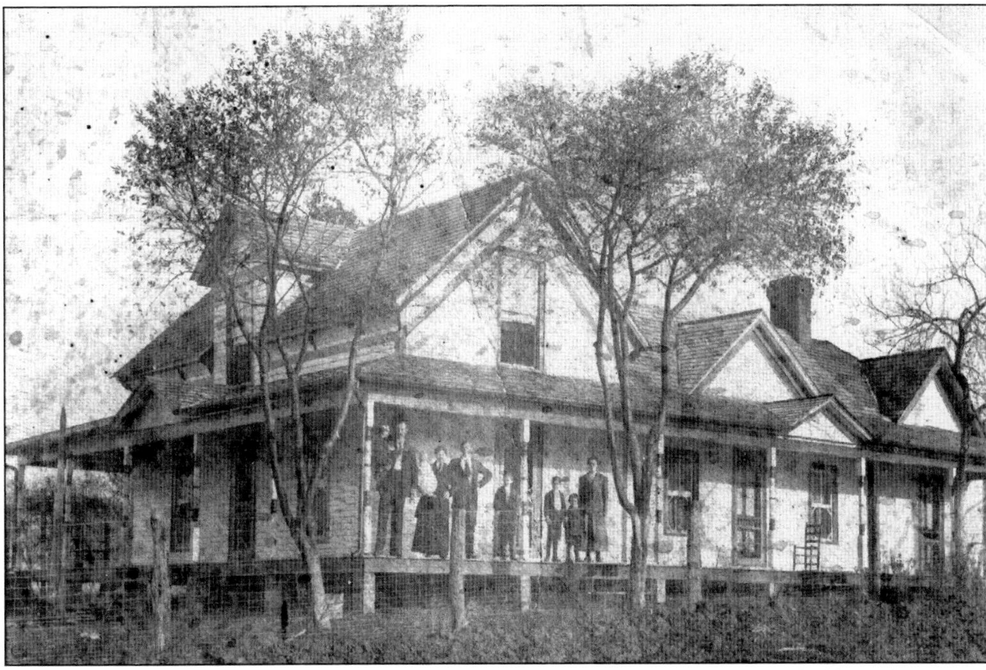

C.M. CHURCH AND HIS FAMILY IN 1910. The photograph was probably taken on a Sunday afternoon.

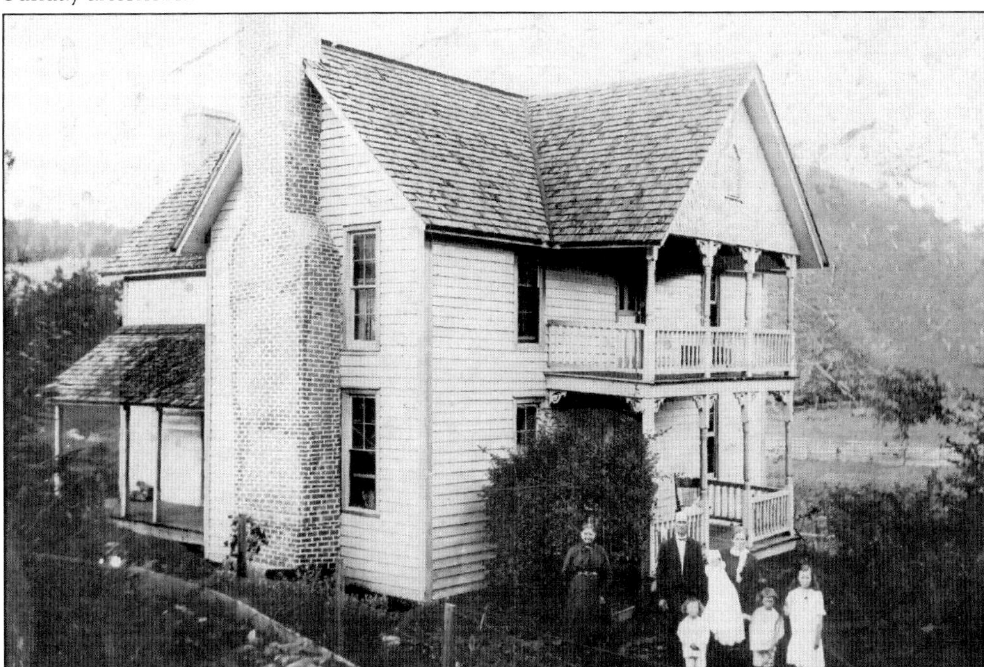

SQUIRE ALLEN CHURCH HOMESTEAD IN IDLEWILD. This picture was taken around 1914. Shown here, from left to right, are Mrs. S.A. Church; Allen H. Church; his wife, Naomi, holding Dwight A. Church; and Felix E. Church standing with Ralph H. and Mildred M. Church.

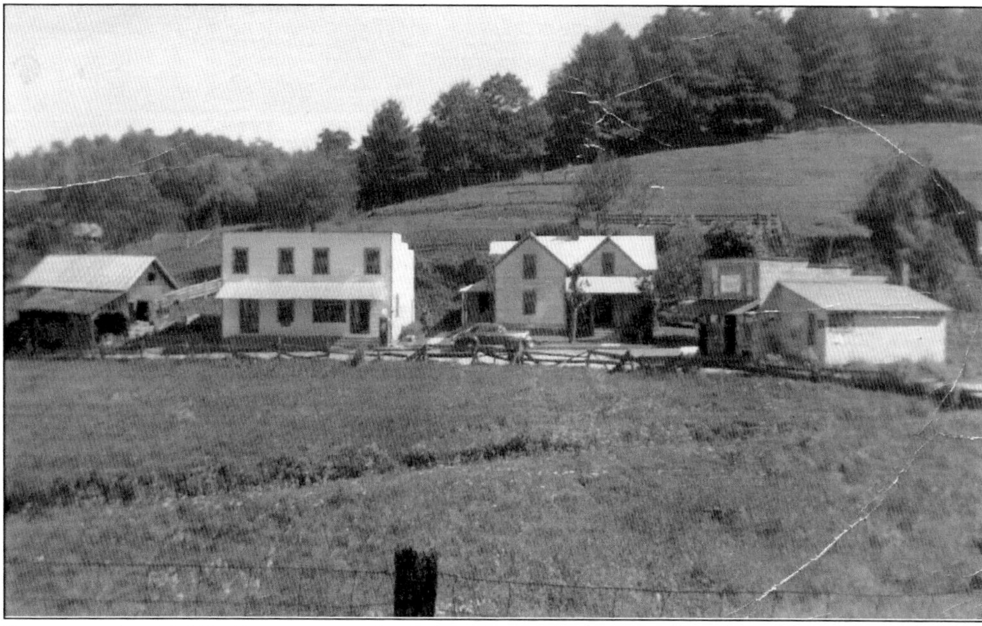

IDLEWILD (C. 1952). Pictured on the left is Dick Phillips Road. The general store is in the center of the photograph, and the old mill is on the right in the back of the picture.

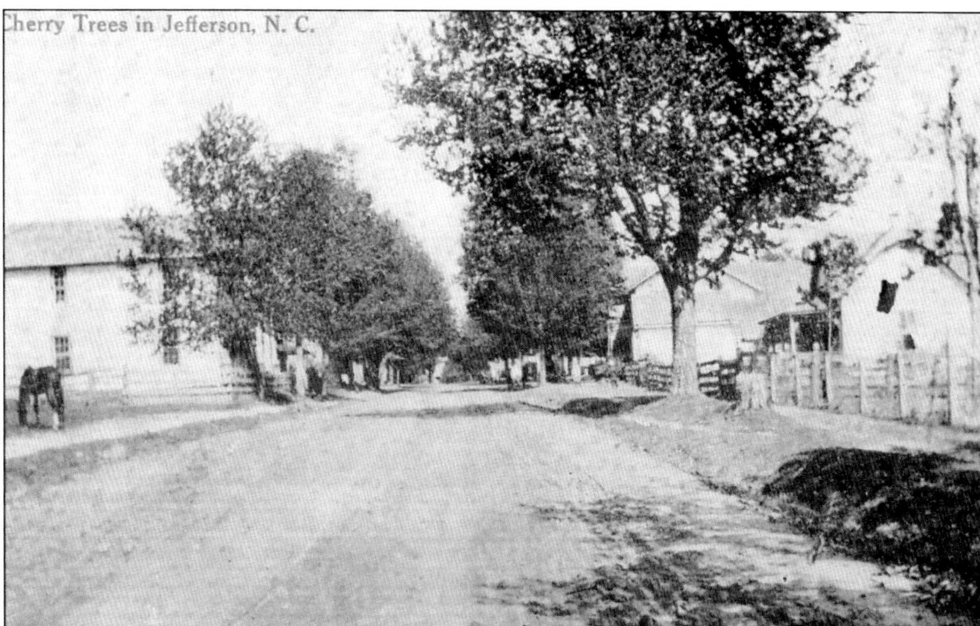

MAIN STREET IN JEFFERSON. Dating from the late 1800s, this picture shows the unpaved street with cherry trees lining both sides. This picture was taken from in front of present Jefferson Methodist Church looking east.

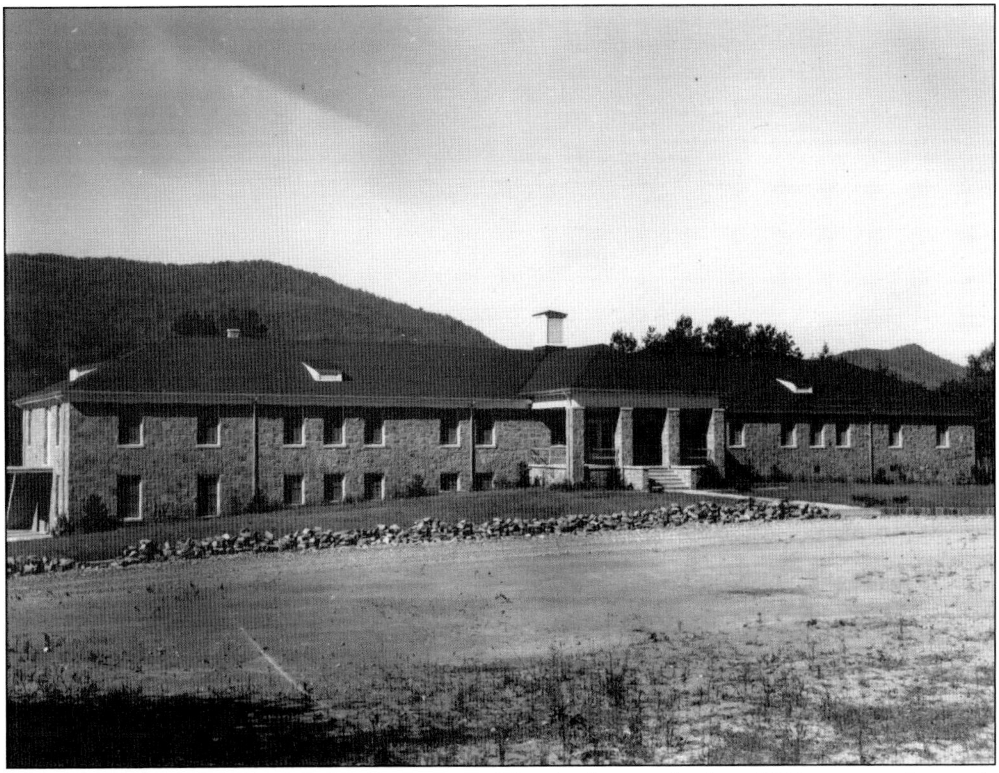

Old Ashe County Hospital in Jefferson. This facility was built in 1941 to serve the needs of Ashe and the surrounding counties.

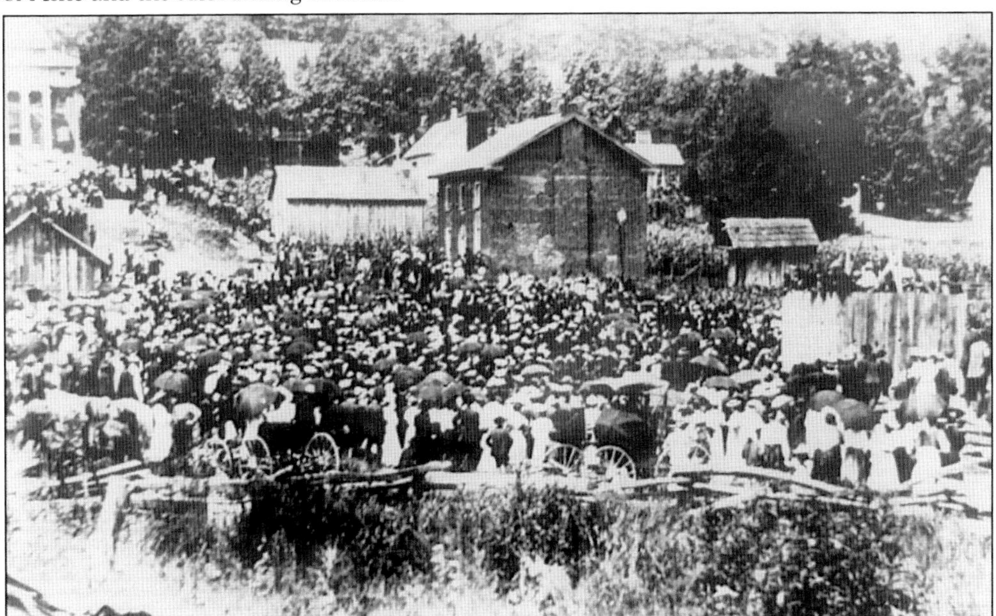

The Hanging of Will Banks. The 1907 hanging of Will Banks was the last hanging in Ashe County. The event drew spectators from three states and was one of the last two public judicial executions in North Carolina.

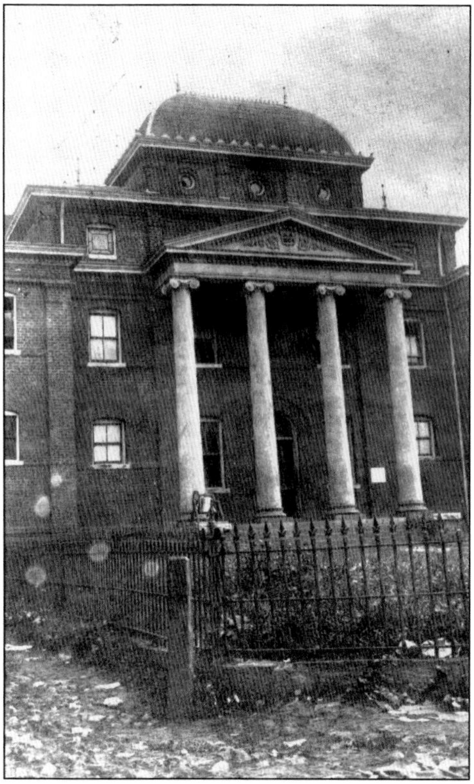

ASHE COUNTY COURTHOUSE (C. 1910). Historical records suggest that court sessions in Ashe County between 1801 and 1904 were held in a log church and log courthouses in several locations.

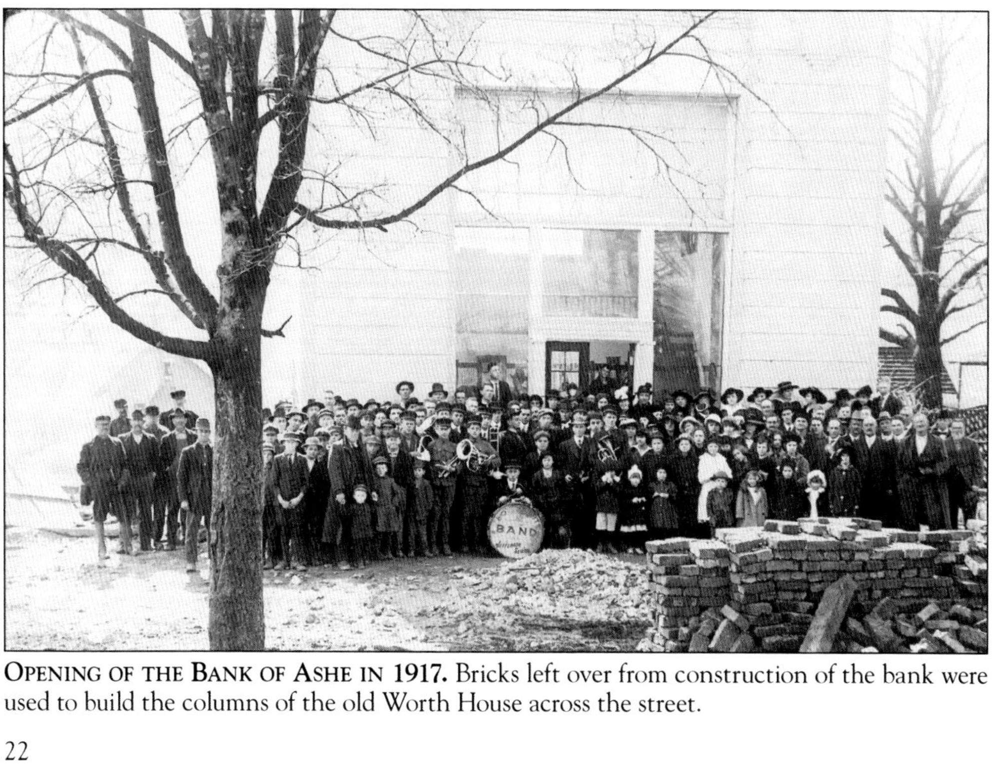

OPENING OF THE BANK OF ASHE IN 1917. Bricks left over from construction of the bank were used to build the columns of the old Worth House across the street.

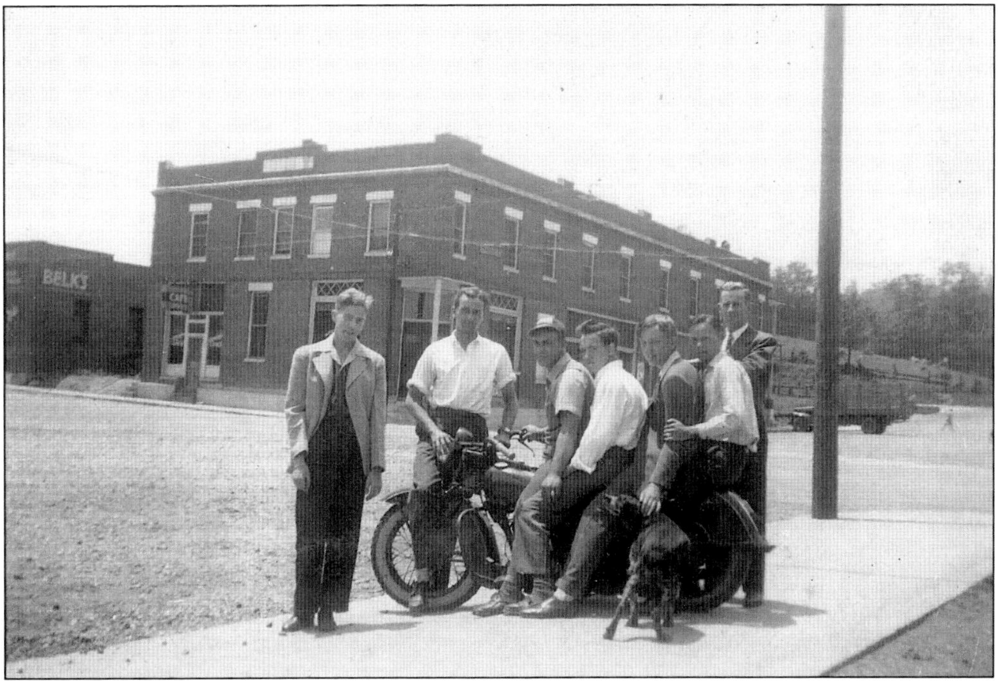

YOUNG MEN RELAXING. Pictured here, from left to right, are Harold Dollar, Edwin Weaver, Jim Miller, Dean Hurley, unidentified, Bill McNeill, and unidentified. This photograph (*c.* 1945) shows the old hotel in the background. Next to the hotel is Belk's Department Store.

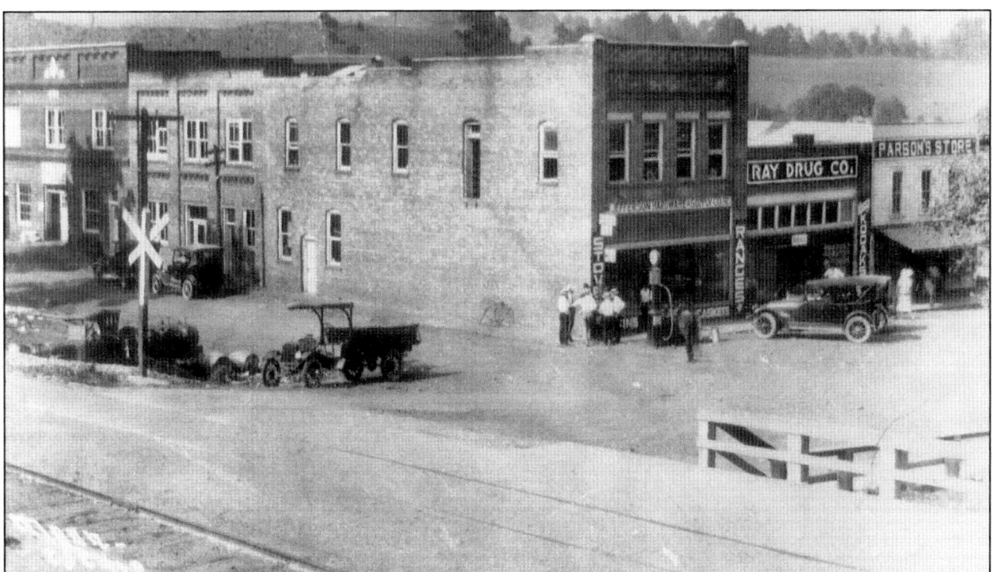

SMITHEY AND MAIN STREETS IN WEST JEFFERSON. In this 1928 photograph, Dr. Gambill's office is shown on the second floor of West Jefferson Hardware. Ray Drug Company later moved to Jefferson Avenue. Note the mail cart in the foreground.

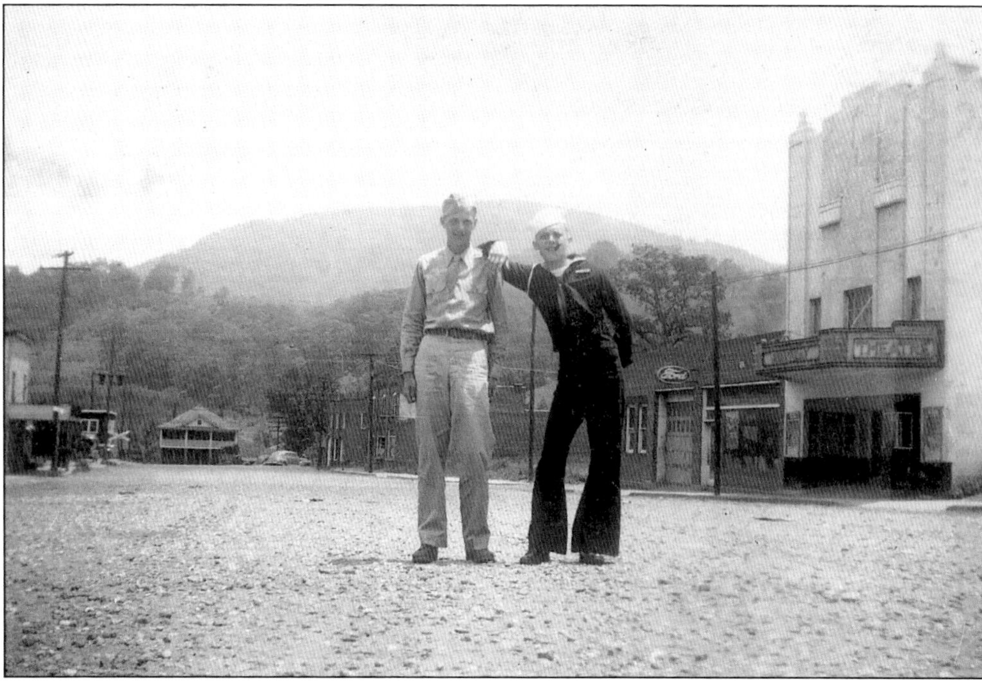

TWO ASHE COUNTY RESIDENTS WHO SERVED IN WORLD WAR II. Carl Jackson (left) and James Leet Vannoy (right) stand at the intersection of Jefferson Avenue and Main Street around 1945. Badger's Funeral Home is visible at the end of Main Street, the Parkway Theater is on the right, and the Bloody Bucket is on the left.

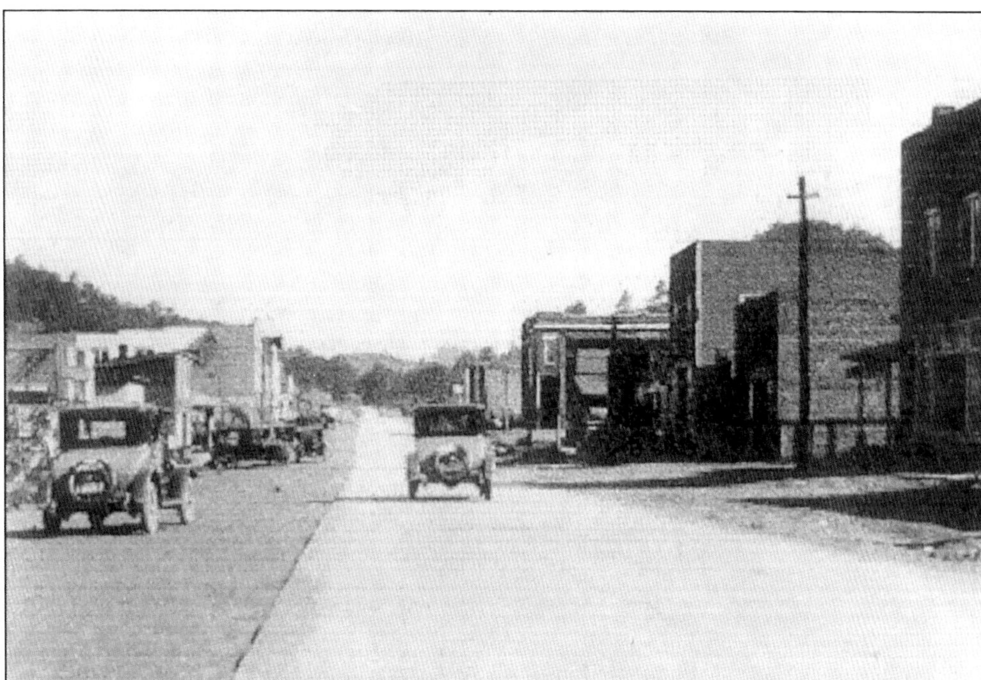

JEFFERSON AVENUE IN WEST JEFFERSON. This view is looking south down Jefferson Avenue.

GRAYBEAL'S DRUG STORE IN WEST JEFFERSON. Dr. B.E. Reeves had his office in the back corner of the pharmacy, and Drs. C.E. Gambill and Jack Hunter had their dentist office on the second floor.

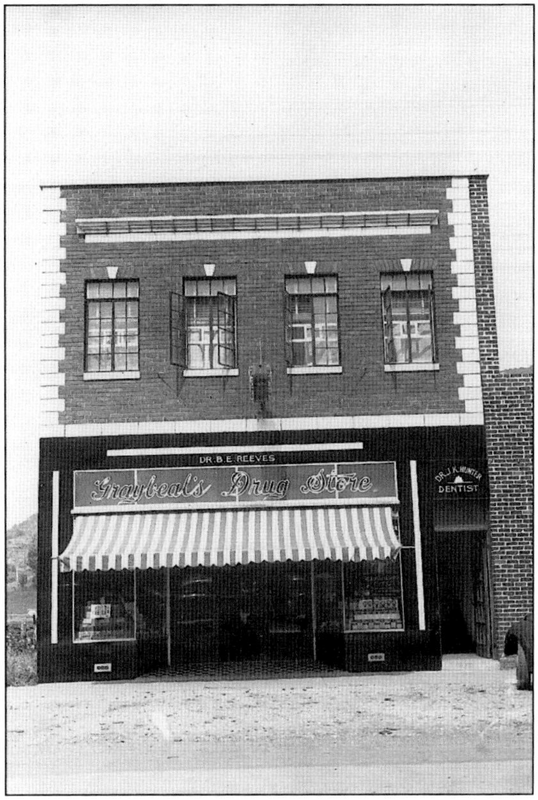

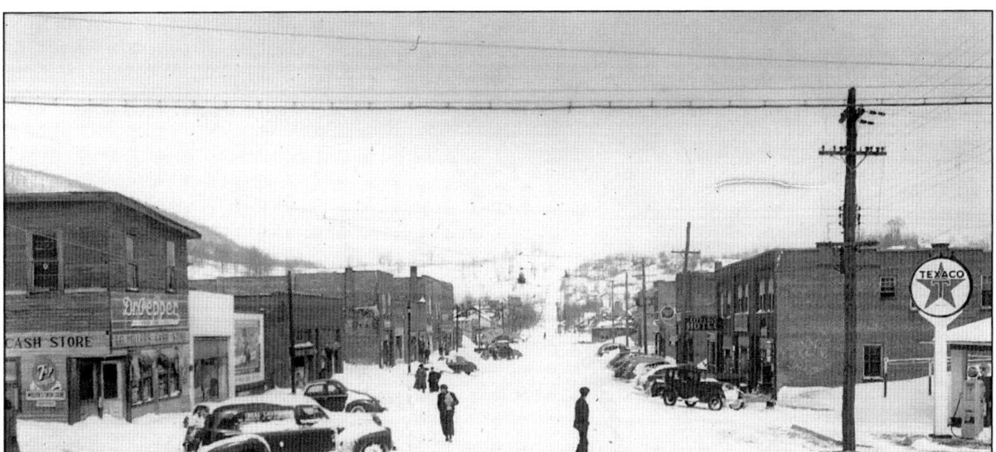

AN EARLY BLIZZARD IN WEST JEFFERSON. The snow is piled up on South Jefferson Avenue.

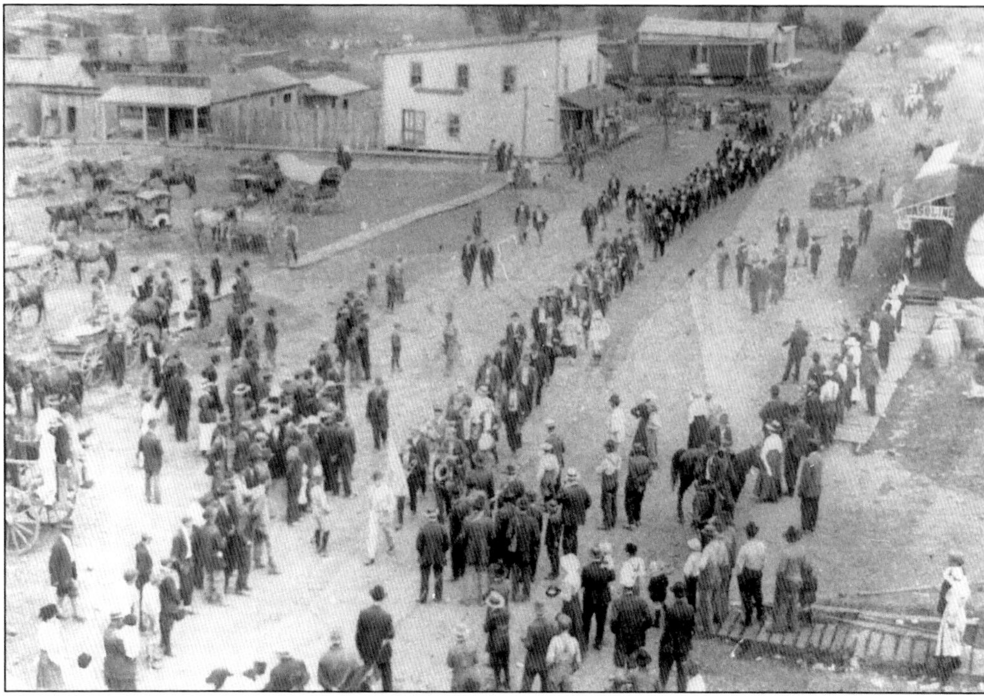

RECRUITS MARCHING TO THE BUSES. In 1915, these young recruits marched from Jefferson to West Jefferson. The large building in the middle background is the Bloody Bucket Restaurant, which occupied the site where Burgess Furniture is now. Wooden sidewalks lined Jefferson Avenue and Main Street. This picture was probably taken from the second floor of the hotel.

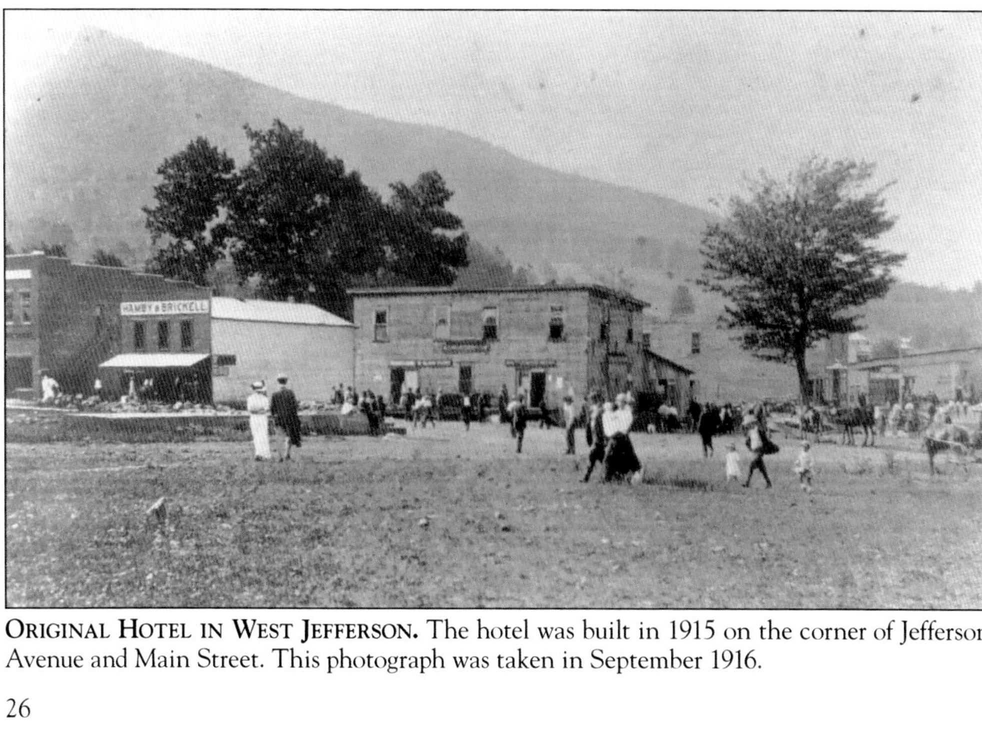

ORIGINAL HOTEL IN WEST JEFFERSON. The hotel was built in 1915 on the corner of Jefferson Avenue and Main Street. This photograph was taken in September 1916.

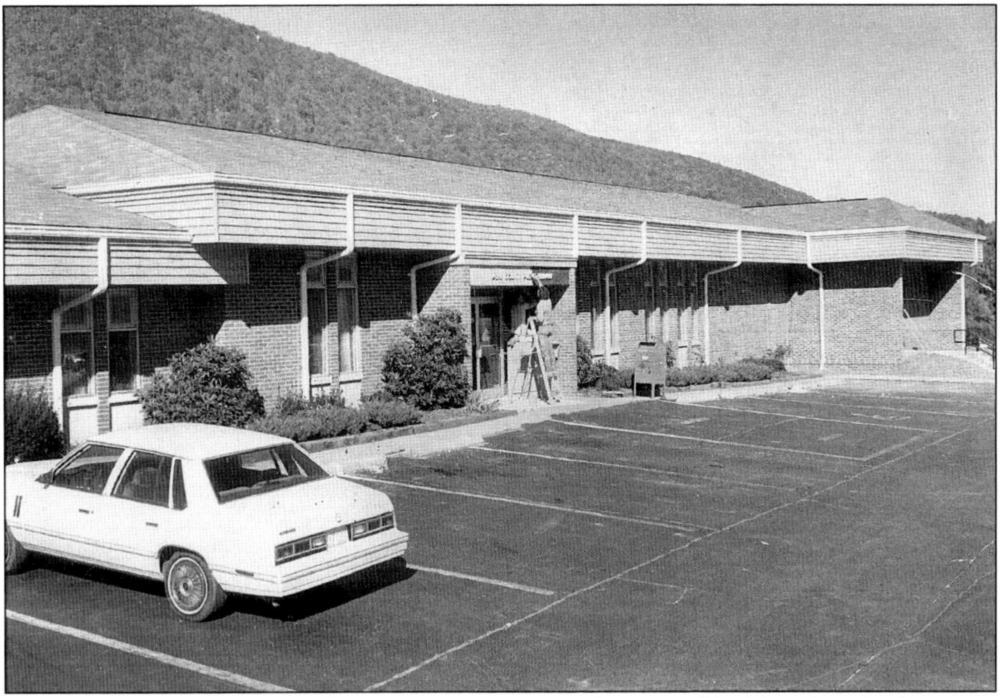

ASHE COUNTY LIBRARY AFTER THE 1987 ADDITION. The original building dates back to 1977. Prior to that, the library was housed in various Jefferson and West Jefferson locations.

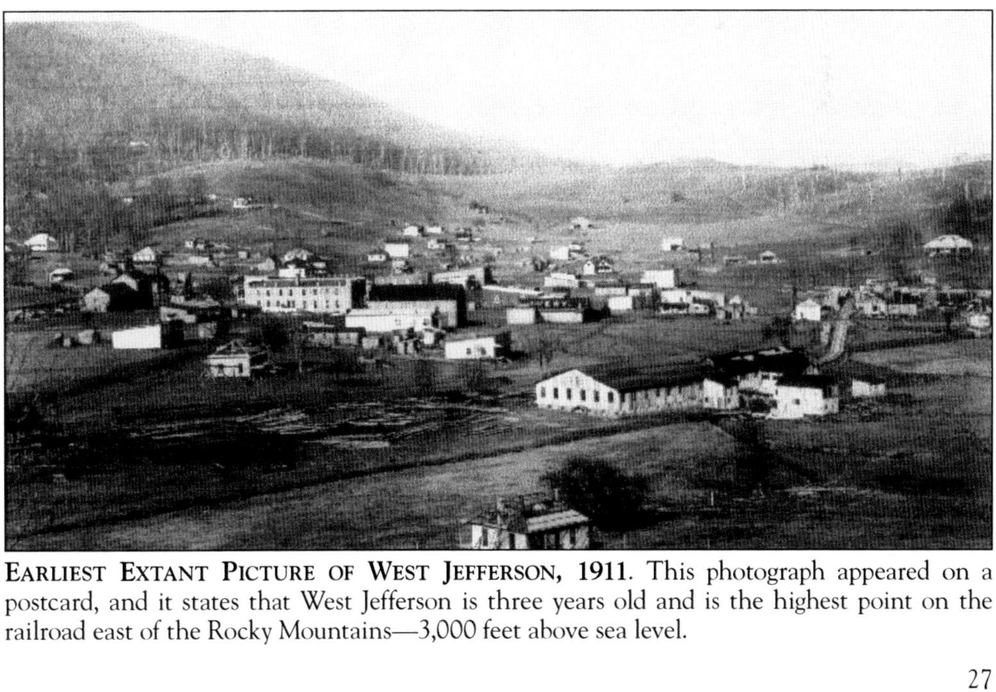

EARLIEST EXTANT PICTURE OF WEST JEFFERSON, 1911. This photograph appeared on a postcard, and it states that West Jefferson is three years old and is the highest point on the railroad east of the Rocky Mountains—3,000 feet above sea level.

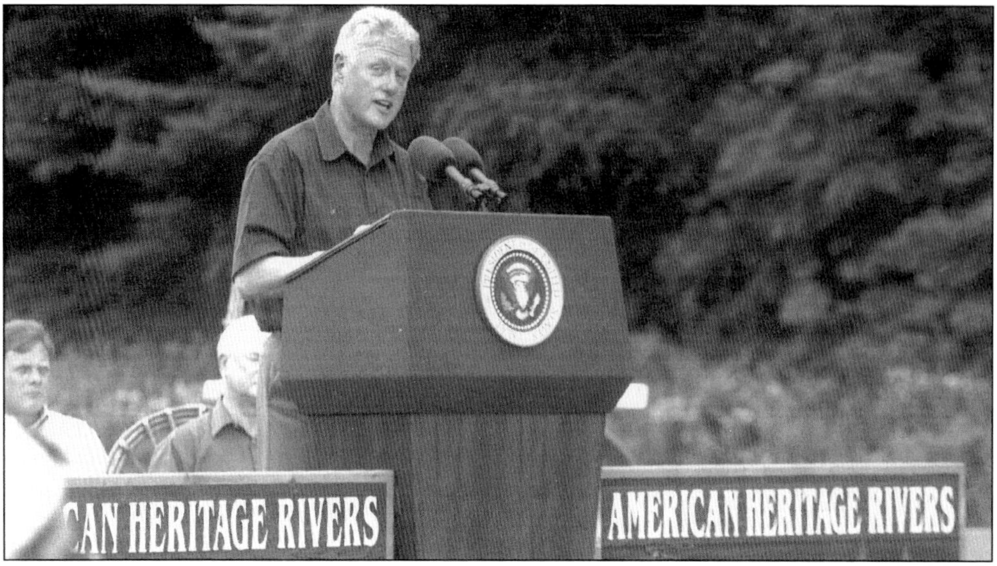

PRESIDENT BILL CLINTON VISITS THE NEW RIVER. The President came to dedicate the first National Heritage River. The 1998 dedication was held on Boggs Road, which borders the South Fork of the New River. National attention has been given to the river since its designation.

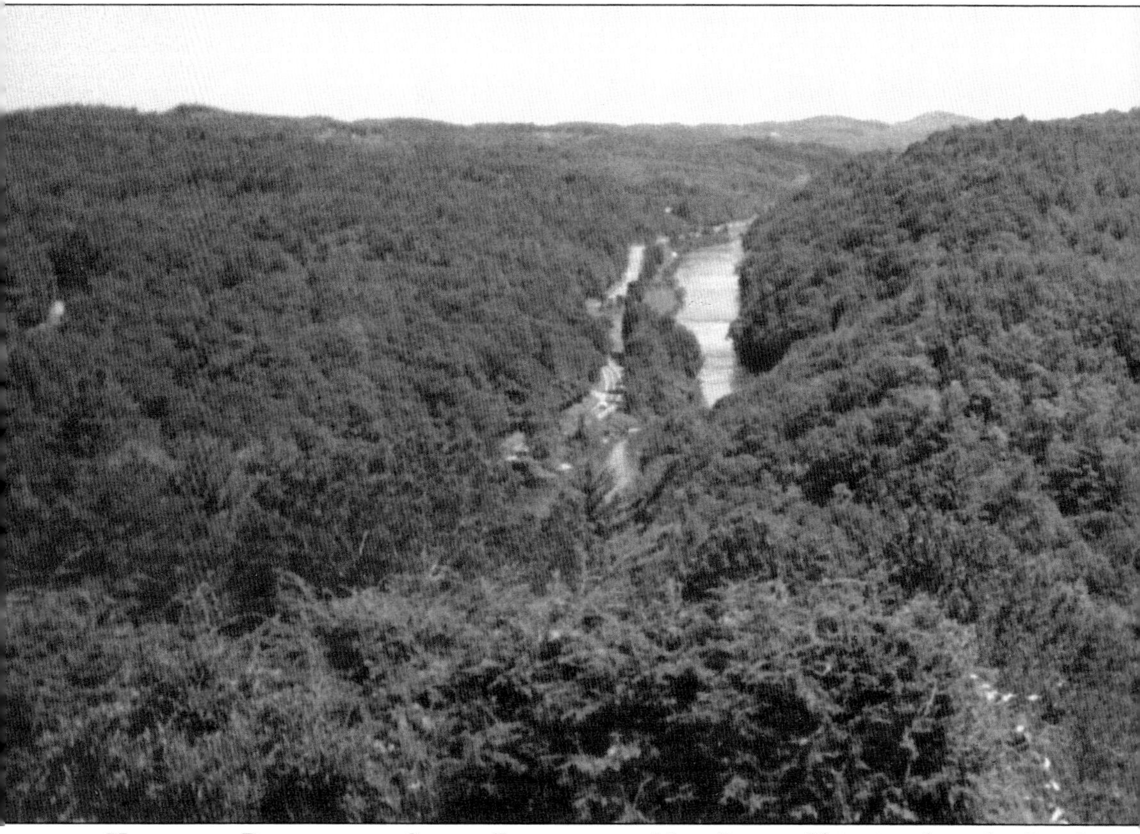

HORSESHOE BEND OF THE SOUTH FORK OF THE NEW RIVER. This view from the Pisgah

BUFFALO CREEK. All creeks and streams in Ashe County flow into either the North or South Fork of the New River.

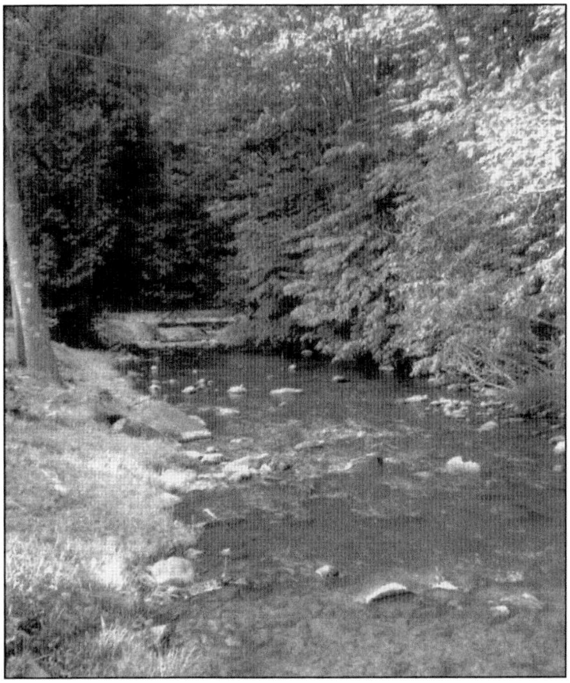

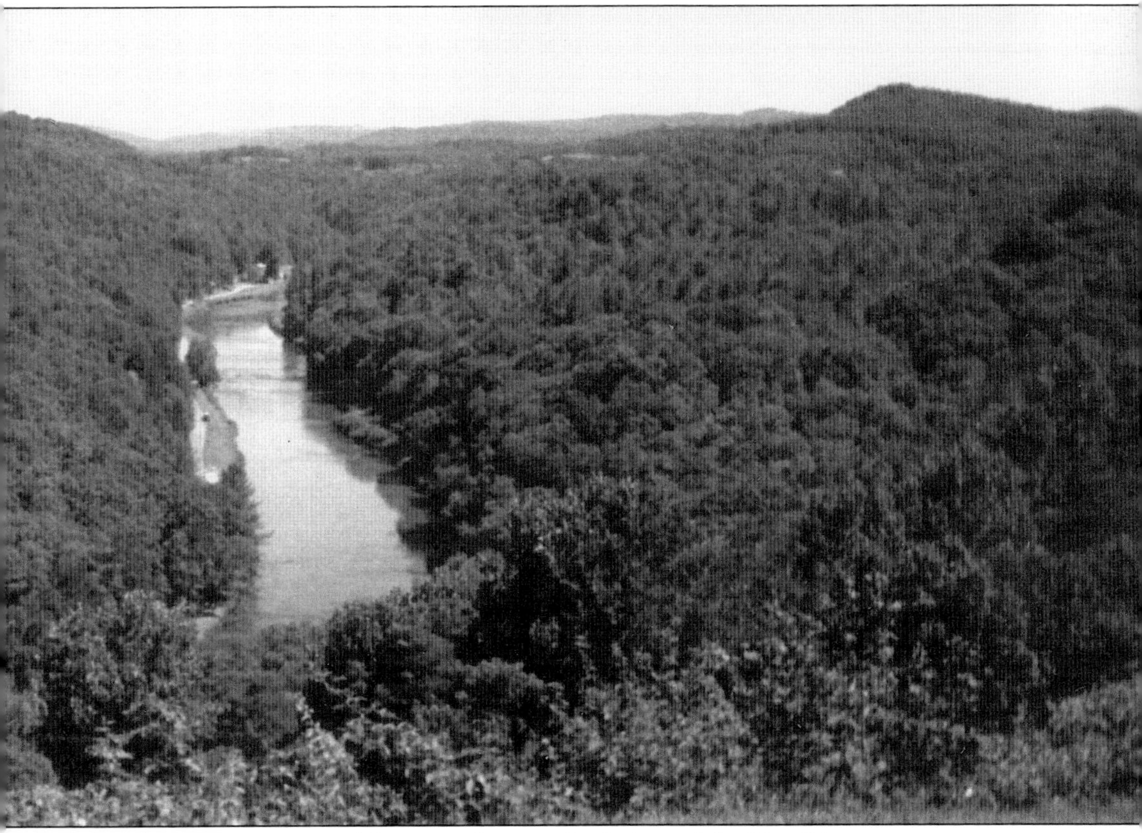

Heights development is one of the most photographed views of the New River.

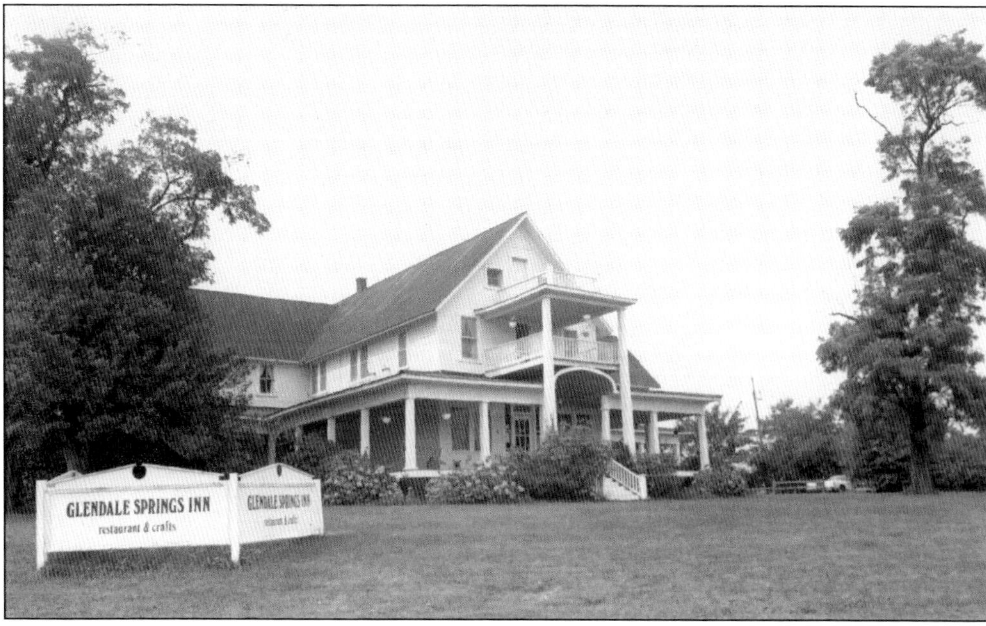

GLENDALE SPRINGS INN. The center portion of the inn was constructed in 1892, with the north and south wings being added between 1902 and 1905. The hotel was in the Bowie family from 1914 until 1968. During construction of the Blue Ridge Parkway from 1936 to 1938, the hotel was leased by the construction company to house its employees. A famous gourmet restaurant is located here.

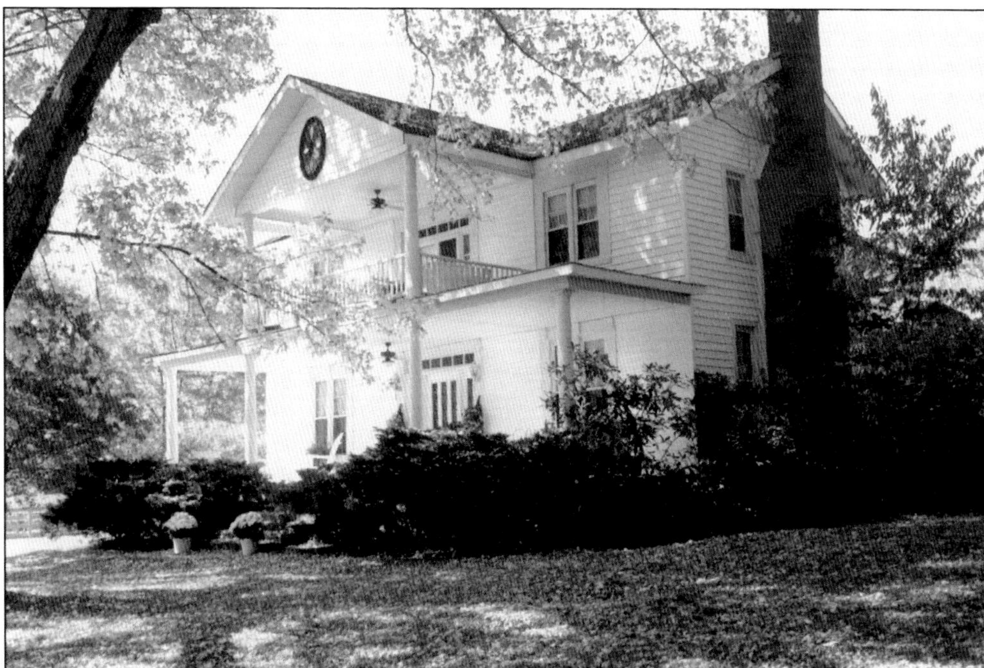

BUFFALO TAVERN. This house, built around 1872, is on the main trail leading from Tennessee into the High Country of North Carolina. In its early days as a tavern, it hosted many travelers, including two governors of North Carolina. It is now a bed-and-breakfast establishment.

Two

FRIENDS AND NEIGHBORS

The people who challenged the wilderness that was to become Ashe County were a hardy breed. They were determined to make homes for themselves and future generations among the beauty of the Blue Ridge.

The first settlers came into Ashe by way of Virginia and Tennessee, a route with no mountain range to conquer. Settlements sprang up at Grassy Creek, Helton, Sutherland, Creston, and gradually spread south and west. By 1800, Jefferson was the center of activity and the logical place for the government of the new county.

Farmers, businessmen, loggers, miners, and others have all contributed to the culture shared today. Thanks to the early residents who faced innumerable obstacles and would have never dreamt of the luxuries we have at this time, people today have a beautiful county with modern conveniences.

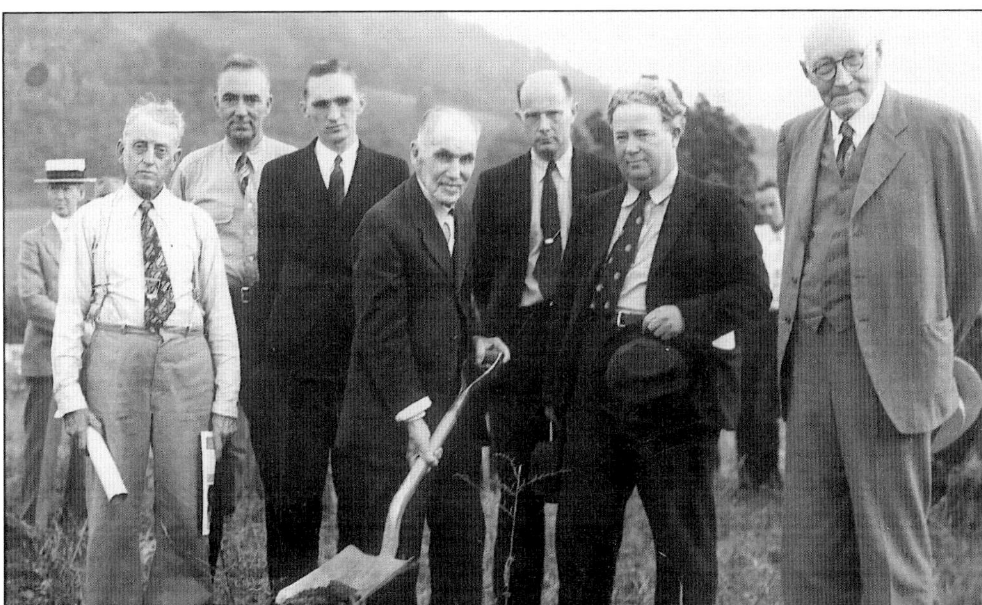

GROUNDBREAKING FOR ASHE MEMORIAL HOSPITAL IN THE LATE 1930S. Pictured here, from left to right, are Charlie Welch, Roy Badger, Guy Badger, Edison Thomas Sr., Dr. Dean Jones Sr., Wade Eller, and Congressman R.L. Doughton.

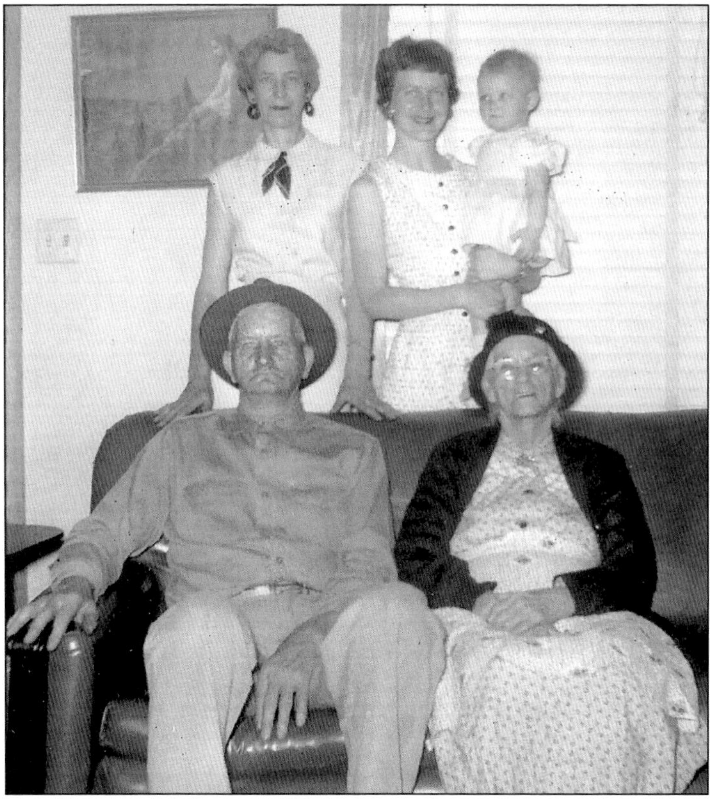

FIVE GENERATIONS OF THE STURGILL FAMILY. Pictured here, from left to right, are the following: (seated) Jim Sturgill, owner and operator of Sturgill's Store, and his mother, Charity Ann Farmer Sturgill; (standing) Zollie Sturgill Phipps, daughter, Mildred Phipps Vannoy, granddaughter, and Patricia Vannoy Inge, great-granddaughter.

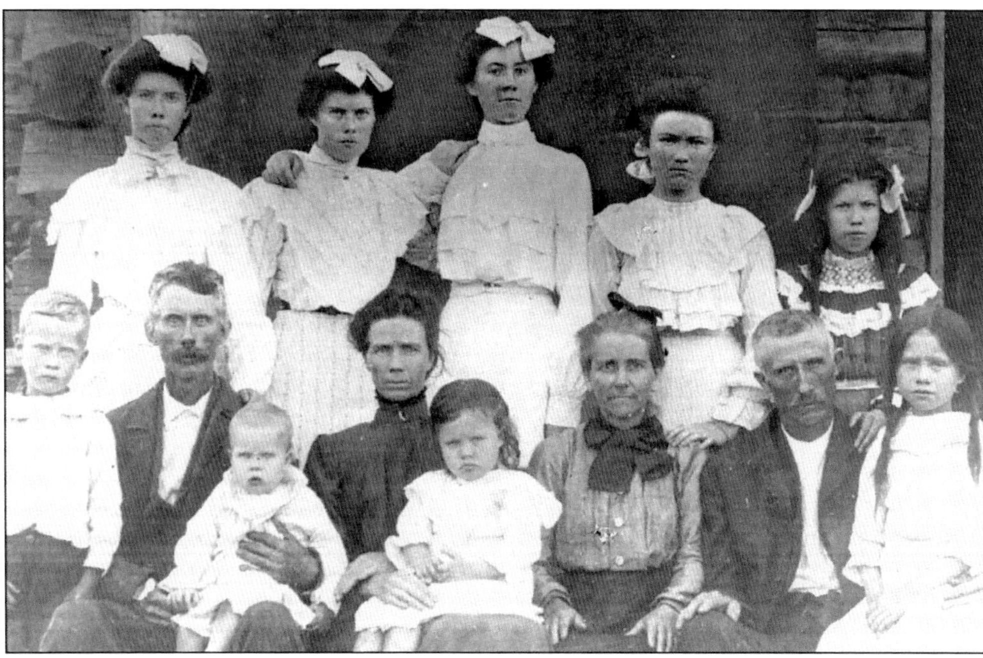

THE MEREDITH GAULTNEY FAMILY. Pictured here, from left to right, are the following: (front row) Charlie, Meredith, Zola, Adaline, Pearl, unidentified, unidentified, and Laura; (back row) Bertha, Cora, Etta, Molly, and Fannie.

POSTMISTRESS ETTA GAULTNEY. She is delivering the mail from Crumpler to Grassy Creek.

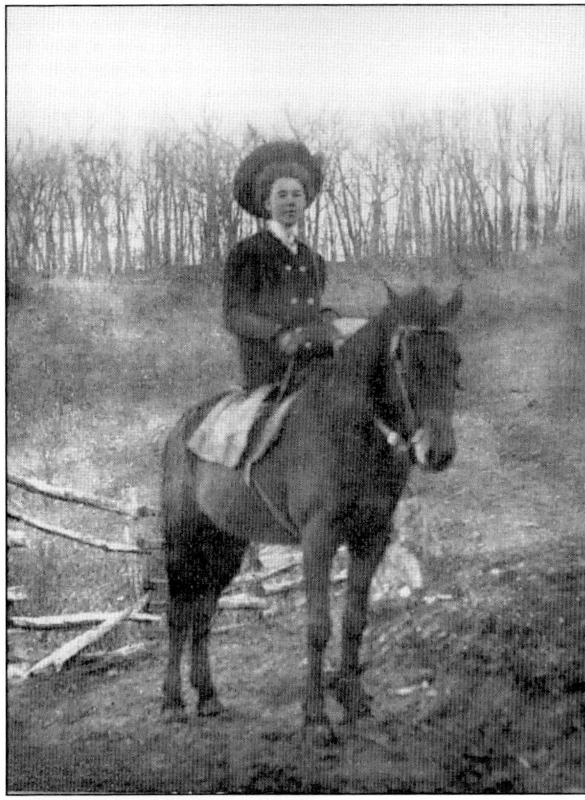

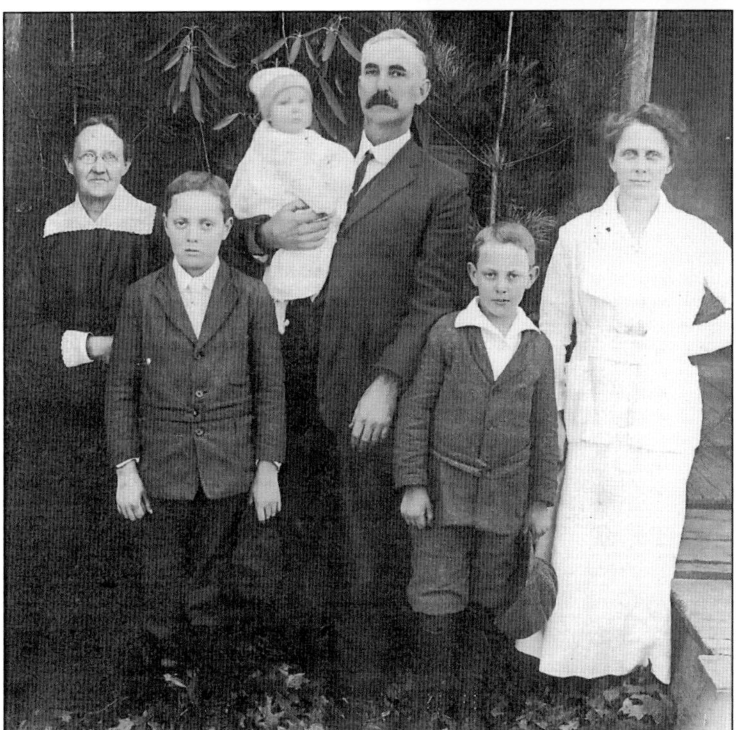

DAVID WAUGH FAMILY (C. 1918). Pictured here, from left to right, are Mary Howell Bledsoe, Joseph Todd Waugh, David Waugh (holding baby Edna Waugh Lawrence), Kendrick Waugh, and Hattie Louise Bledsoe Waugh. David Waugh was born in 1869 in Jefferson.

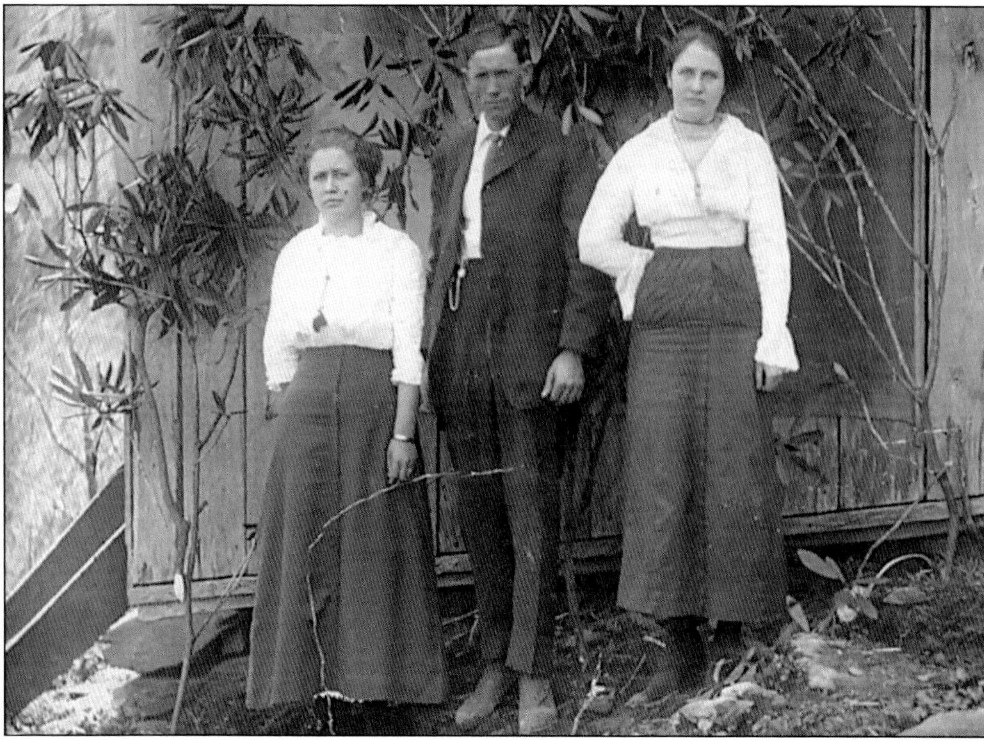

Maude Mahaffey, Little Am Clark, and Rettie Stansberry (c. 1915). The threesome were residents of the Little Horse Creek area of Ashe County.

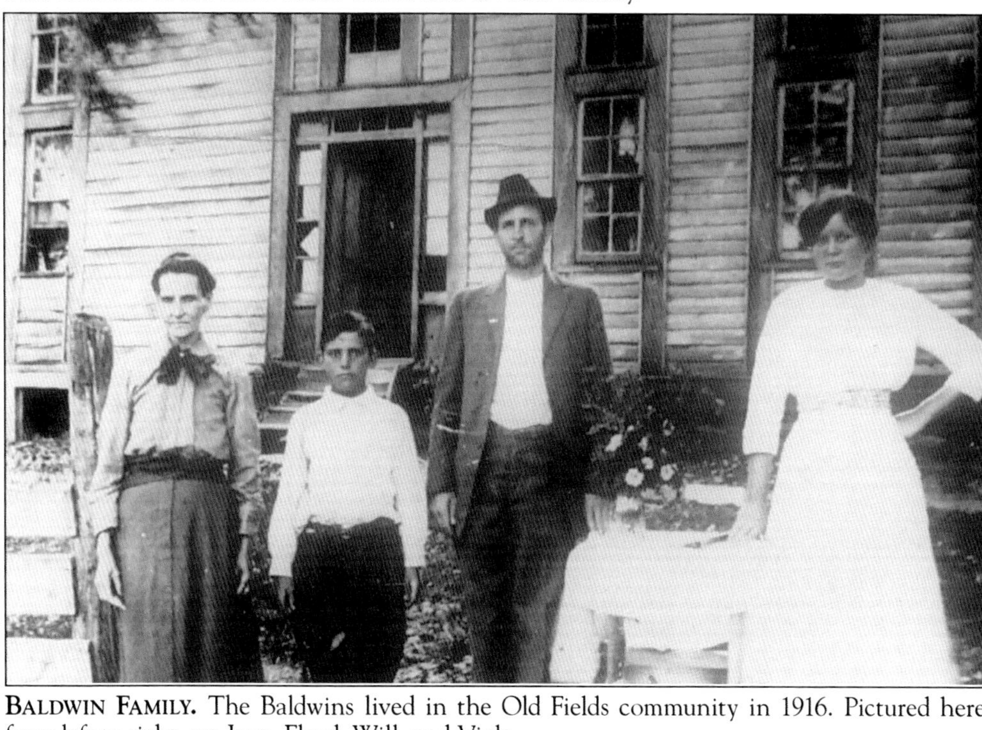

Baldwin Family. The Baldwins lived in the Old Fields community in 1916. Pictured here, from left to right, are Jane, Floyd, Will, and Viola.

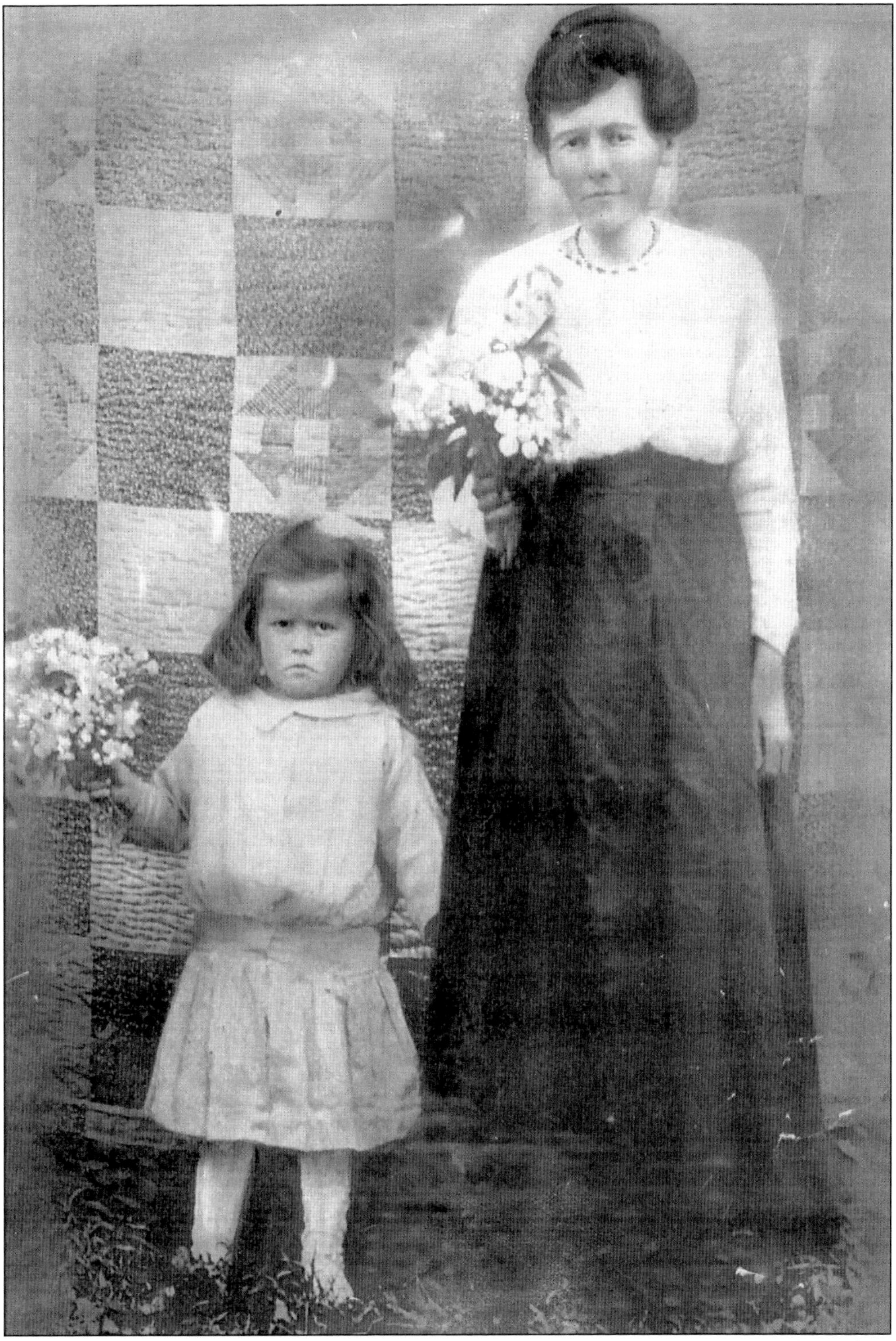

Alice Finely Miller and Viller C. Miller Goss of the Nella Community. The quilt in the background is an example of the churn dash pattern.

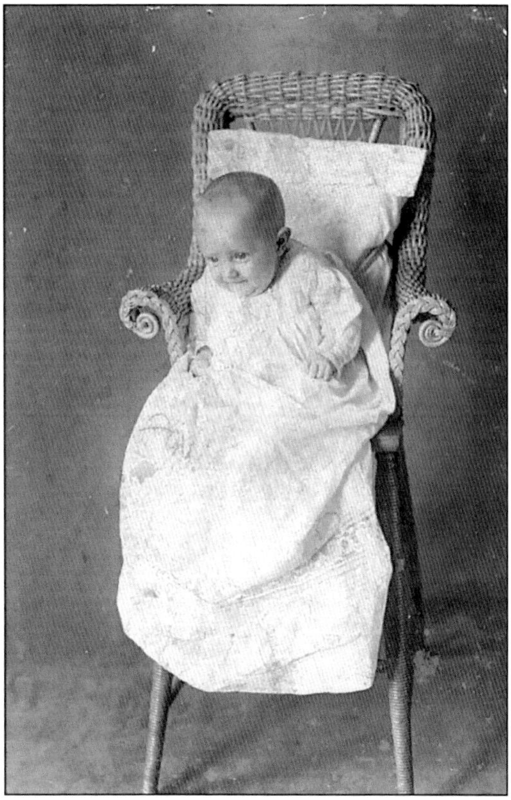

ELLA SUE VANNOY. Born in Wilkes County in 1915, she later moved to Ashe County, where she met and married Carl F. Colvard.

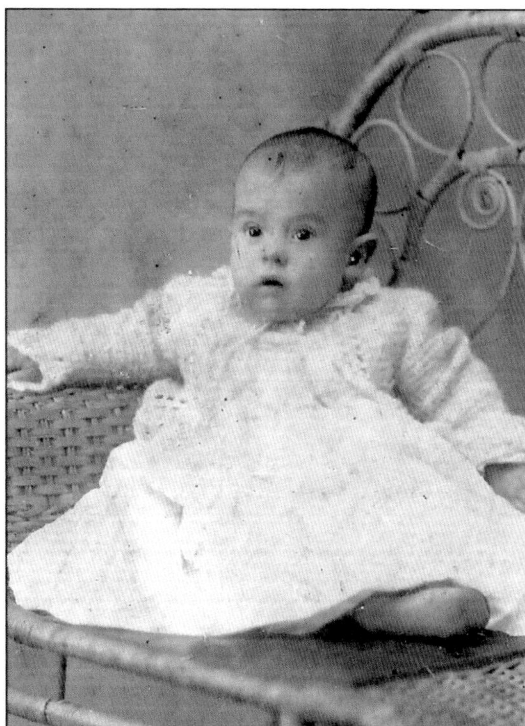

CARL FRANKLIN COLVARD SR. Born in Wilkes County in 1908, he moved to Ashe County in the early 1930s.

NINA GOSS (C. 1910). She died in childhood after accidentally falling into a vat of molasses.

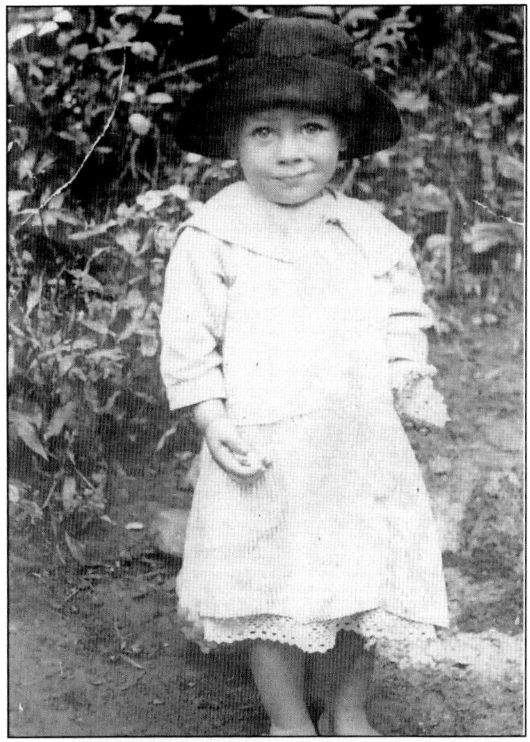

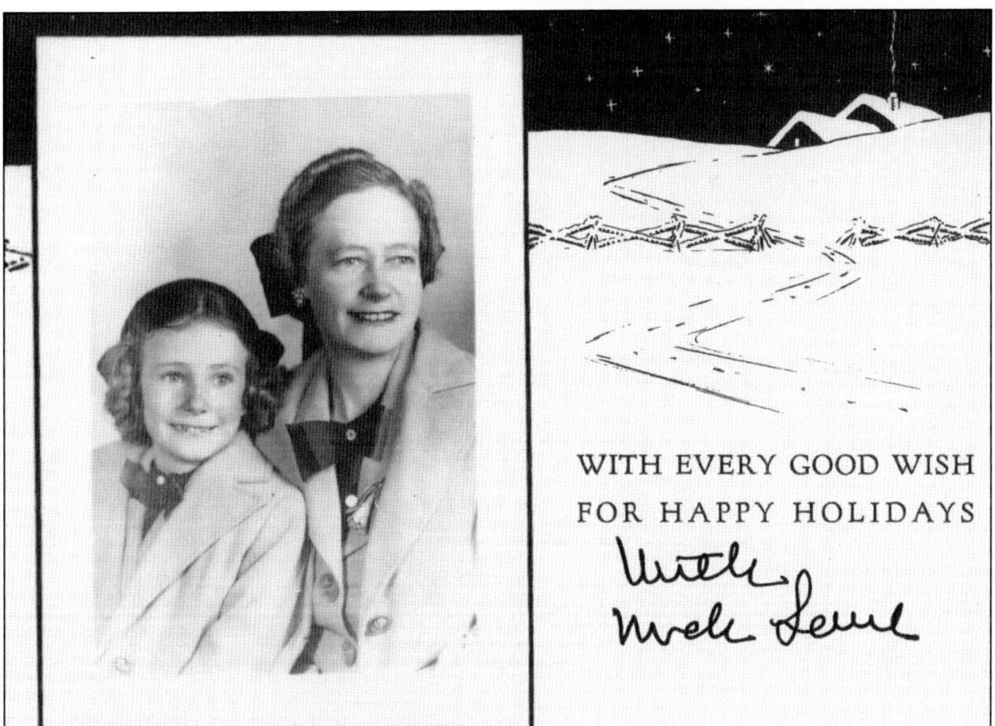

A 1940S CHRISTMAS CARD. This Christmas greeting was from Mrs. Ed M. Anderson and her daughter Stella.

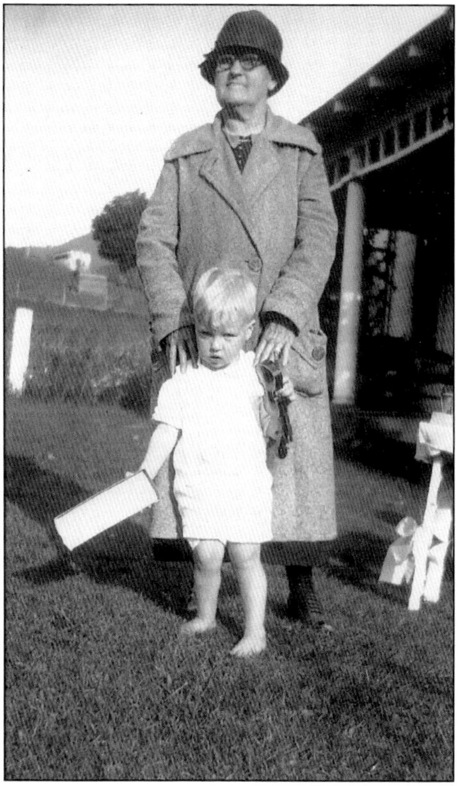

MRS. VORHEES AND YOUNG LEET VANNOY IN 1928. Leet Vannoy was born in this family home on East Fourth Street in West Jefferson.

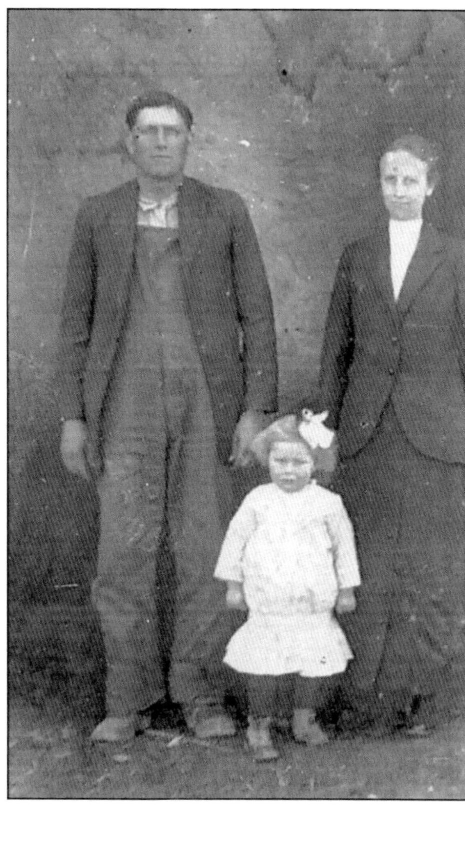

SHEPHERD FAMILY. This picture was taken around 1940 in Tuckerdale, across the creek from the Wilburn Waters Cemetery. Pictured here, from left to right, are Andrew Jackson Shepherd, Cina Low Ham Shepherd, and their daughter Lucy Shepherd Sharpe.

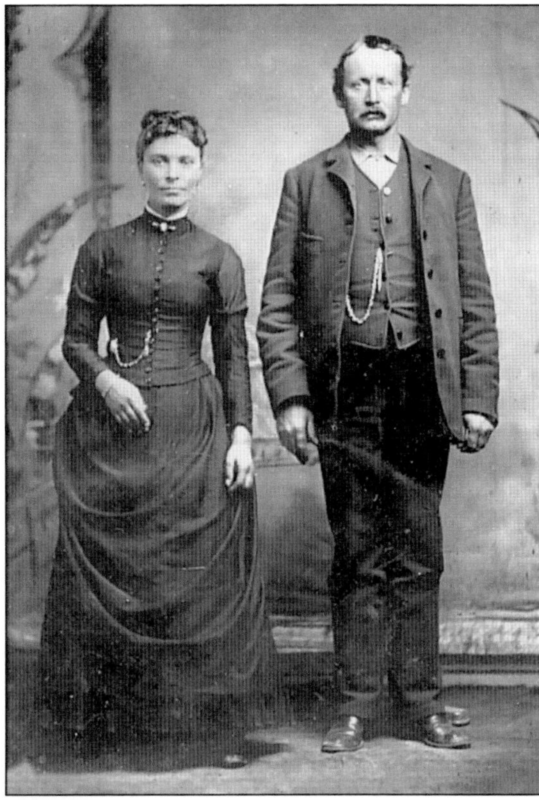

Sarah Fine and Will Vannoy. The Vannoys lived in Tuckerdale in 1875.

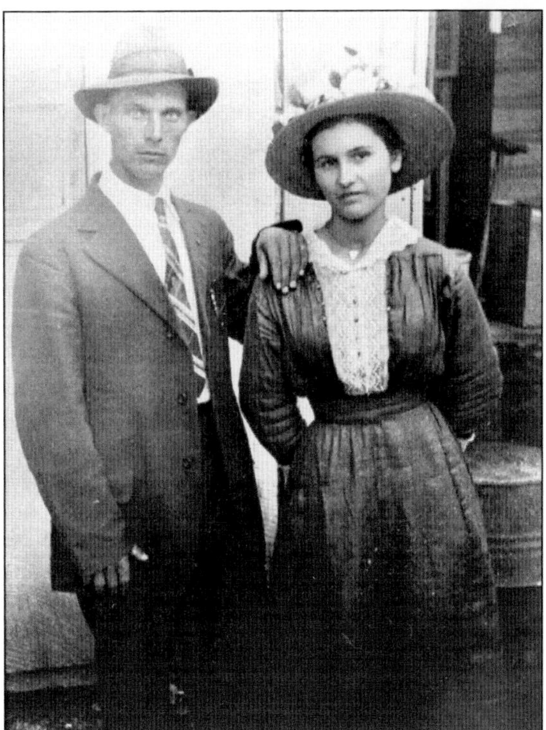

Lucy and Sherman Moretz of the Buffalo Community. This photograph is of their 1917 wedding.

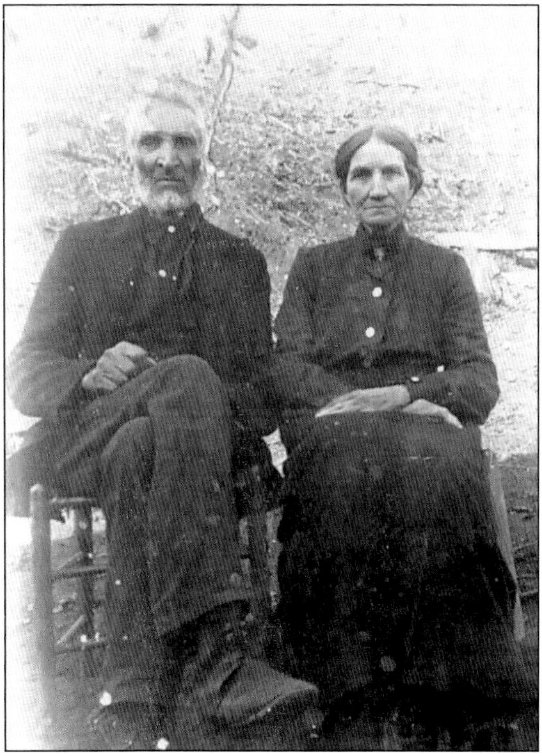

Hiram and Phoebe Miller of Little Horse Creek. Hiram was the son of Isaac and Eva Stanley Miller, who were among the earliest settlers of the Little Horse Creek area.

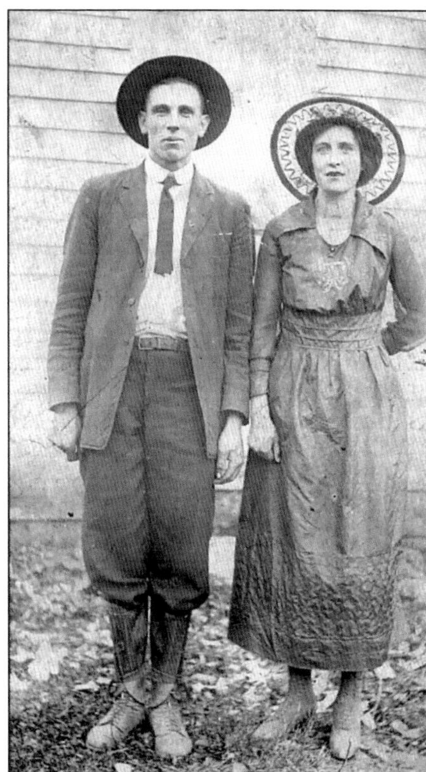

Wade and Rettie Stansberry. They were living in their home on Little Horse Creek in 1919.

ISHAM THOMPSON AT AGE 93. At the time of this photograph, he was the last surviving Confederate veteran in Ashe County. Though the 1860 census recorded the population of Ashe as less than 8,000, approximately 600 men served in the Confederate Army from 1861 to 1865.

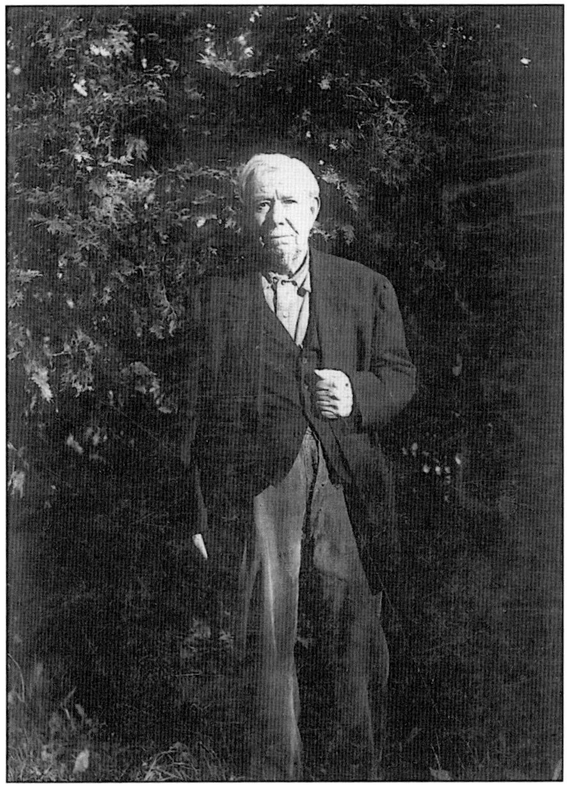

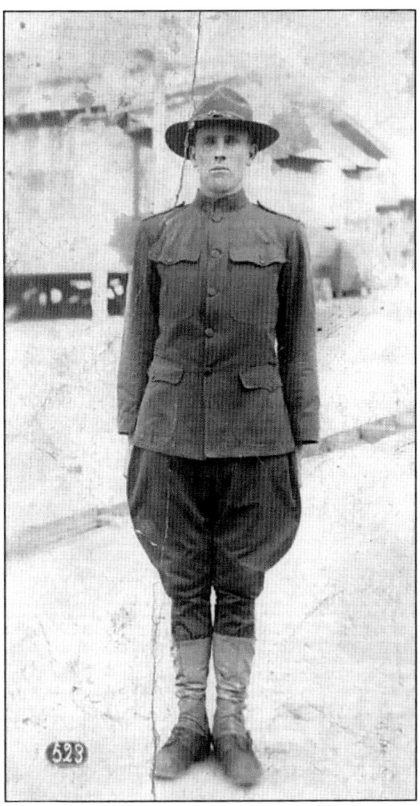

WADE STANSBERRY. This photograph was taken just before Wade shipped out to France during World War I.

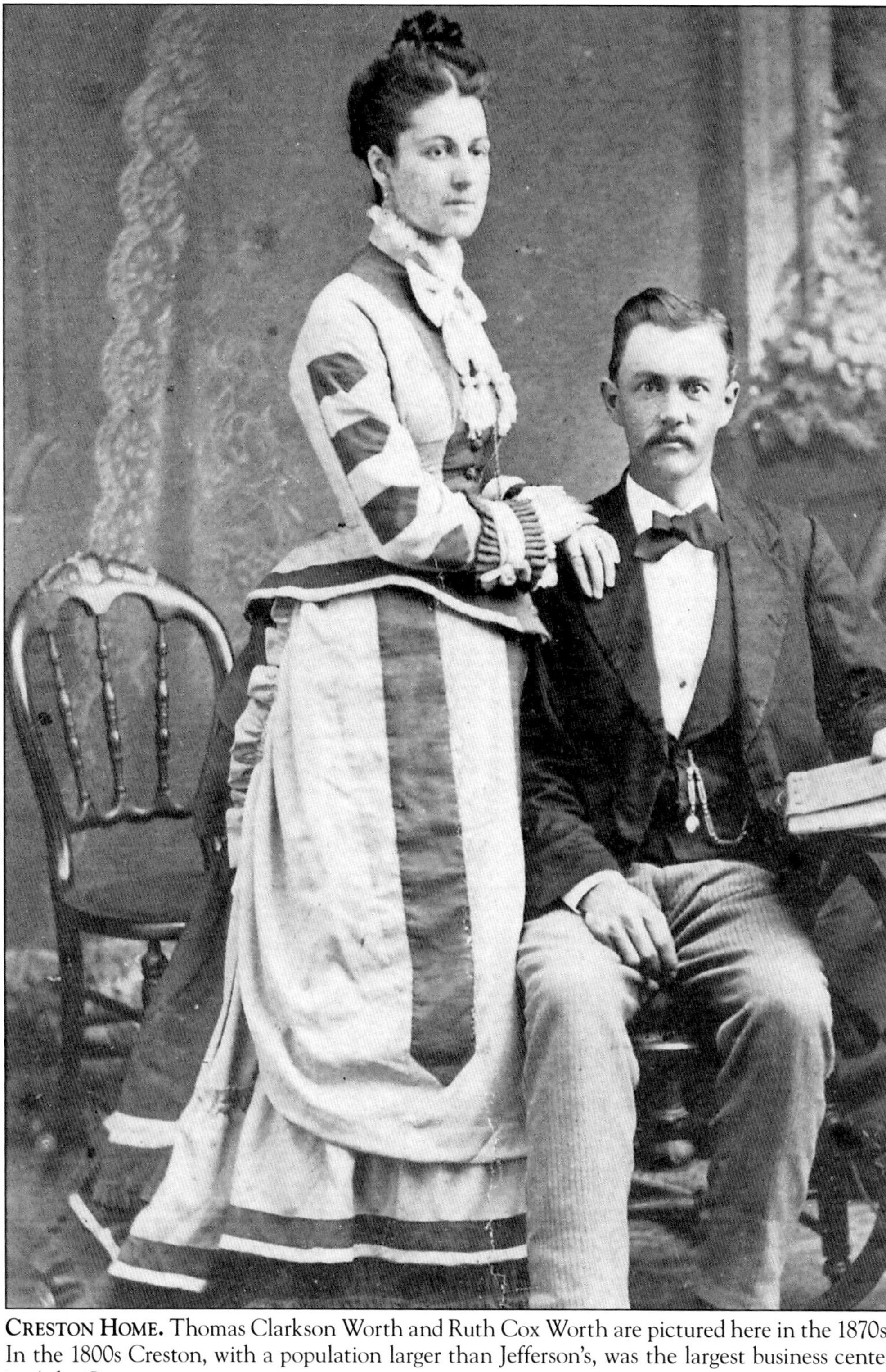

CRESTON HOME. Thomas Clarkson Worth and Ruth Cox Worth are pictured here in the 1870s. In the 1800s Creston, with a population larger than Jefferson's, was the largest business center in Ashe County.

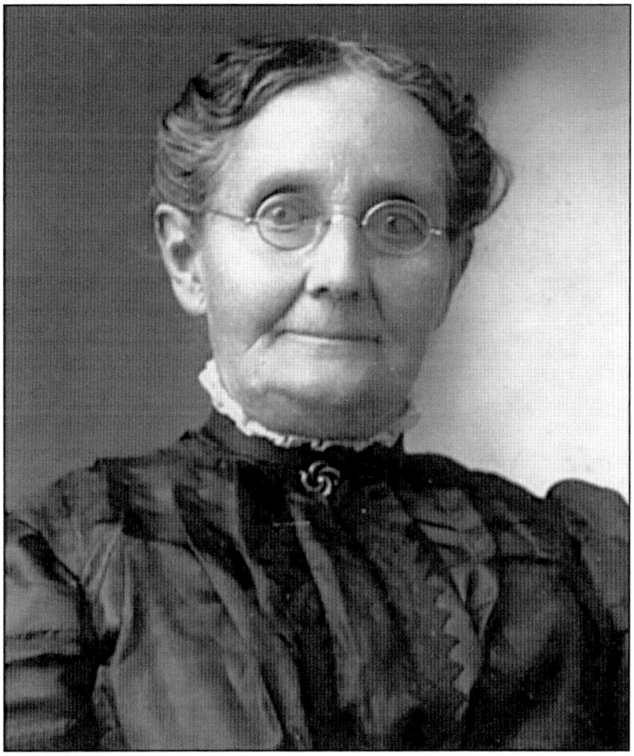

MARY HOWELL BLEDSOE (C. 1905). Mary, who wedded James Bledsoe, was born in 1856 and died in 1942.

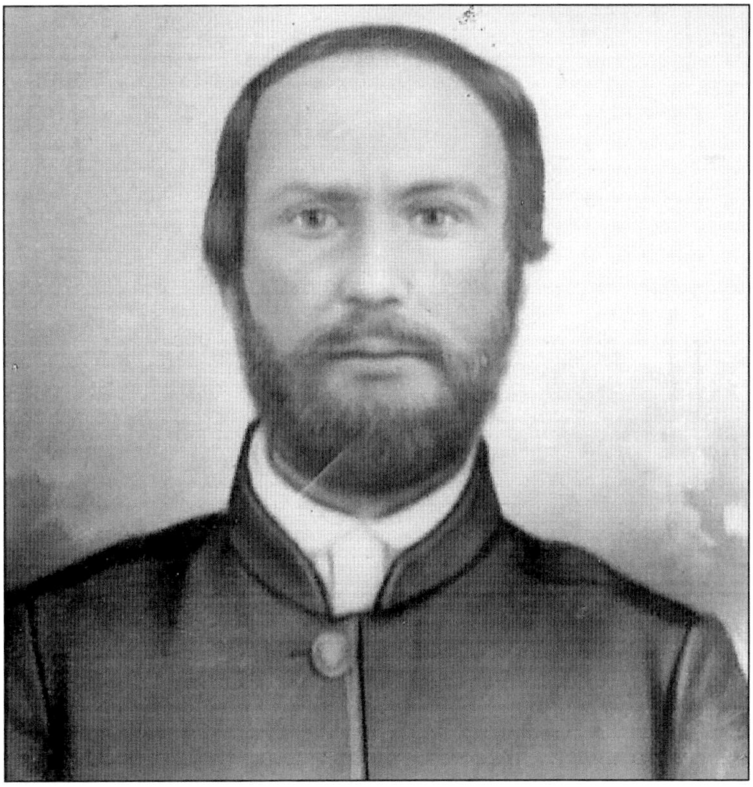

JOHN BARE (C. 1800). John was related to the Waughs, the Jones, and other old Ashe County families.

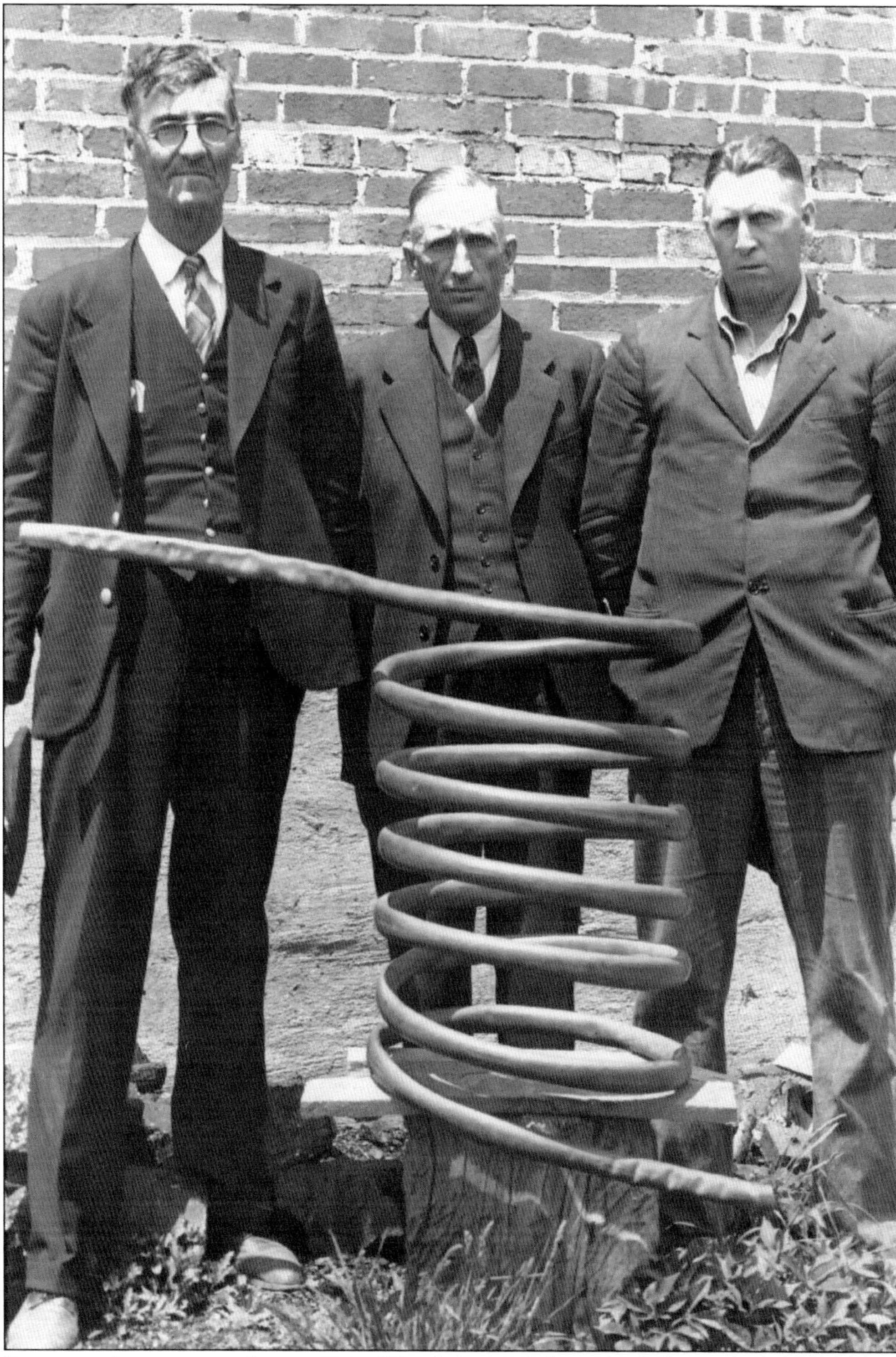

SEIZING A STILL IN THE LATE 1930S. West Jefferson Police Chief Charlie McMillan (on the left) displays the seized coil. Constable Bob Watson stands on the right.

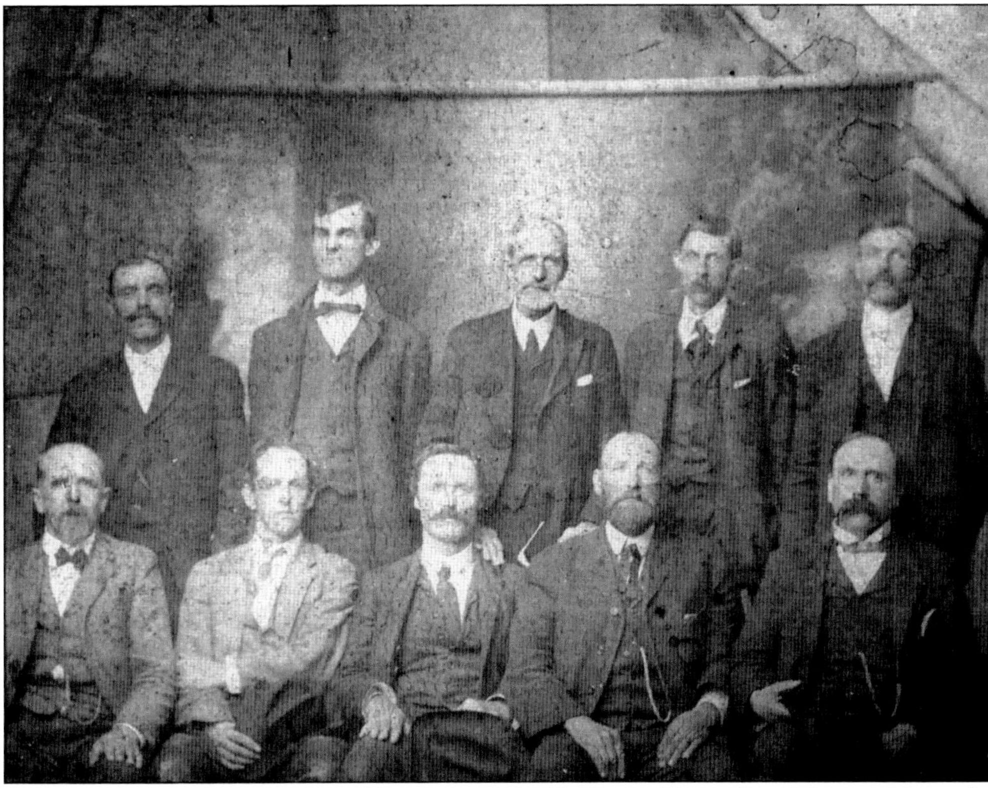

CANDIDATES FOR ASHE COUNTY ELECTION IN 1906. Pictured here, from left to right, are the following: (front row) J.A. Jones, register of deeds; Walter H. Worth, clerk of the superior court; D.A. Osborne, clerk of the superior court; G.B. Austin, sheriff; and Ambrose Clark, sheriff; (back row) R.K. Elliott, register of deeds; G.L. Park, representative; Hiram Weaver, representative; L.S. Vannoy, treasurer; and M.M. Lewis, treasurer.

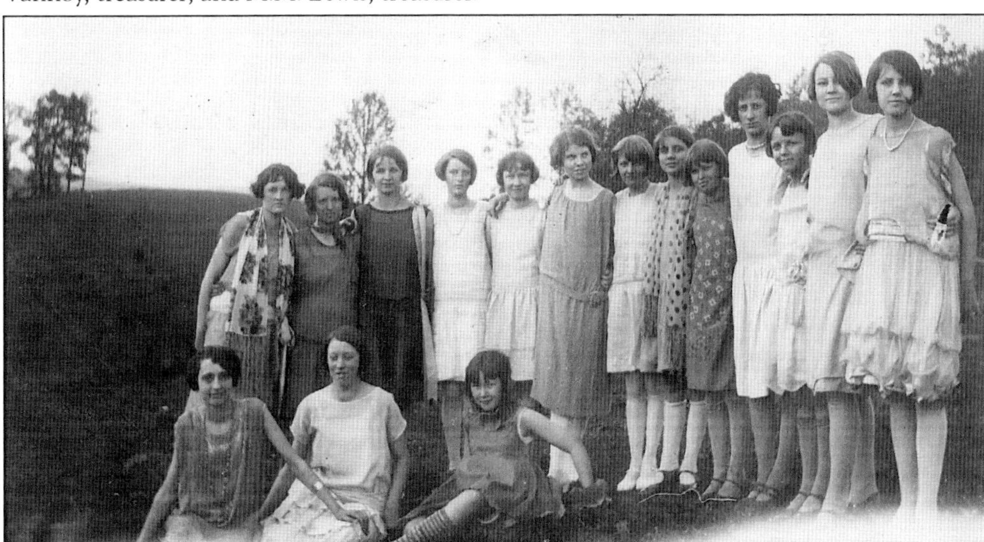

FASHIONABLE WEST JEFFERSON LADIES IN THE 1920S. These young ladies were close friends from early childhood.

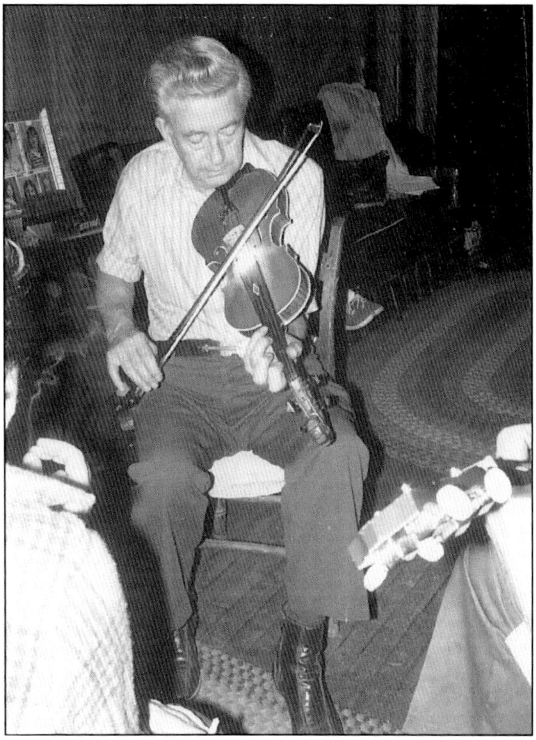

ALBERT HASH. Hash was an early mountain musician, instrument maker, and composer. A music festival has been named in his honor.

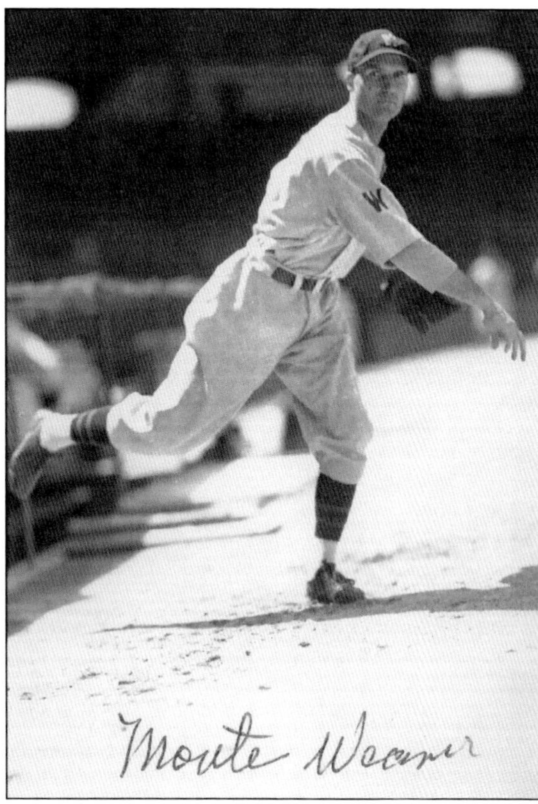

MONTE WEAVER, PROFESSIONAL BASEBALL PLAYER. Born in Helton in 1906, Monte graduated from Emory and Henry College and the University of Virginia. He became a pitcher with the Washington Senators after a teaching career at the University of Virginia. He pitched a World Series game in 1933 while with the Senators. Later he pitched for the Boston Red Sox. His military service in World War II ended his professional baseball career. Weaver died in 1994.

JUDGE TUCKER AND HIS BLOODHOUNDS. Pictured in front of West Jefferson Hardware, from left to right, are C.O. Parsons, Walt Tucker, unidentified, Charles McNeil, unidentified, Harrison Tucker, and unidentified.

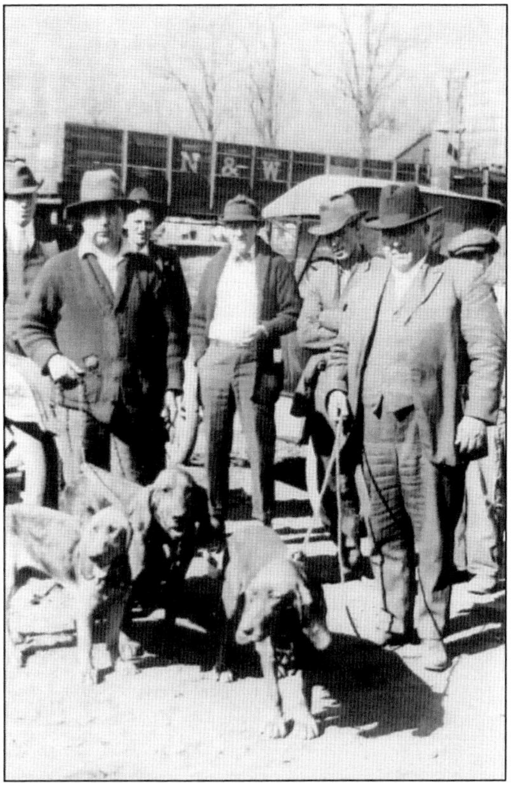

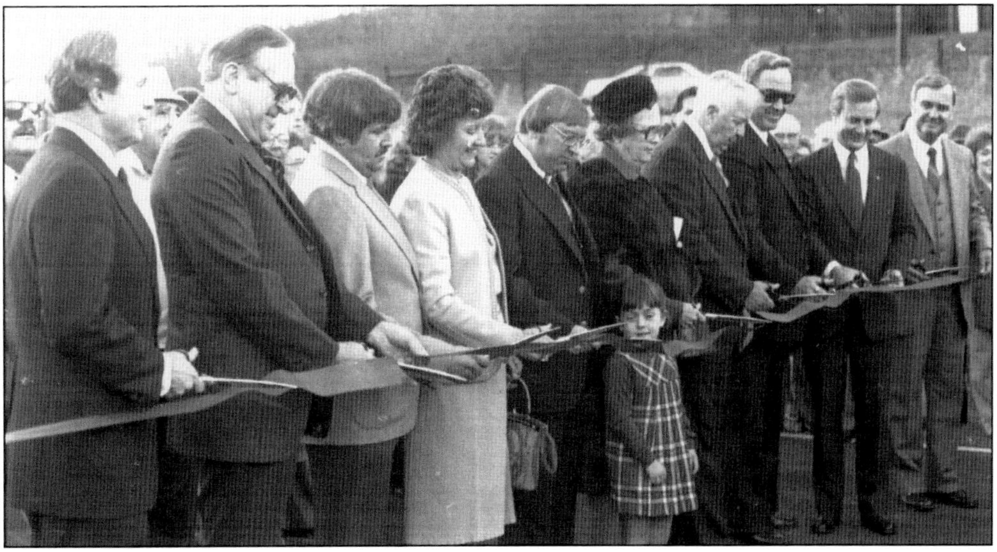

RIBBON CUTTING FOR THE ROBERT G. BARR EXPRESSWAY. The ceremony took place between Baldwin and West Jefferson in October 1981. Pictured here, from left to right, are the following: Congressman Steve Neal; Jefferson mayor Tom Cockerham; Bob McCoy, chairman of the Ashe County Commissioners; West Jefferson mayor Virginia Myers; Winston H. Baldwin, president of the Ashe County Chamber of Commerce; Alexandra Reeves; Mrs. Chattie Barr; Robert G. Barr; former North Carolina governor Bob Scott; North Carolina governor Jim Hunt, and North Carolina transportation member Ranny Phillips.

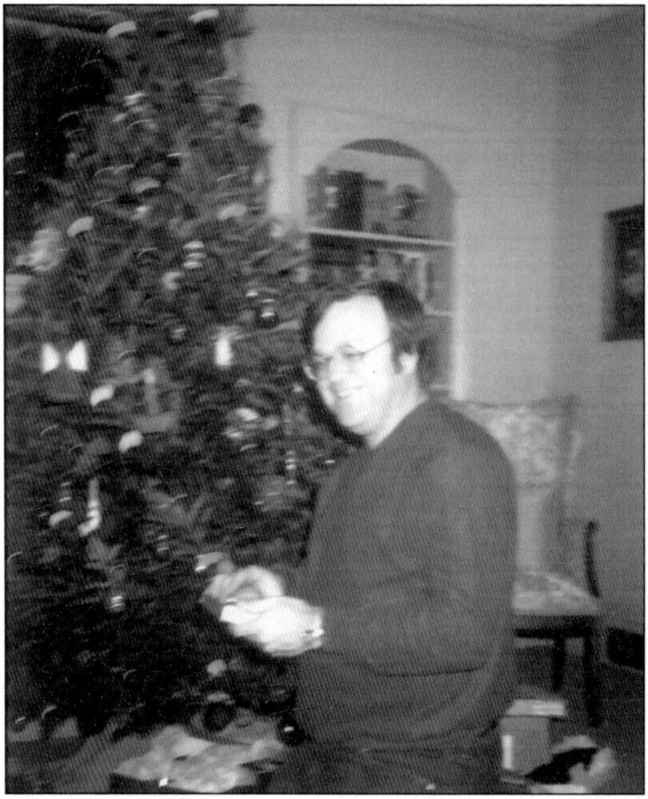

J. Kennith Morris in 1974. Morris was celebrating his first Christmas as minister at the West Jefferson First Baptist Church.

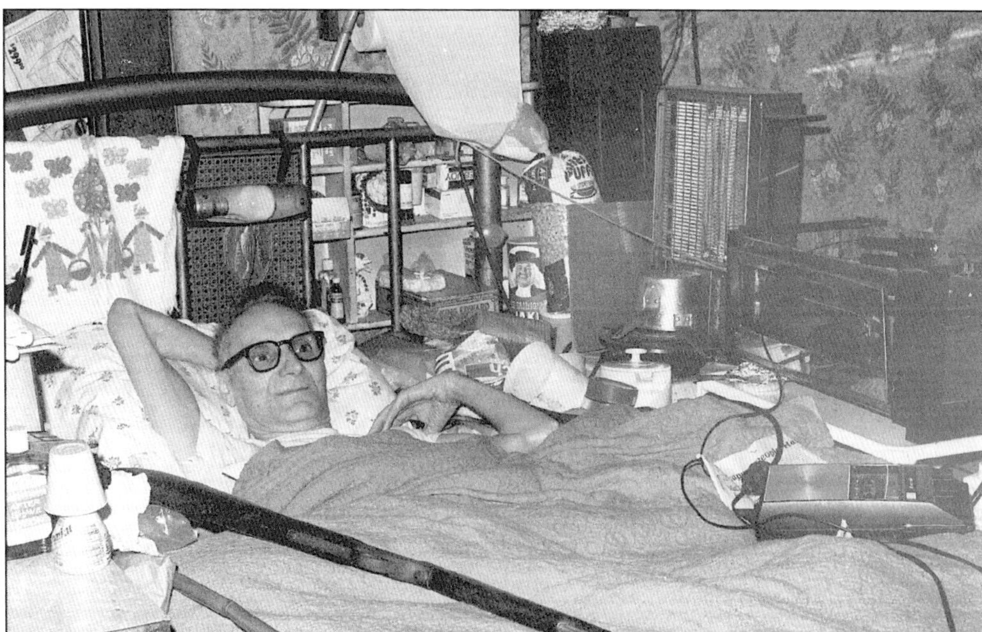

Johnny Richardson of the Cranberry Creek Area. Richardson became ill and bedridden around 16 years of age. Following the death of his mother, he lived alone for 30 years with mechanical conveniences and a daily visit from his sister to meet his needs.

BERNARD WAYNE GOSS. Bernard was active in youth and church activities and was one of the models for the Glendale Springs fresco, *The Last Supper.*

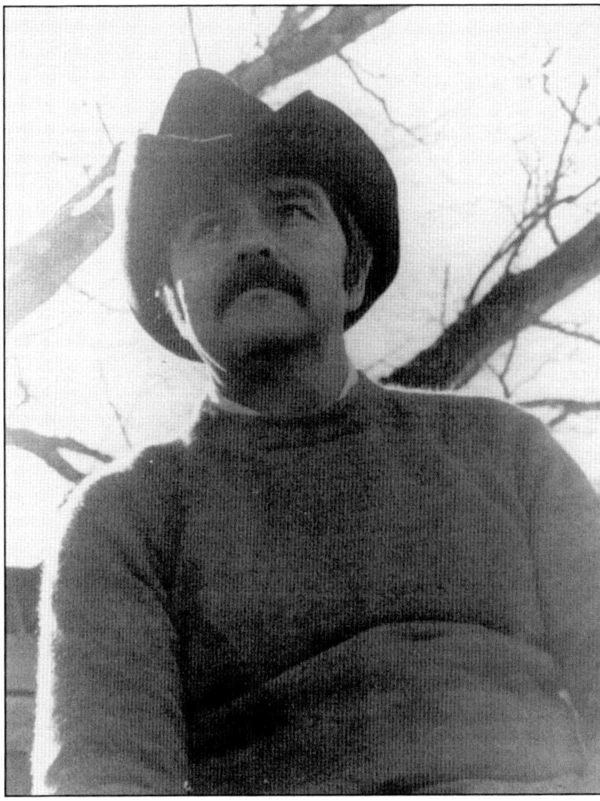

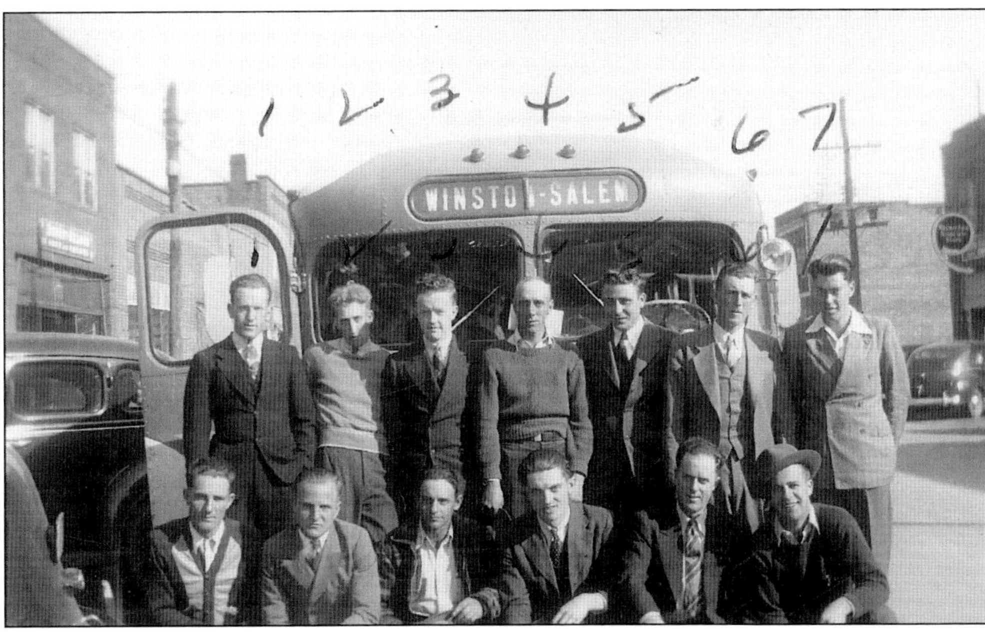

WEST JEFFERSON WORLD WAR II DRAFTEES. Shown here heading off to boot camp, from left to right, are the following: (front row) Raymond L. Barker, Phil Houck, Mack Holman, John C. Nickles, Bertie Lee Bare, and Blank Eller; (back row) Robert Lee Cox, Leonard Bare, Fred Parsons, John W. Farrington, Leonard Shepherd, Preston Pennington, and Jasper Walker.

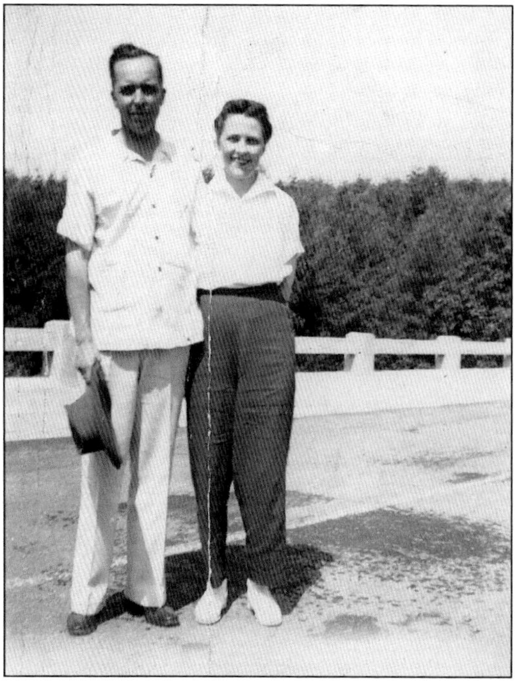

Robert and Chattie Barr. In 1944 many Sunday afternoons were spent motoring the new Blue Ridge Parkway.

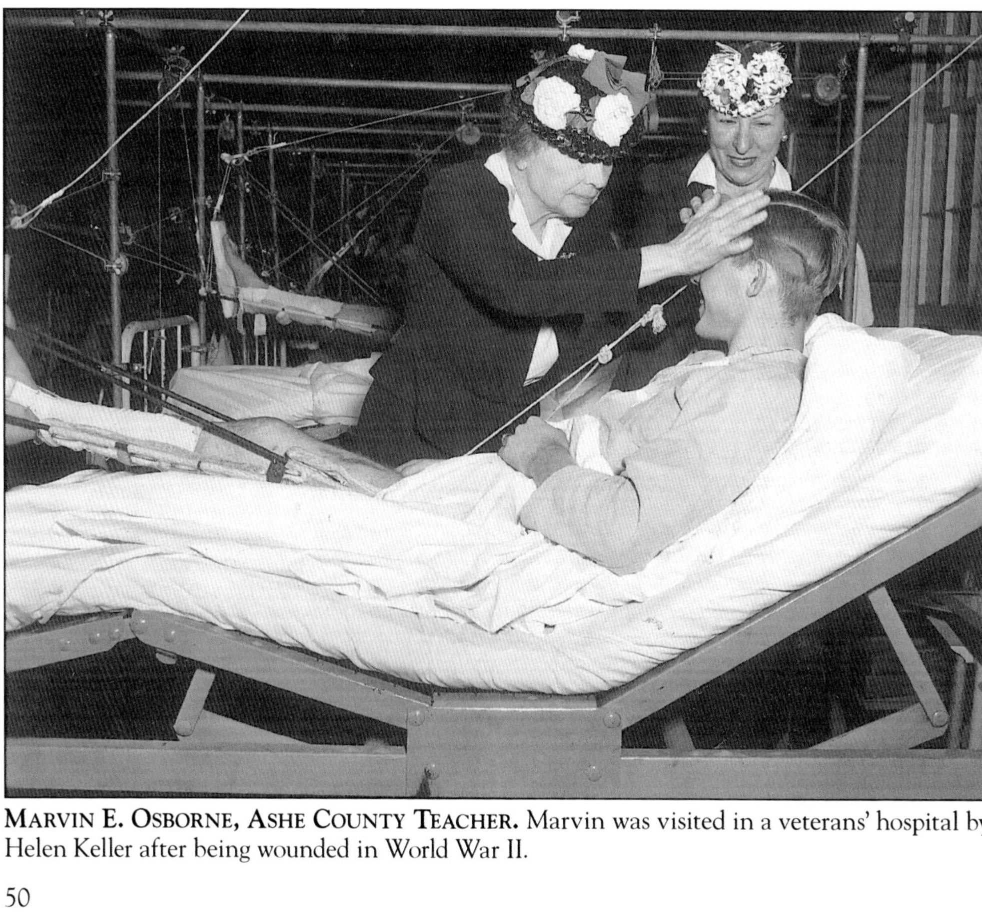

Marvin E. Osborne, Ashe County Teacher. Marvin was visited in a veterans' hospital by Helen Keller after being wounded in World War II.

Three

WORK

Survival. Lifestyle. Work. These three words have always meant the same thing to the people of Ashe County. People cleared the land to plant crops and raise livestock to feed their families. Sometimes chickens or eggs were bartered for coffee, tea, or shoes. Extra crop yield was sold for cash to pay property taxes.

With the arrival of the railroad and the increased demand for building lumber and extract timber, sawmilling became a common occupation. After World War II, Ashe County residents did their part to help build a strong national economy. First, they raised buckwheat, then beans and potatoes, and most recently cattle, chickens, tobacco, and Christmas trees.

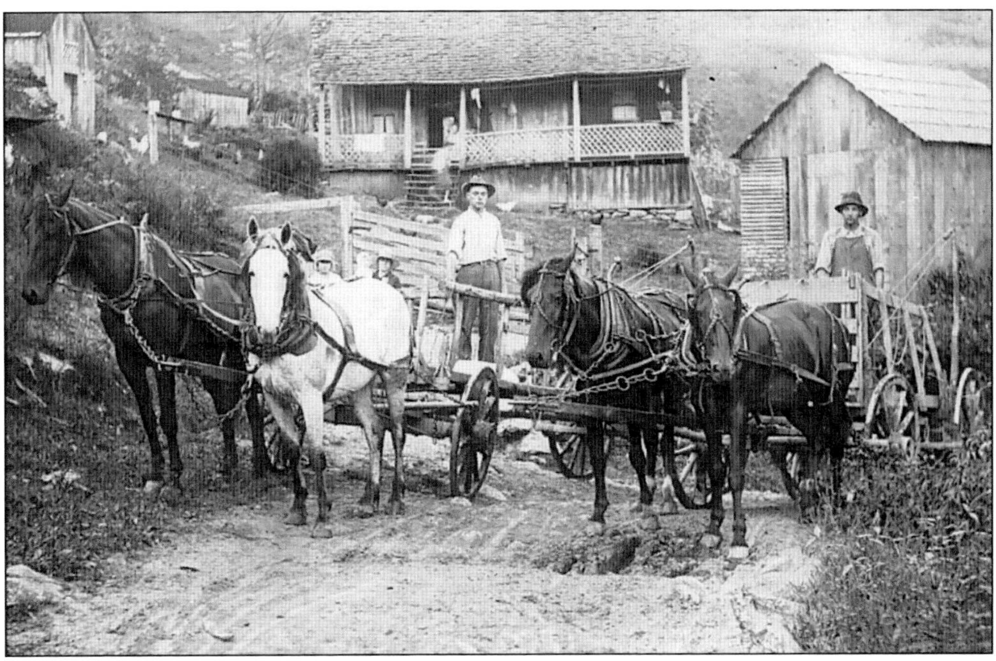

OFF FOR A DAY'S WORK IN THE FIELDS. Victor Clark stands in the middle of this photograph taken in the 1920s.

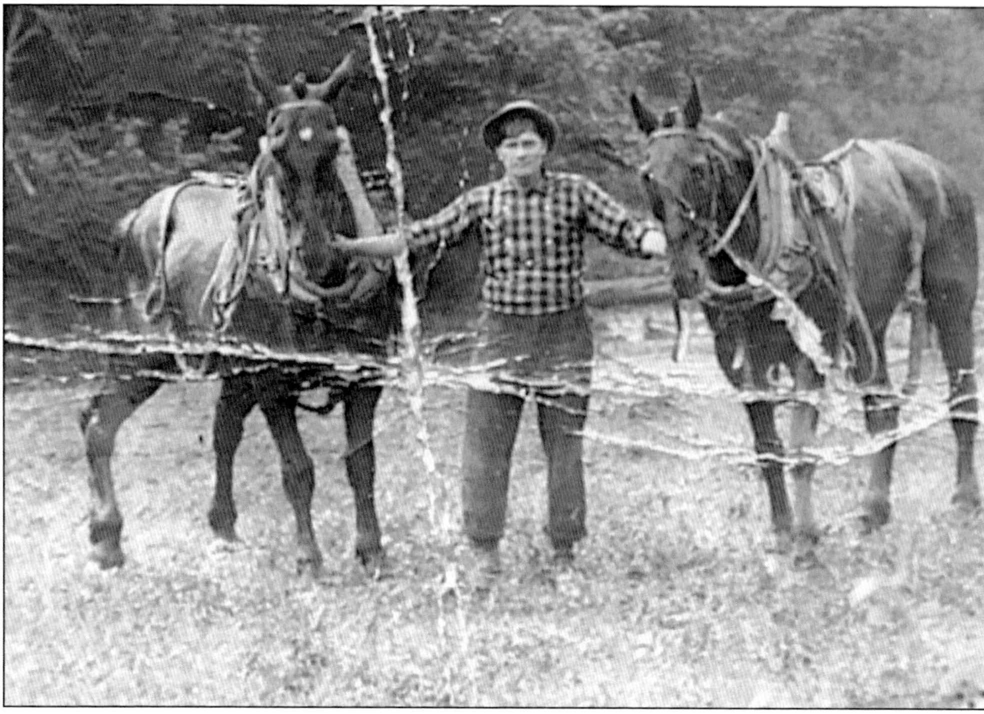

WALTER WYATT WITH HIS HORSES. Walter lived in the Flatwoods area of Ashe County.

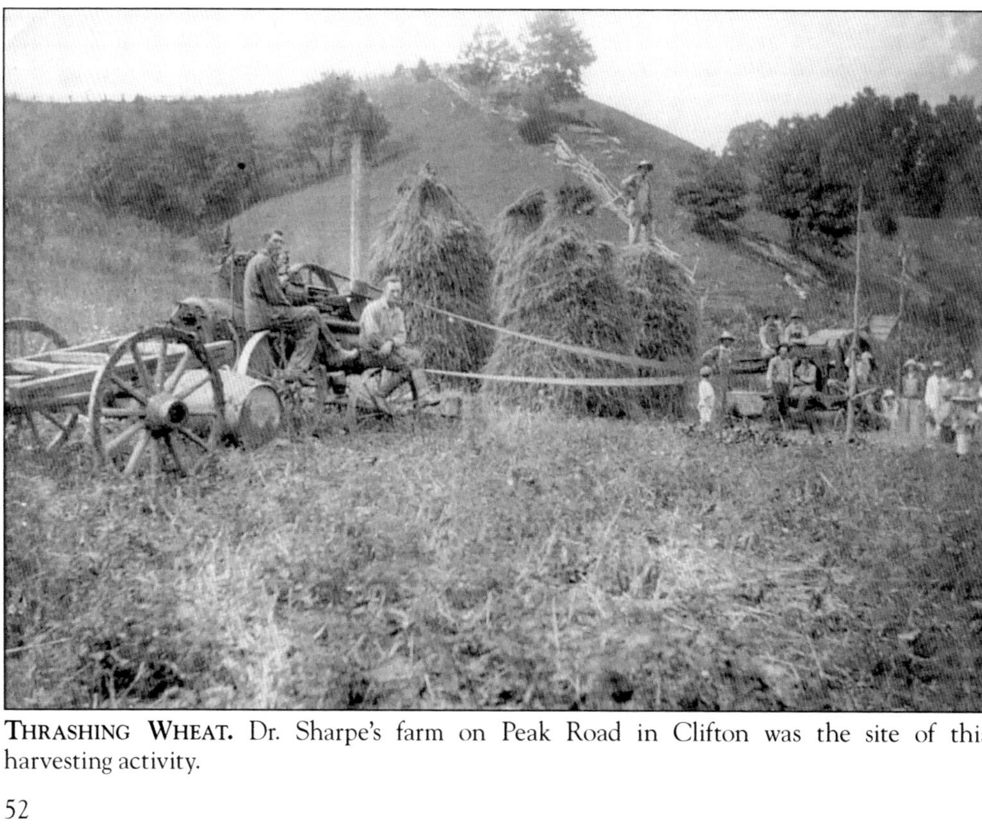

THRASHING WHEAT. Dr. Sharpe's farm on Peak Road in Clifton was the site of this harvesting activity.

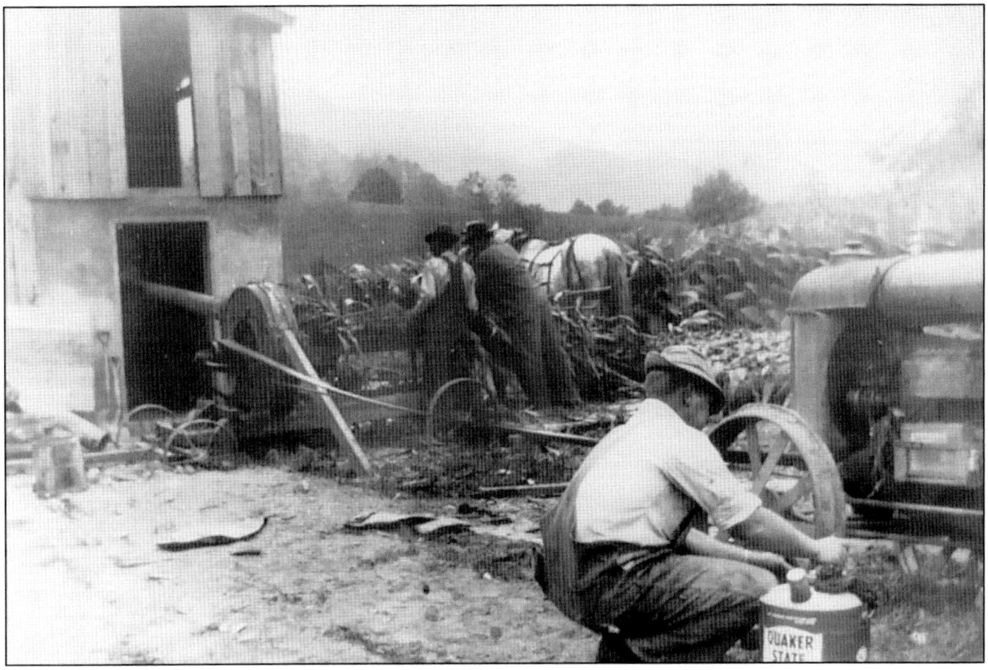

CUTTING SILAGE. Robert Faw of Teaberry Road fuels the generator that runs the cutting machine on the W.O. Ashley farm.

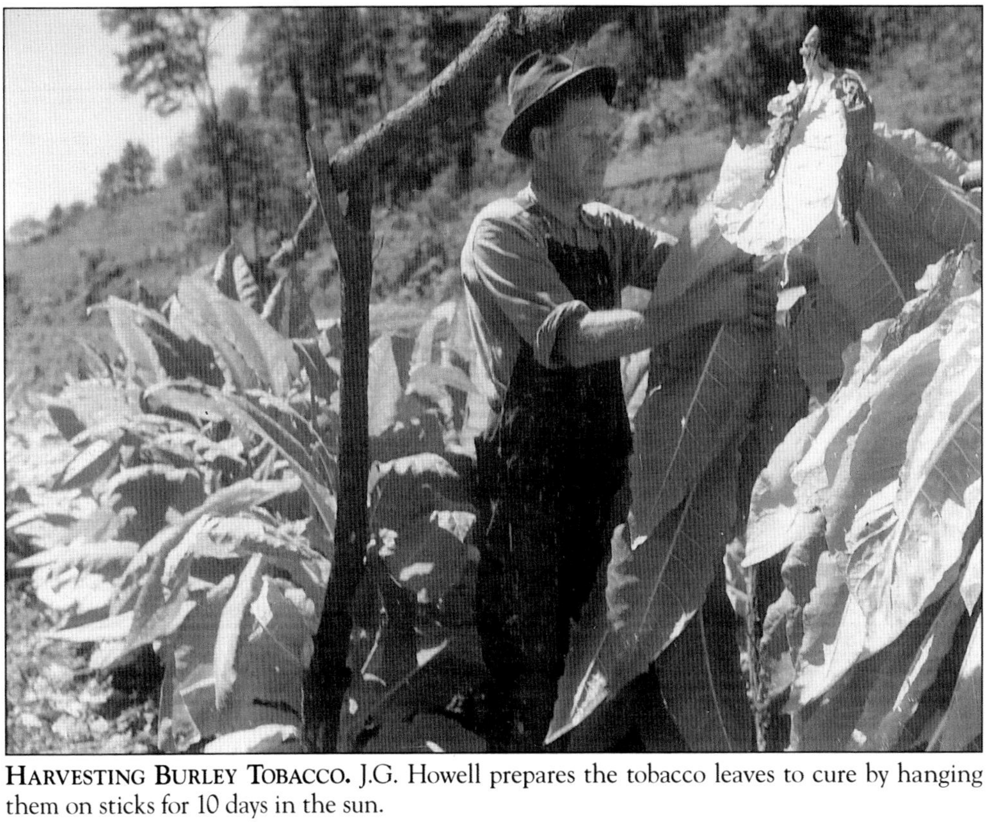

HARVESTING BURLEY TOBACCO. J.G. Howell prepares the tobacco leaves to cure by hanging them on sticks for 10 days in the sun.

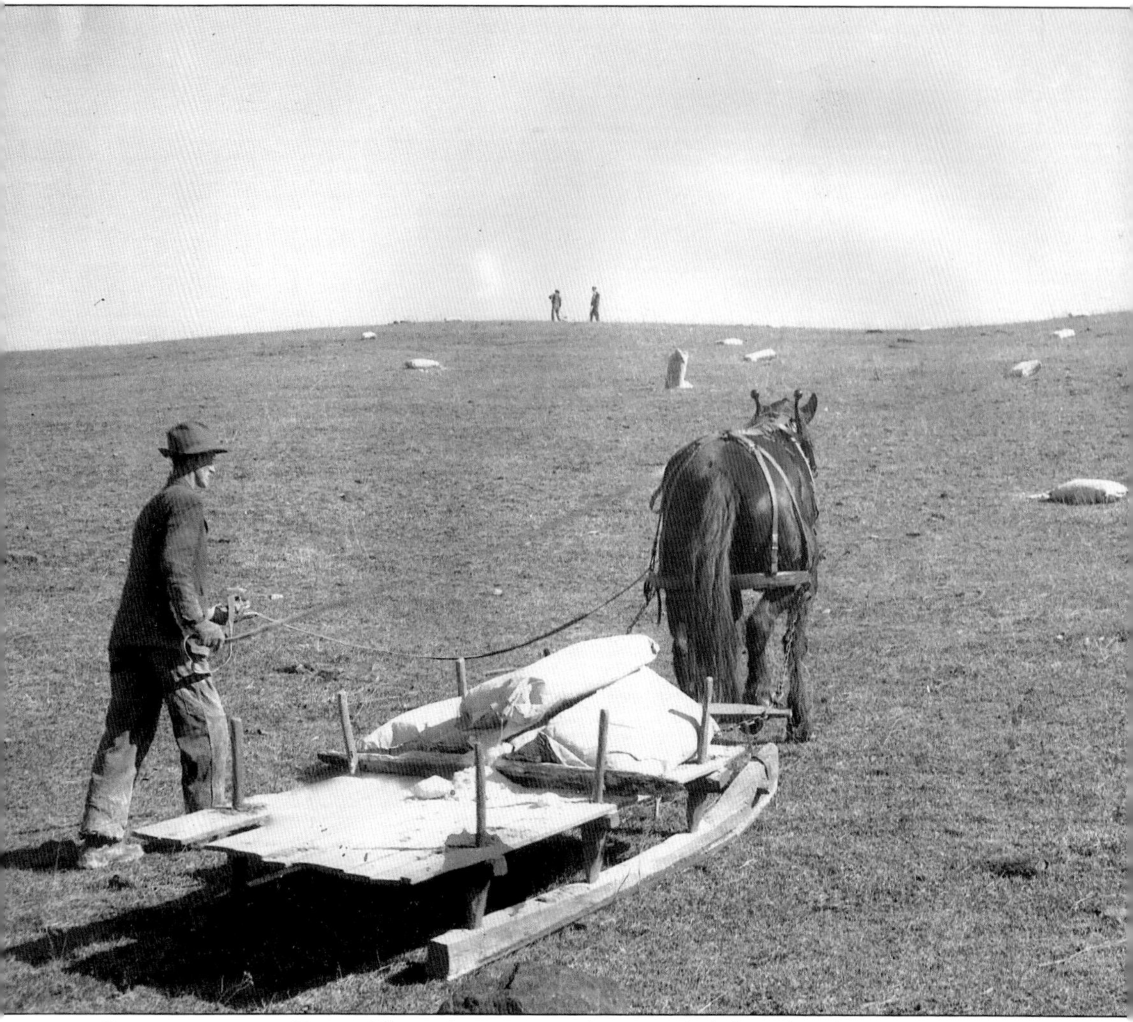

FERTILIZING THE FIELD. These farmers use a horse and sled to distribute fertilizer to various areas of the field.

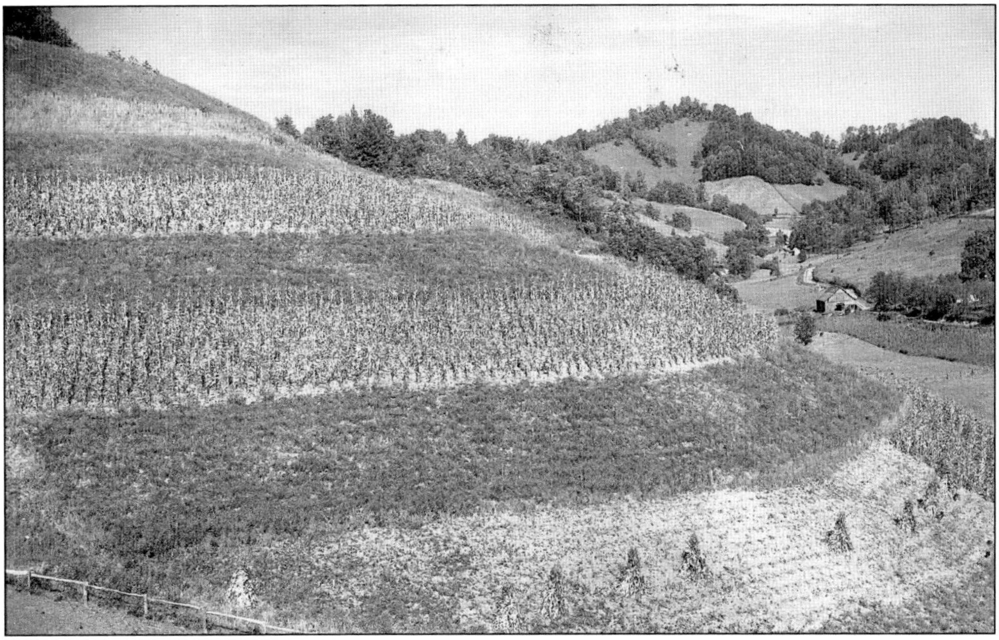

Soil Rotation on the W.W. Miller Farm in Warrensville. This rotation method features strips of soil, pasture grasses, and legumes. No terracing was used on this 55-degree slope.

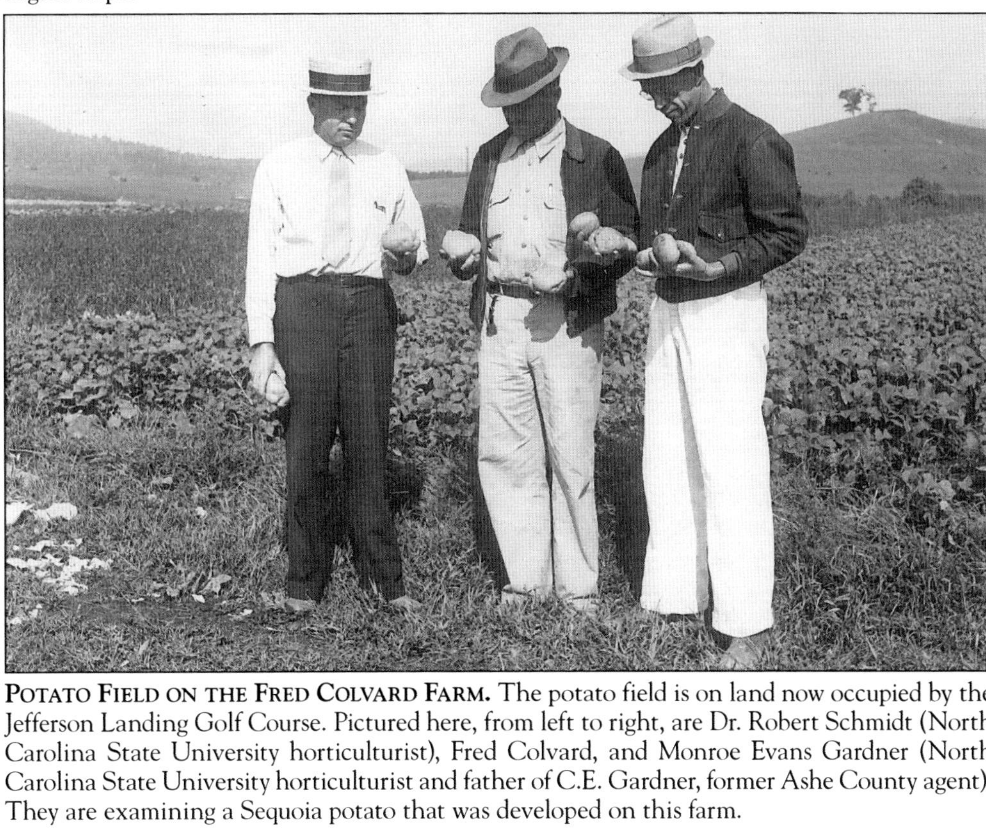

Potato Field on the Fred Colvard Farm. The potato field is on land now occupied by the Jefferson Landing Golf Course. Pictured here, from left to right, are Dr. Robert Schmidt (North Carolina State University horticulturist), Fred Colvard, and Monroe Evans Gardner (North Carolina State University horticulturist and father of C.E. Gardner, former Ashe County agent). They are examining a Sequoia potato that was developed on this farm.

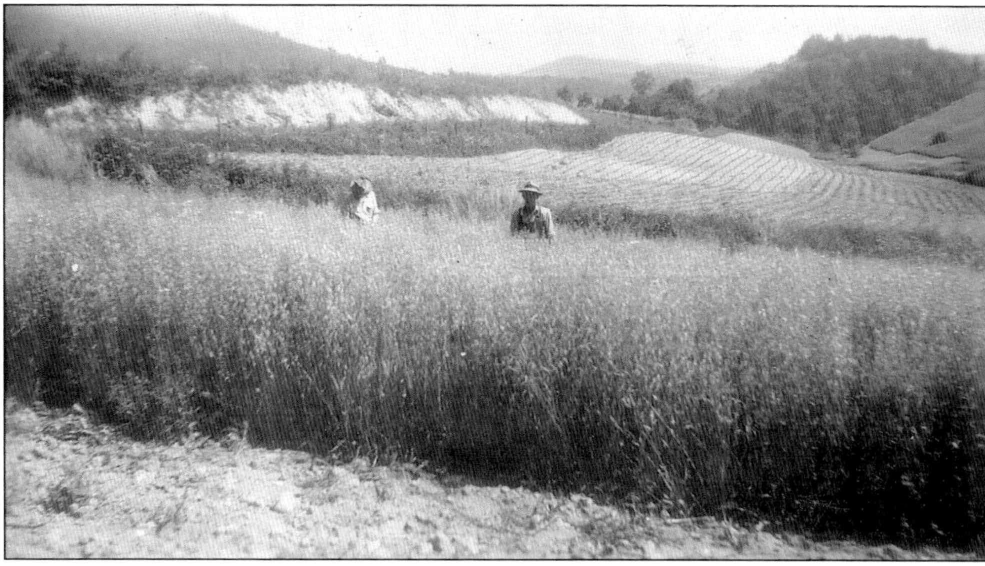

FIELD OF "LETORIA" OATS. This oat field on the G.H. Pugh farm in Crumpler was seeded in 1945.

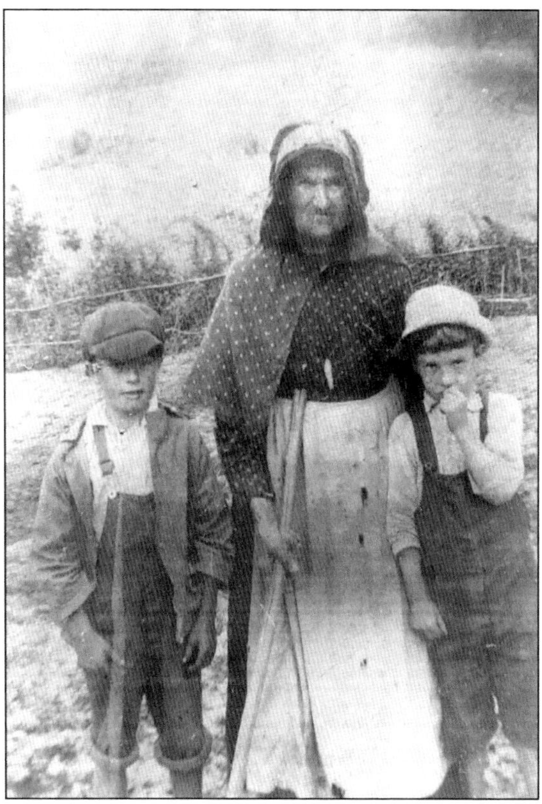

HEADING FOR THE FIELDS. Mary Paisley and her two great-grandsons are ready to hoe a Fairview garden in this 1917 photograph.

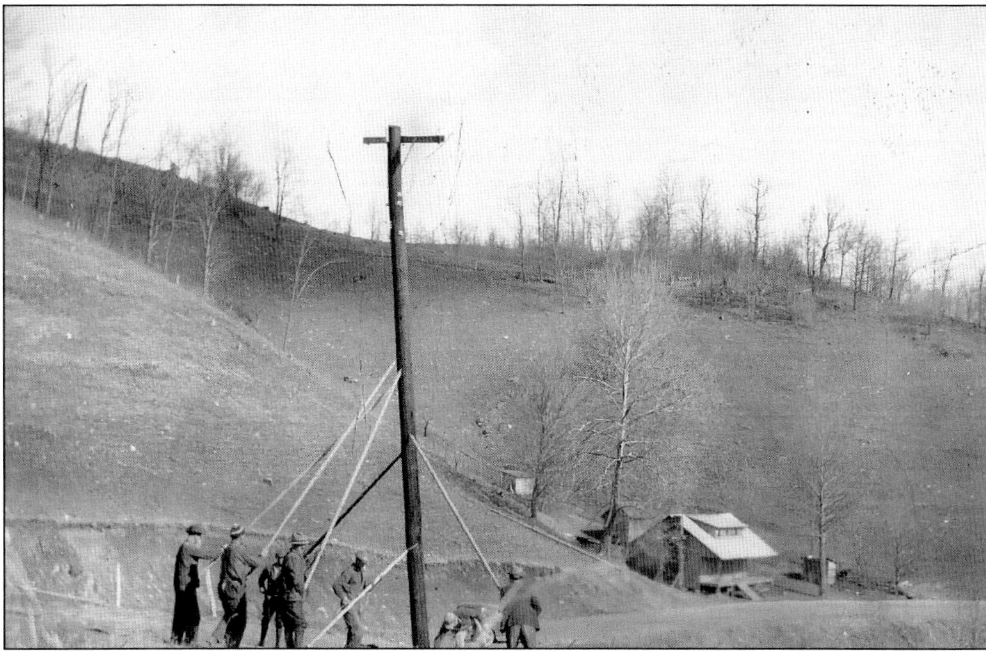

BREMCO Sets a Pole. Blue Ridge Electric Membership Corporation (BREMCO) set its first pole in Ashe County in March 1939. Electricity was made available to the outlying areas of the county in the mid-1940s. Notice the boards used to hold the pole erect in the prepared hole.

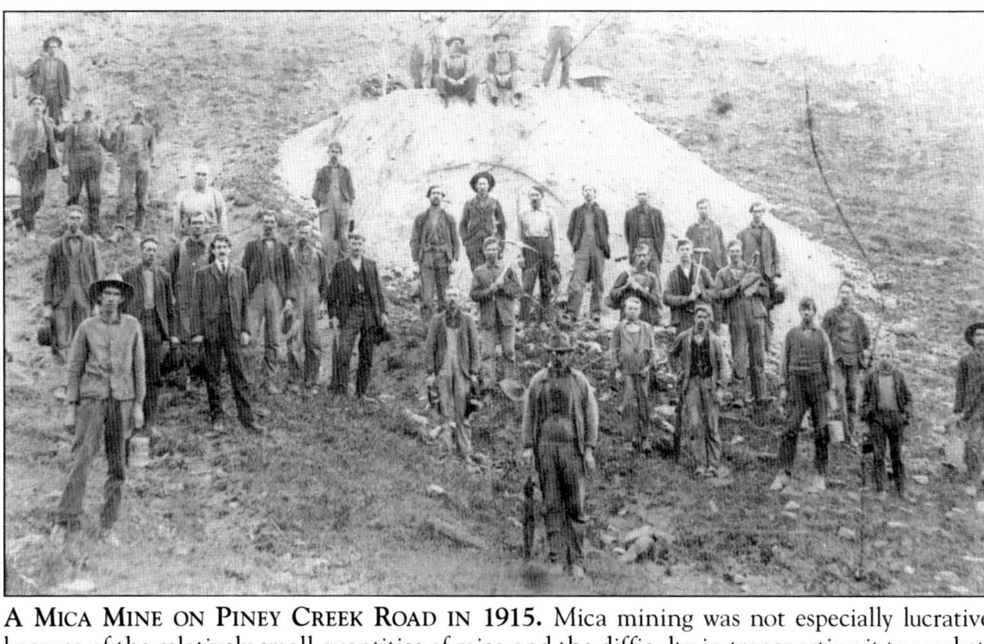

A Mica Mine on Piney Creek Road in 1915. Mica mining was not especially lucrative because of the relatively small quantities of mica and the difficulty in transporting it to market. Robie Stike is standing center front; his son Luther Stike is standing to the left holding a lunch bucket; and Winfield Jones is seen at back left, standing with his legs crossed.

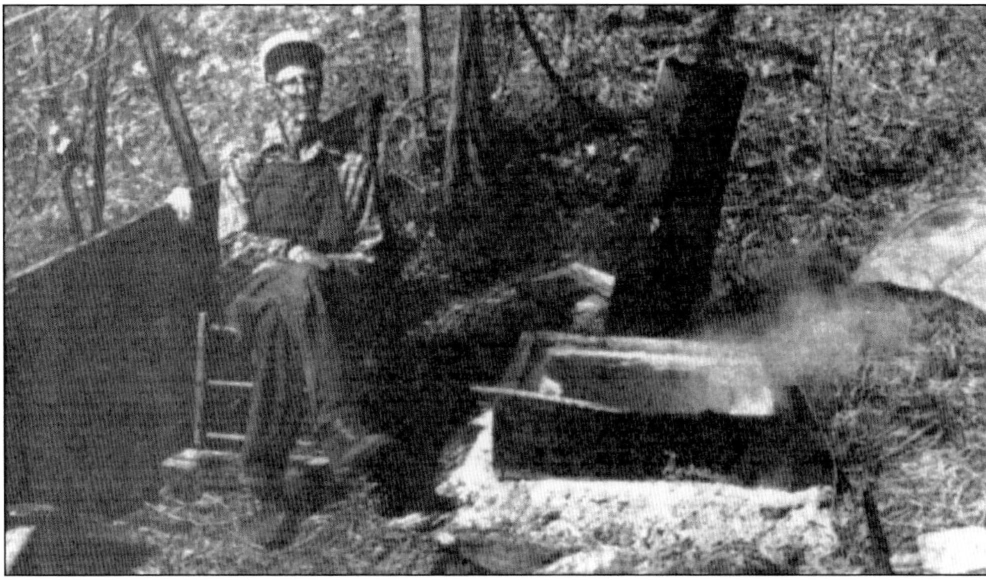

JIM HARLESS MAKING MAPLE SYRUP IN THE BUFFALO COMMUNITY. It typically took 40 gallons of tree sap to make 1 good gallon of syrup.

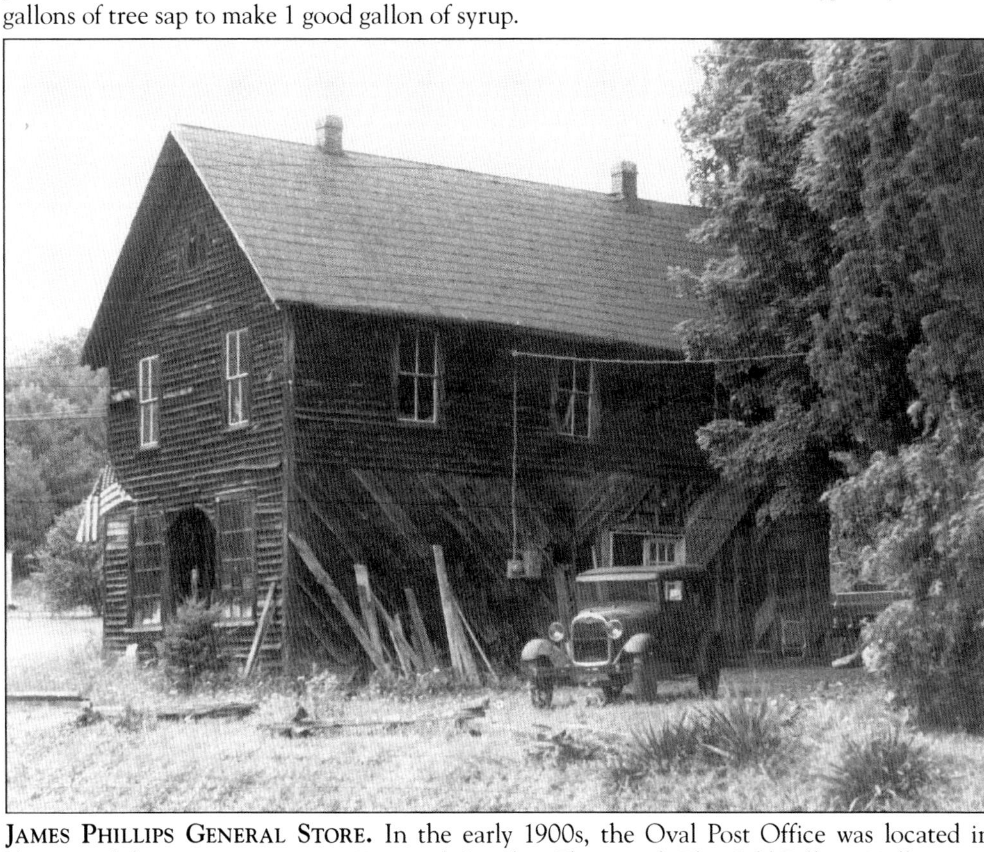

JAMES PHILLIPS GENERAL STORE. In the early 1900s, the Oval Post Office was located in the rear of this store on present Watertank Road in Fleetwood. The Odd Fellows Hall was on the second floor, and Mount Olive Baptist Church was organized here prior to constructing a church building.

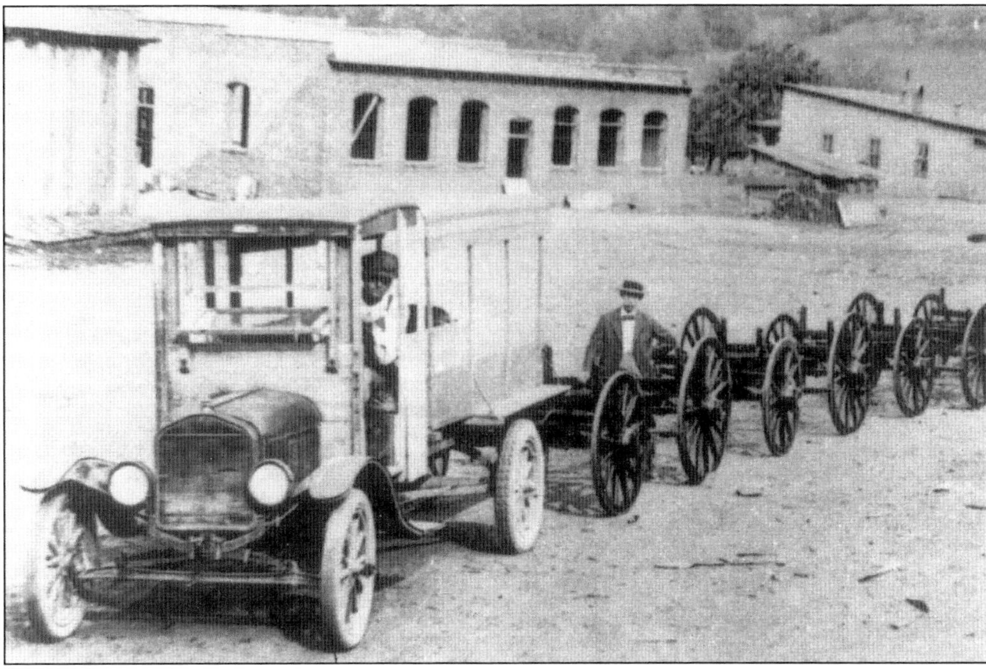

H.H. GRIGGS DELIVERS THE MAIL. The Scarborough Mail Service operated between Jefferson and West Jefferson.

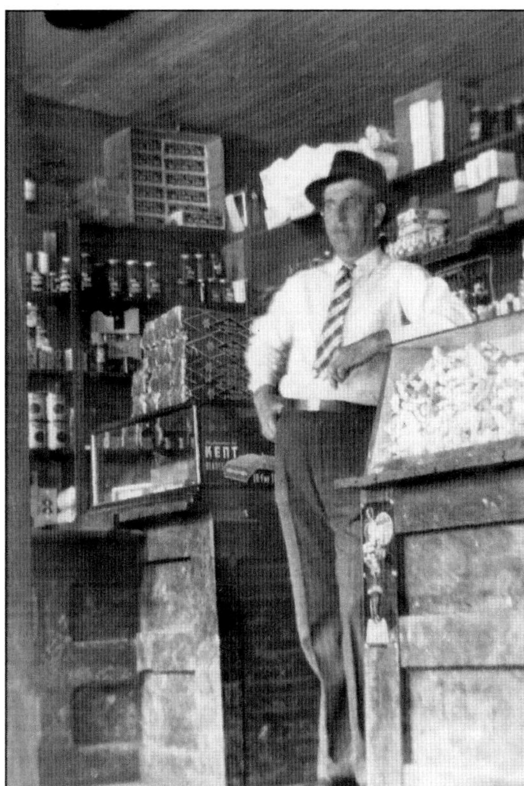

CLAUDE WILCOX IN HIS COUNTRY STORE. This store, operated by Wilcox and his father before him, occupied the same spot for 46 years. The site is at the top of Laurel Knob on Mill Creek Road.

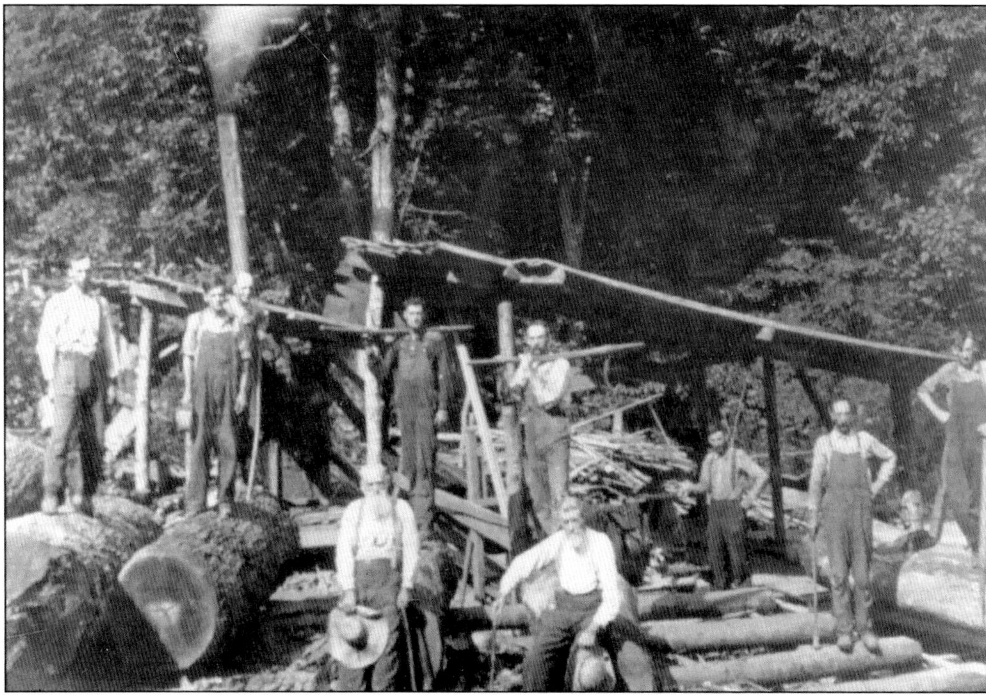

SAWMILL IN OPERATION. This 1920 photograph pictures a bearded Thomas Jefferson Baldwin at center front.

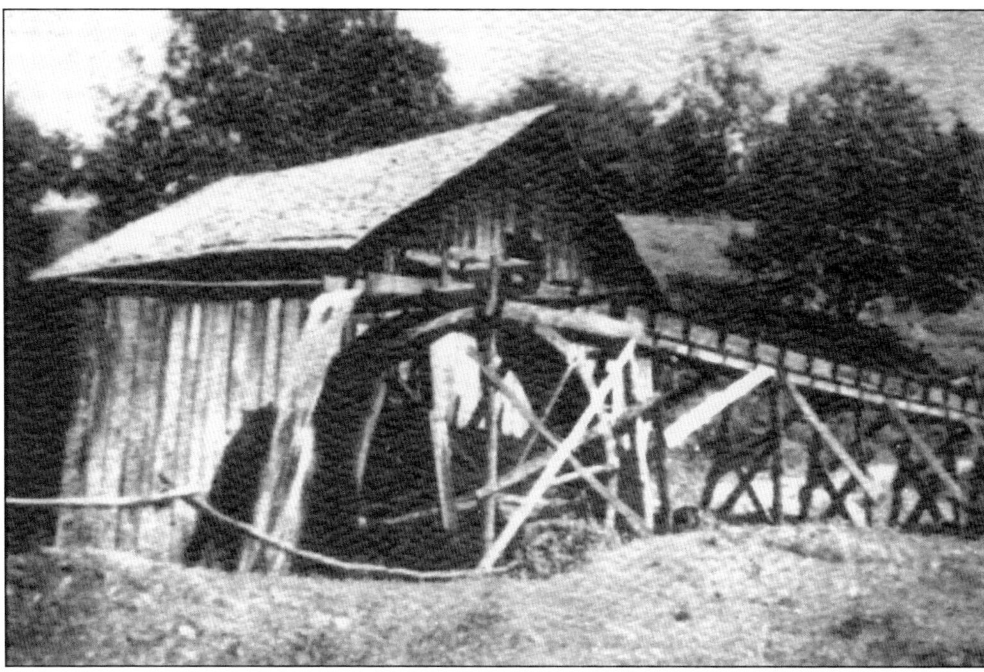

COMMUNITY MILL IN IDLEWILD. The mill, run by Casey Jones and several other members of the community, was located near an intersection of Phillips Gap Road. The millpond washed away in the 1940 flood.

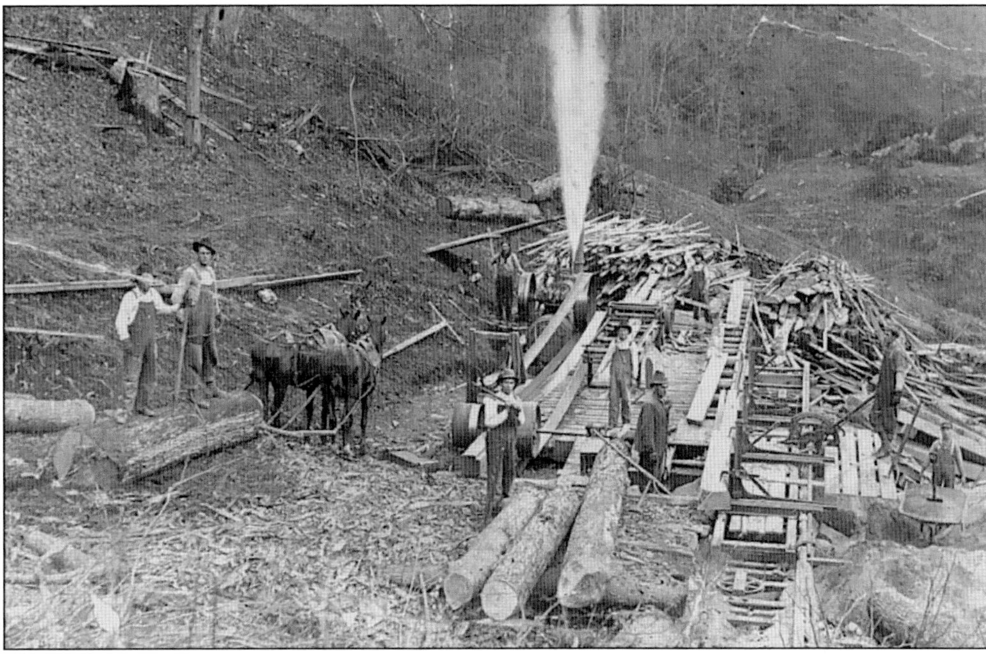

SAWMILL AT LITTLE HORSE CREEK. This 1920s photograph pictures the sawmill owned by Ambrose Clark, former Ashe County sheriff.

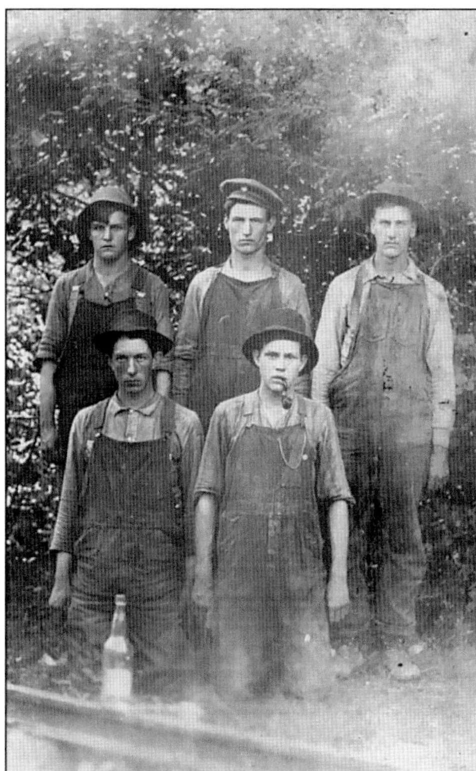

RELAXING AT MELLICOO. These workers at the lumbering spur take a break from cutting virgin timber in the Flatwoods area.

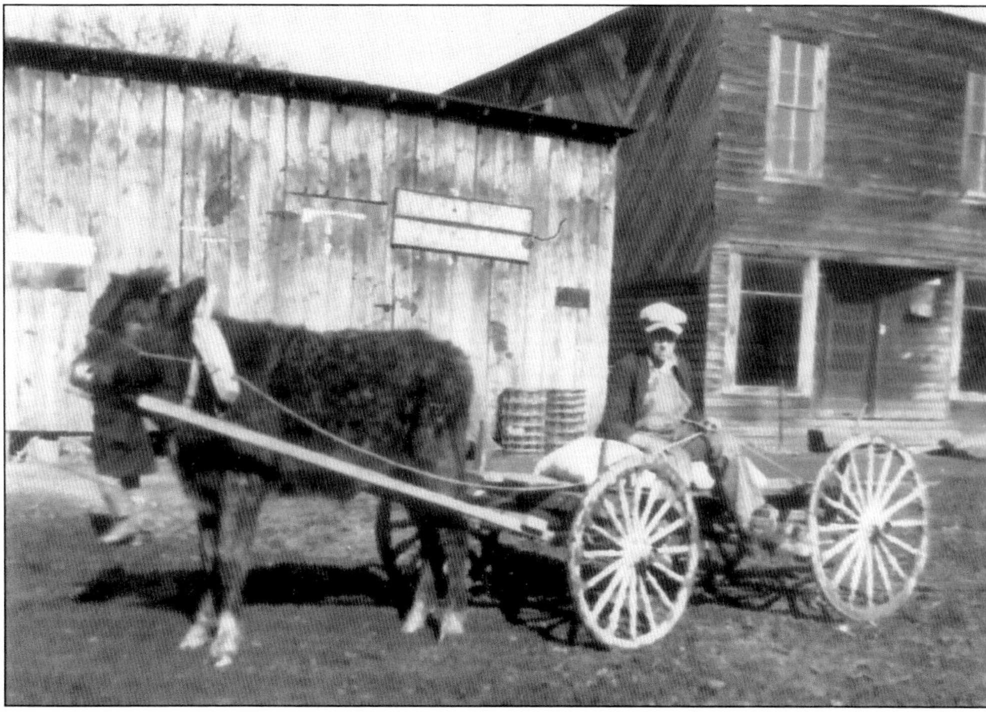

JOE LAWRENCE IN FRONT OF HIS STORE. This Fleetwood store later burned.

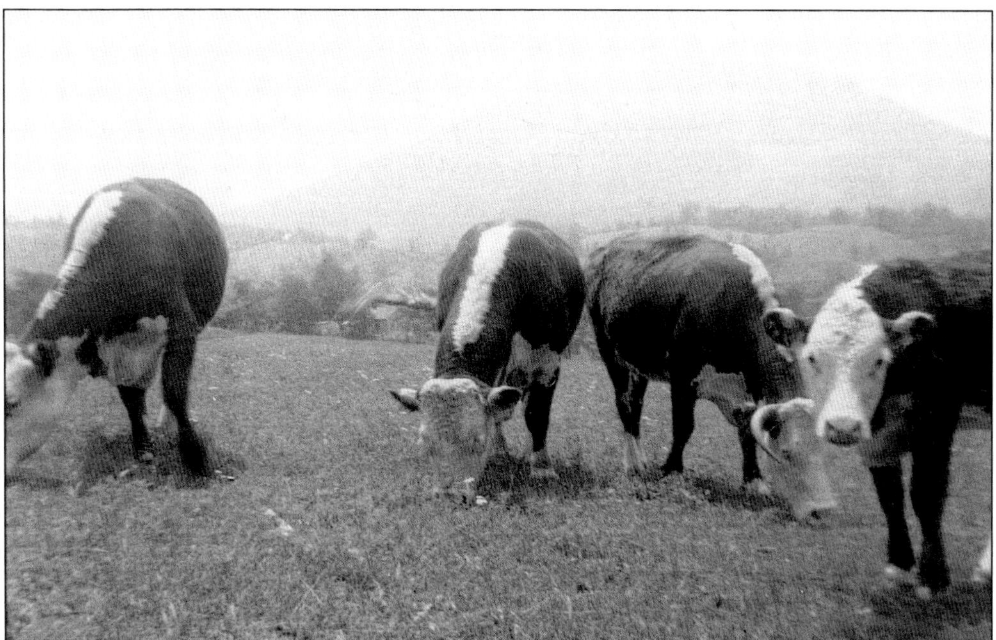

CATTLE GRAZE WITH MOUNT JEFFERSON IN THE BACKGROUND. Cattle have been important to Ashe County in both the dairy and beef industries.

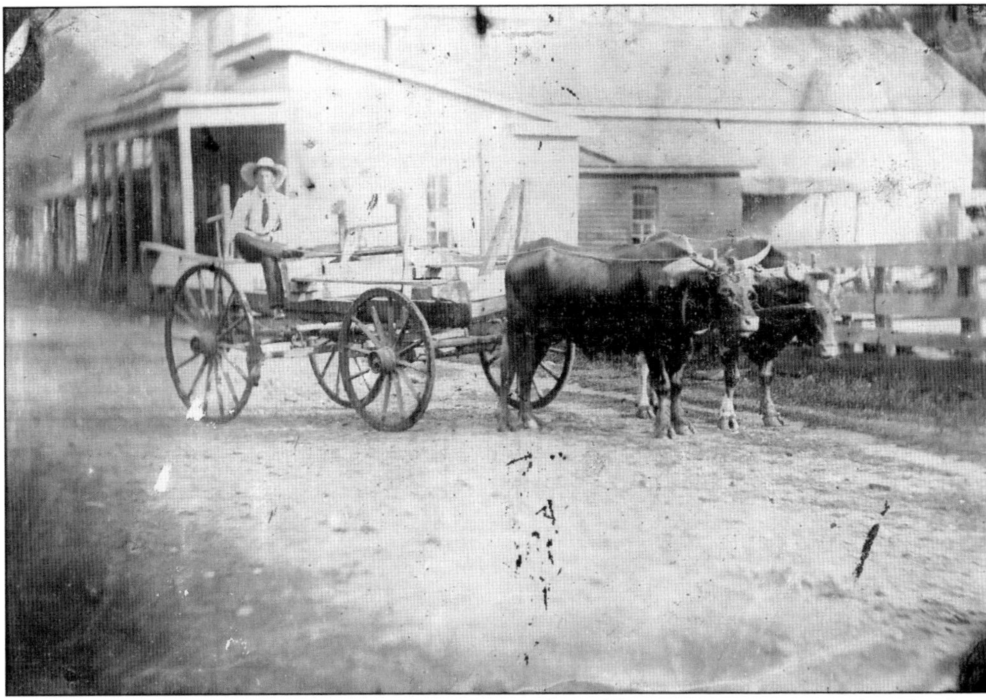

The Worth Store in Creston. Walter H. Worth and his ox cart are pictured in this late-1800s photograph. The cart was used to transport merchandise from the Piedmont to Creston.

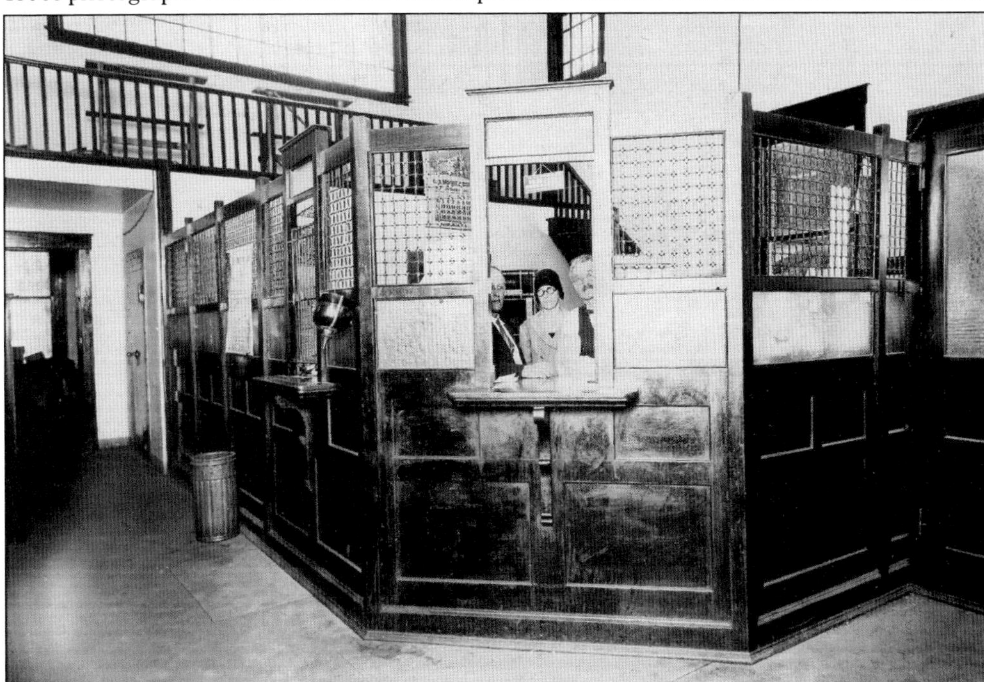

Interior of Bank of Ashe. Behind the teller's window in this 1925 photograph, from left to right, are Walter H. Worth (founder and first cashier), Hattie Ham, and Ed Johnson (both employees).

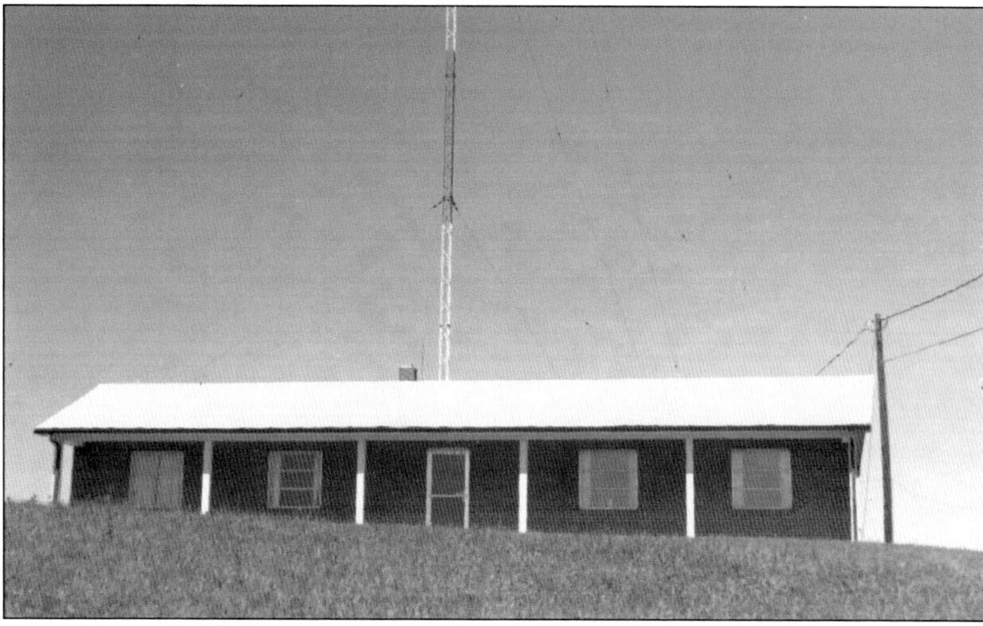

RADIO STATION WKSK. Mr. and Mrs. Jimmy Childress founded the radio station on May 27, 1959. It has been owned by Mr. and Mrs. Jan Caddell since the mid-1960s, when this photograph was taken of the new building.

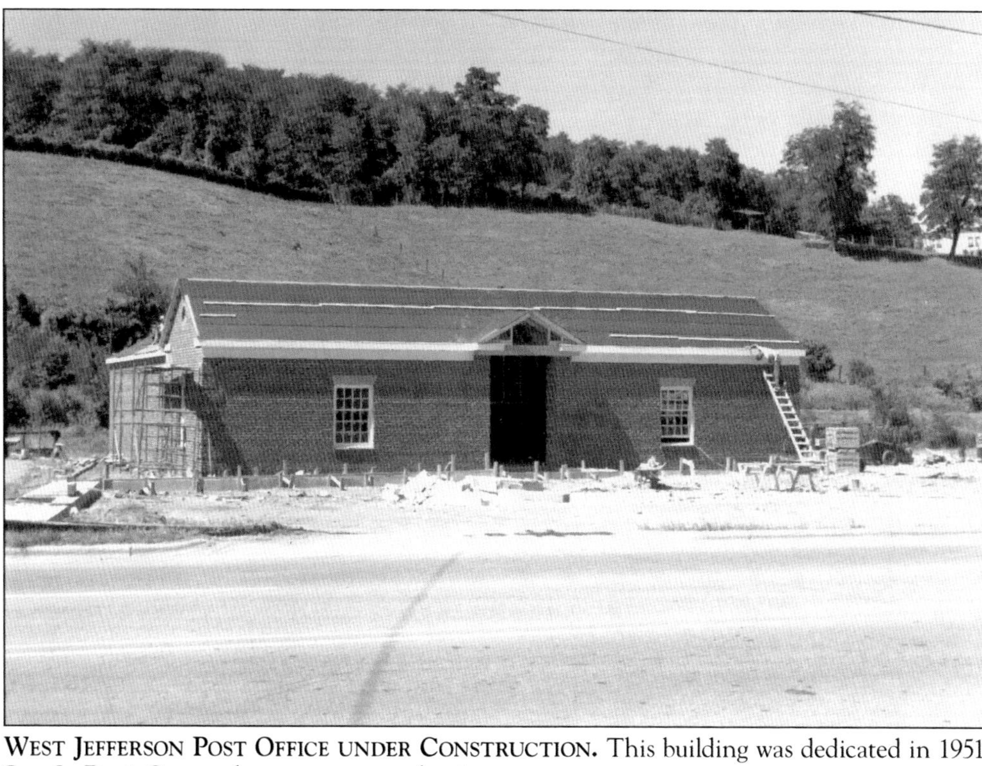

WEST JEFFERSON POST OFFICE UNDER CONSTRUCTION. This building was dedicated in 1951. Sam L. Davis Sr. was the postmaster at the time.

Four

Business and Commerce

Since its earliest days, citizens of Ashe County traded goods amongst themselves. Because of the limited access to surrounding communities, local stores were necessary and many businesses opened to respond to people's needs. Most goods were either homemade or homegrown, and bartering was commonplace.

When the railroad came into the county in 1914, a link to the outside world and manufactured goods was established. Towns such as Todd, West Jefferson, and Lansing evolved and thrived as a result of rail access. Transport by train opened the county to other parts of the country, and industries such as timbering, textiles, furniture, and electronics flourished throughout the region.

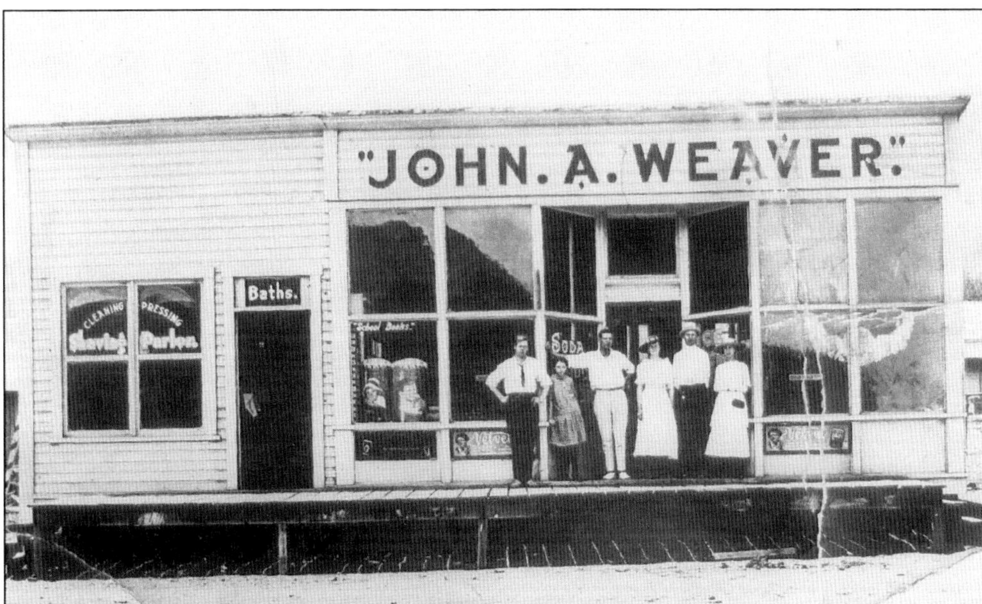

The John Weaver Store in West Jefferson. The Weaver store stands at the site now occupied by the Lenore Depree Gallery. John Weaver is leaning against the doorframe in this 1913 photograph.

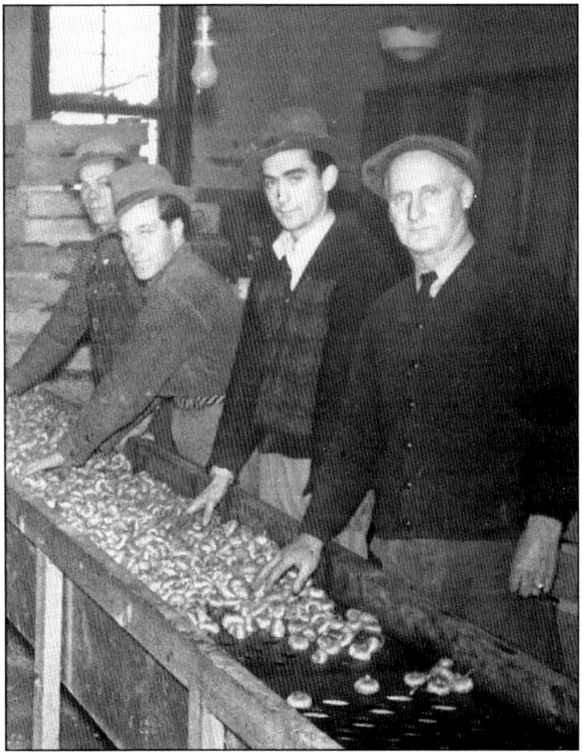

SORTING GLADIOLI BULBS. For several years around 1939, gladioli bulbs were grown on a 10-acre field owned by Lloyd Witherspoon on the site of the new consolidated high school. Bulbs were sold to the Vaughn Seed Company. Pictured here, from left to right, are Jim Colvard, Pell Bowers, John Witherspoon, and Lloyd Witherspoon.

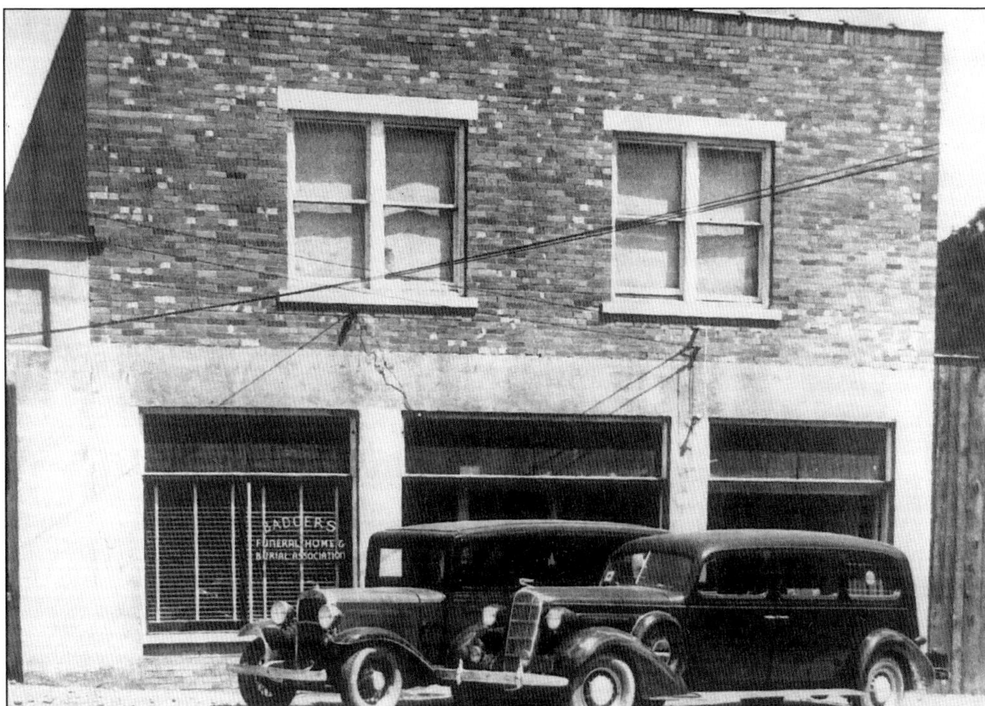

ORIGINAL BADGER FUNERAL HOME. The funeral home stands on the site now occupied by the Dollar Tire Store in West Jefferson.

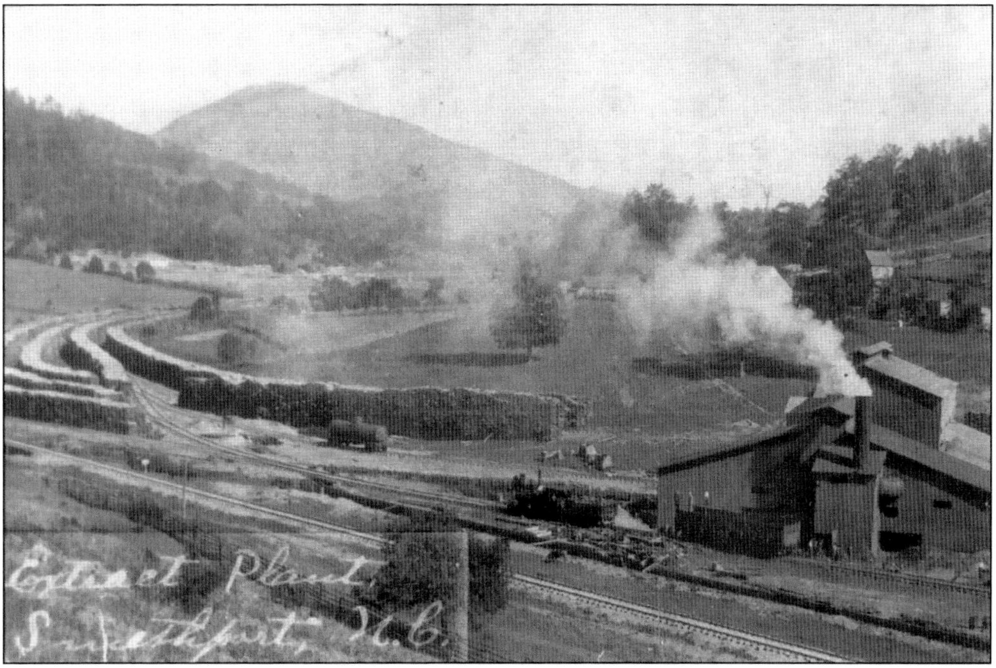

EXTRACT PLANT IN SMETHPORT. The plant came to Ashe County from Smethport, Pennsylvania, in 1914 to extract acid from the bark of the chestnut tree, an abundant crop at the time. The acid was used in the tanning industry, and at the height of the operation, the industry was a major employer. Around 1920, the plant was dismantled and moved to Helen, Georgia.

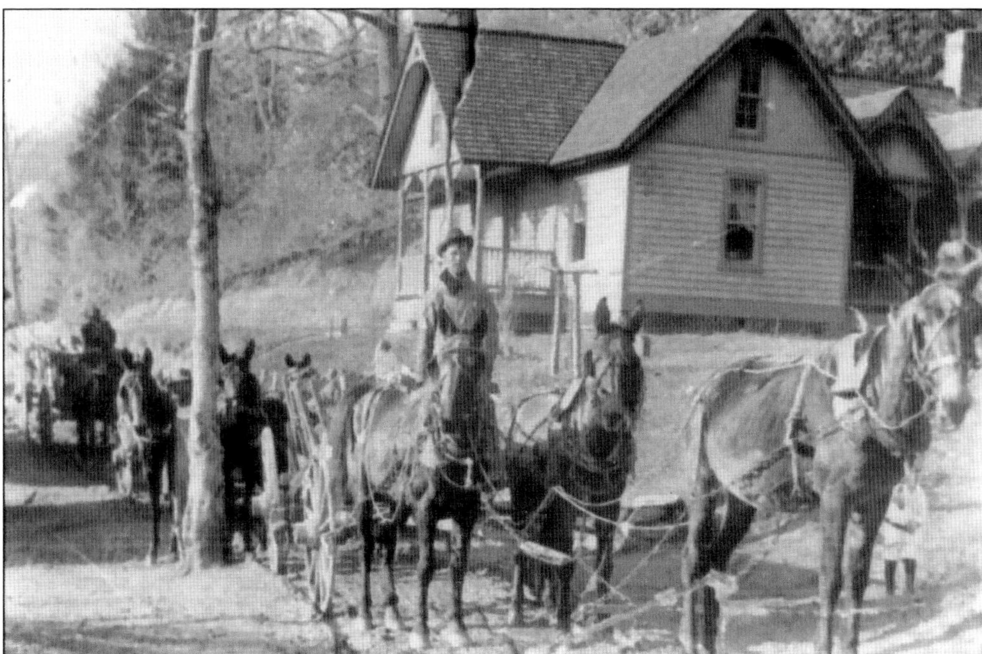

WOOD FOR THE EXTRACT PLANT. Joe Lawrence and his mules pulled wood from the Fleetwood area. Note the use of a three-mule team instead of a more conventional two- or four-mule team.

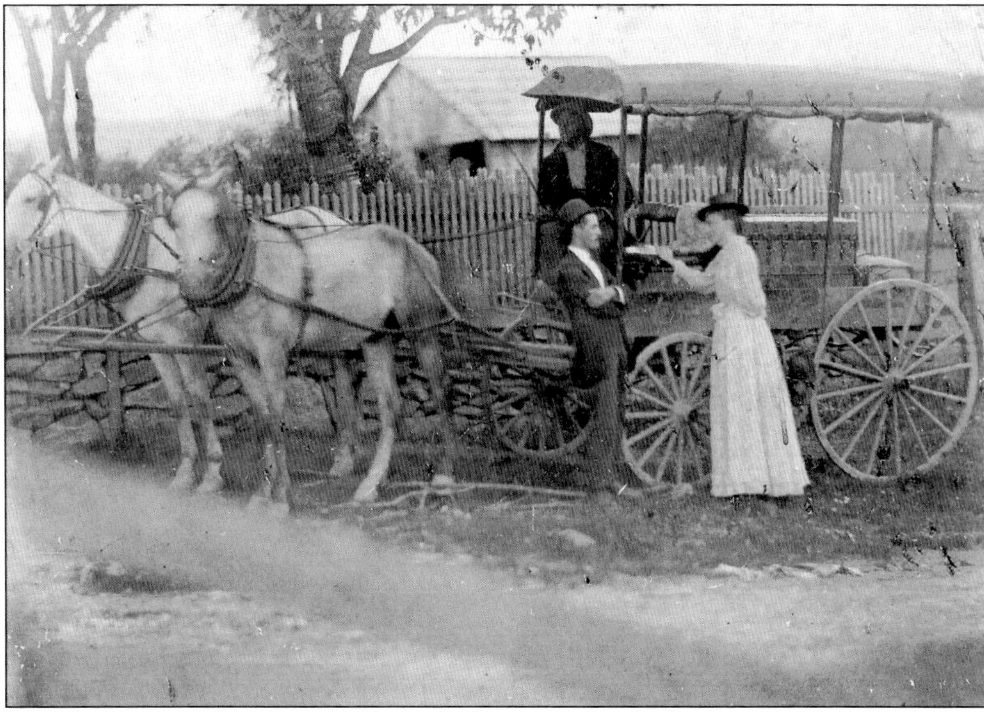

WAGON FACTORY. In the early 1900s, Walter H. Worth owned and operated this Creston wagon factory.

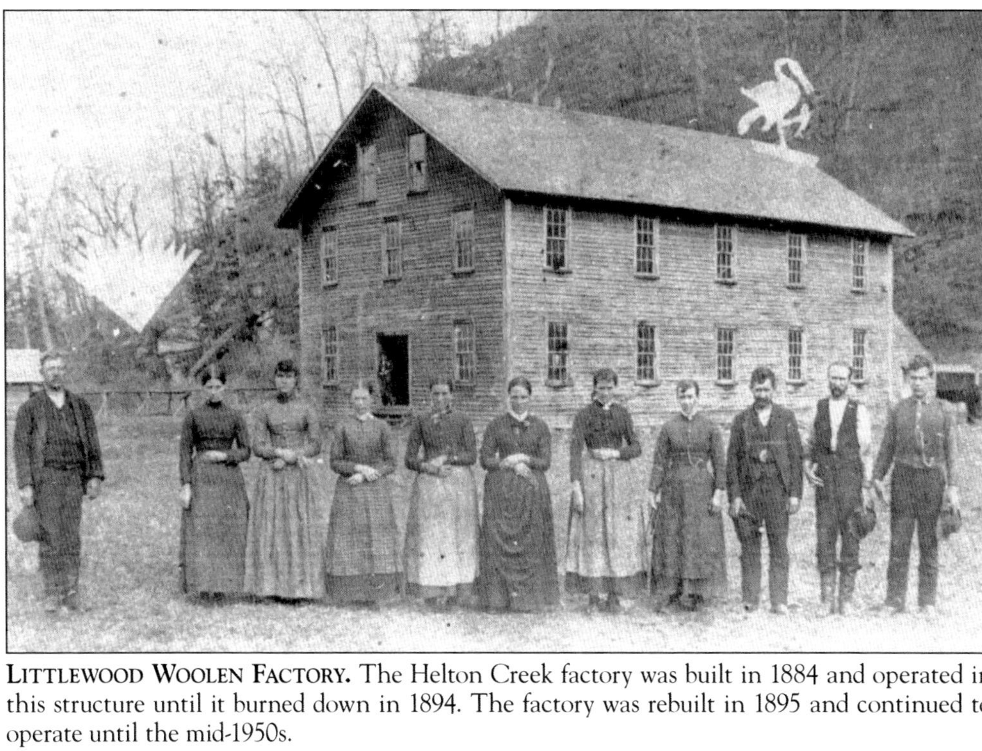

LITTLEWOOD WOOLEN FACTORY. The Helton Creek factory was built in 1884 and operated in this structure until it burned down in 1894. The factory was rebuilt in 1895 and continued to operate until the mid-1950s.

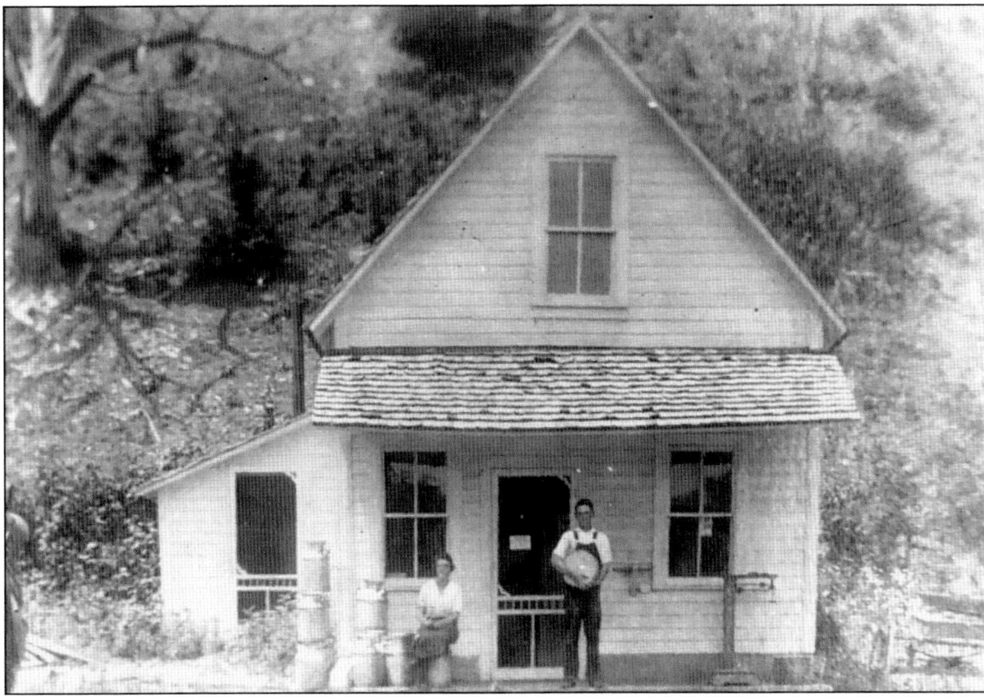

GENERAL STORE. The milk cans piled in front suggest that this store was an outlet for a local dairy farm.

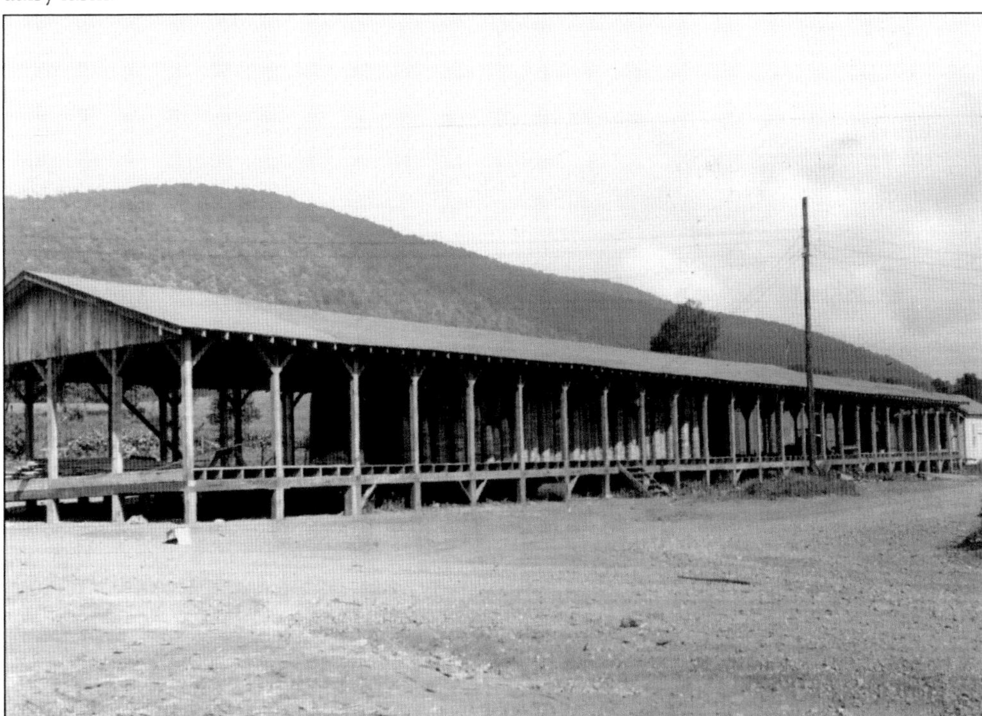

BEAN MARKET IN SMETHPORT. In the 1940s, beans grown in Ashe County were taken to this open-air facility for sorting and packing.

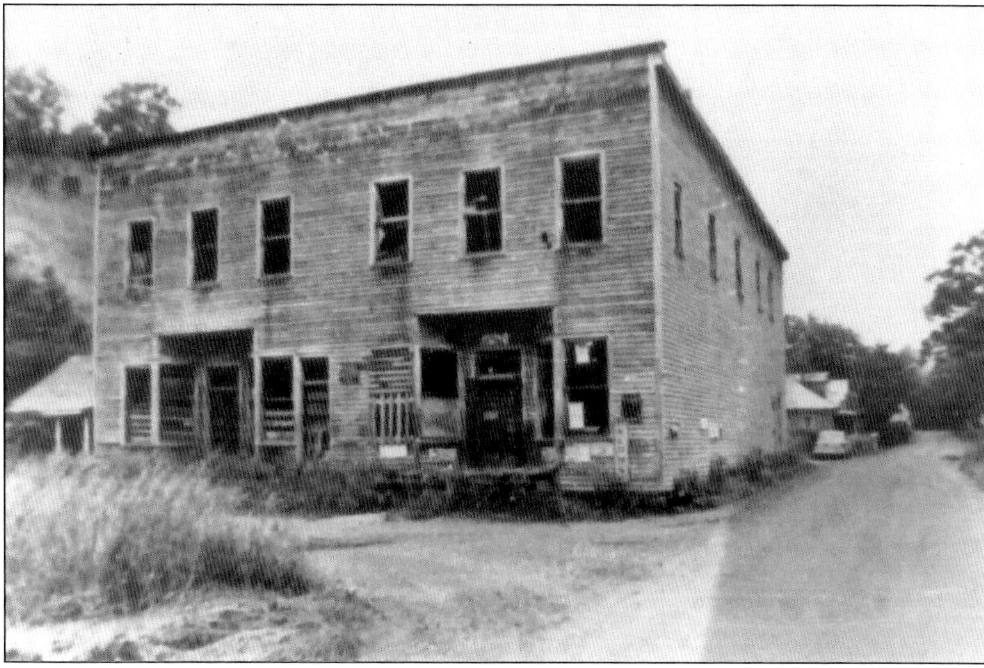

OLD TUCKERDALE HOTEL. A store operated on the first floor, which included the office of Dr. Joe Tucker. Hotel rooms were on the second floor. The hotel was torn down in the early 1940s.

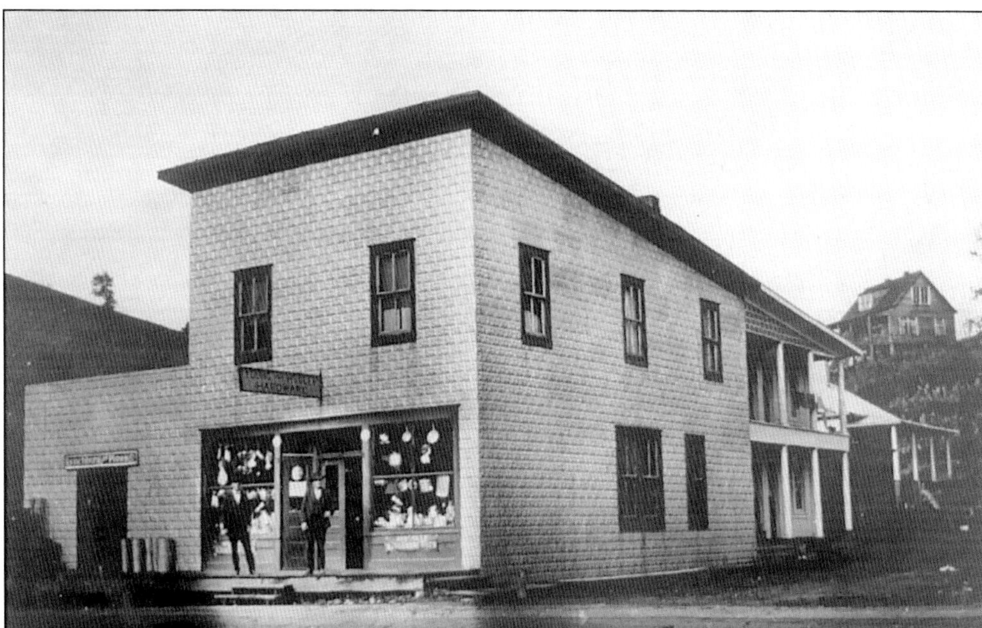

YOUNG AND HUDLER HARDWARE STORE IN LANSING. The new Lansing Bank now occupies this site.

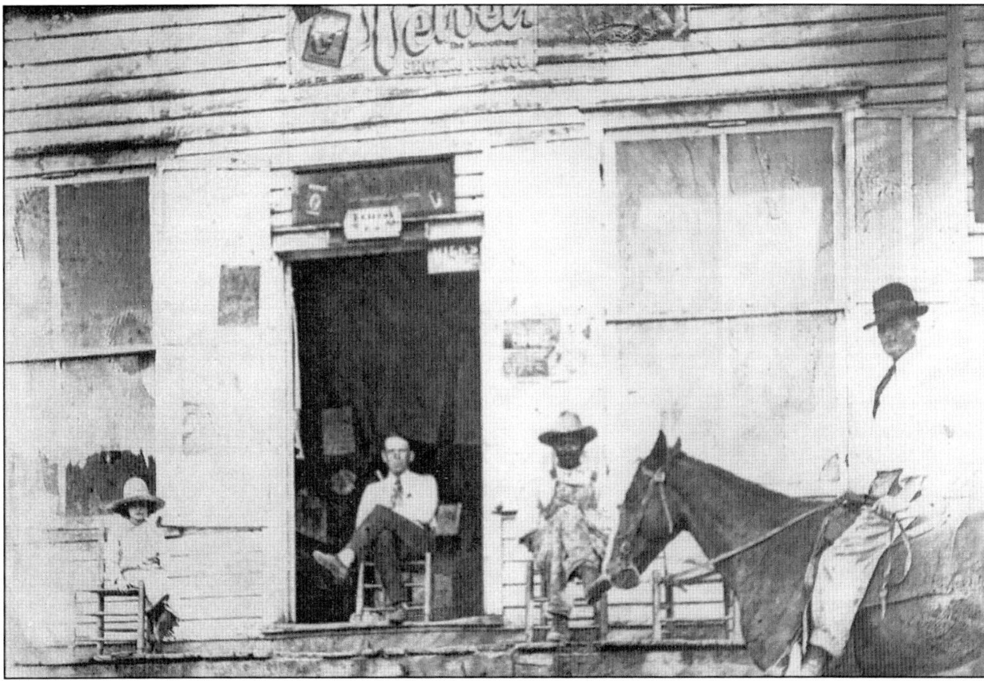

General Store in the Clifton Area (c. 1911). Pictured here, from left to right, are Ruth Jones, Carl Eastridge, Bill Horton, and unidentified.

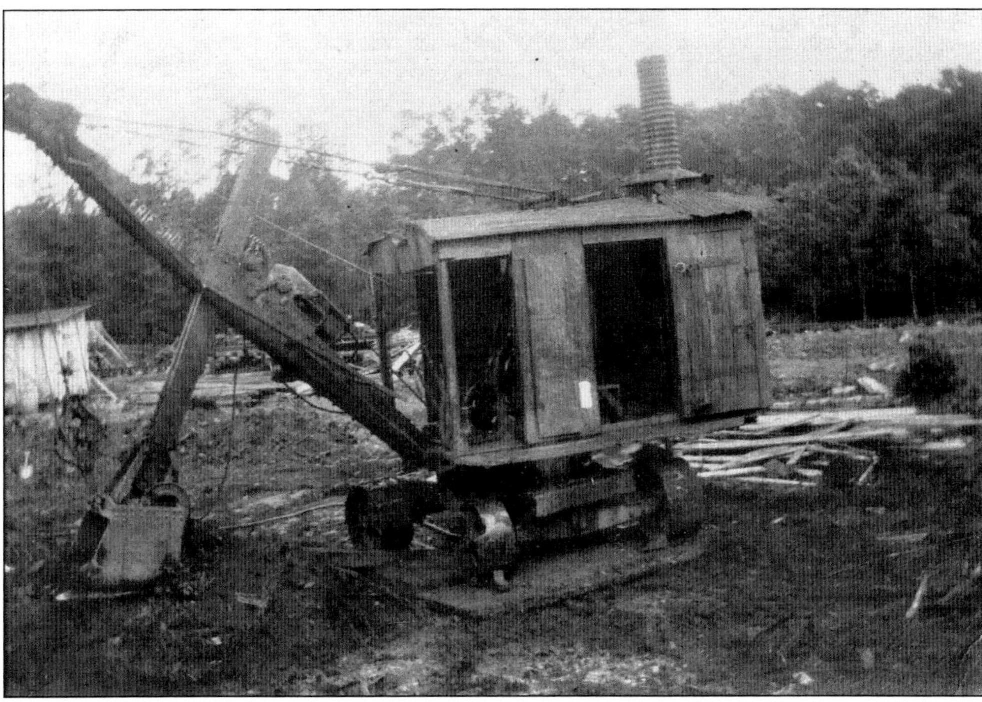

Soapstone Factory in Beaver Creek. Soapstone was quarried from land near Black Bear Inn Road. American Indians had known of this resource for centuries and used soapstone to create bowls and other useful utensils.

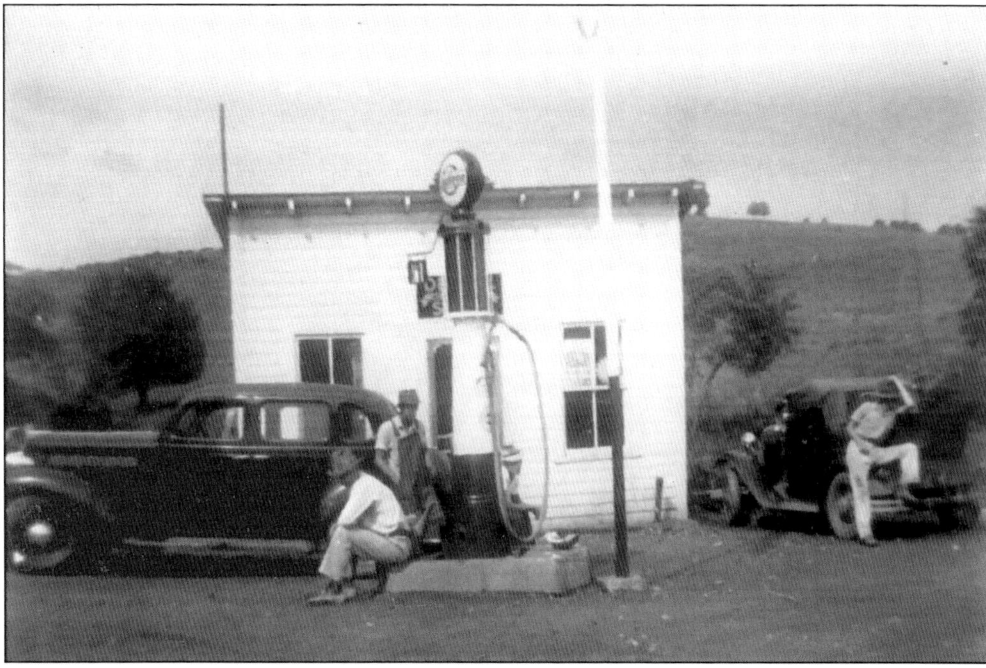

Lee Bower's 1930 Esso Station. This gas station, located near the present-day Vannoy offices on SR 16, sold only one kind of gas.

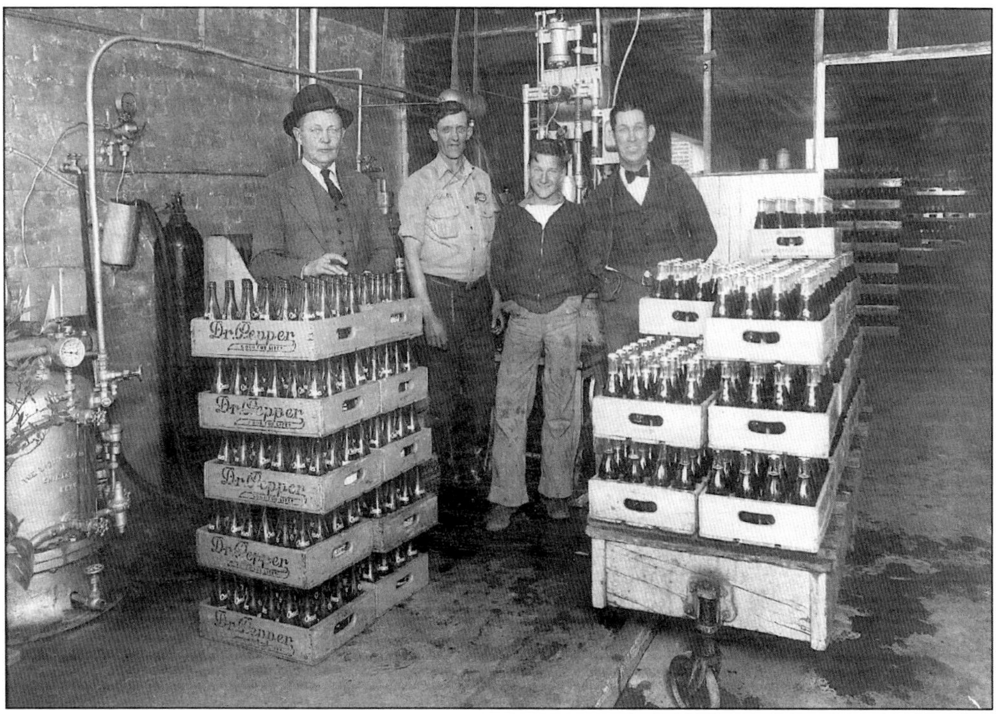

Interior of the Dr. Pepper Bottling Plant. Empty bottles on the left go through the filling machine in the back. Pictured here, from left to right, are H.R. Vannoy, Claude Blevins, Pete Blevins, and Norman Hege.

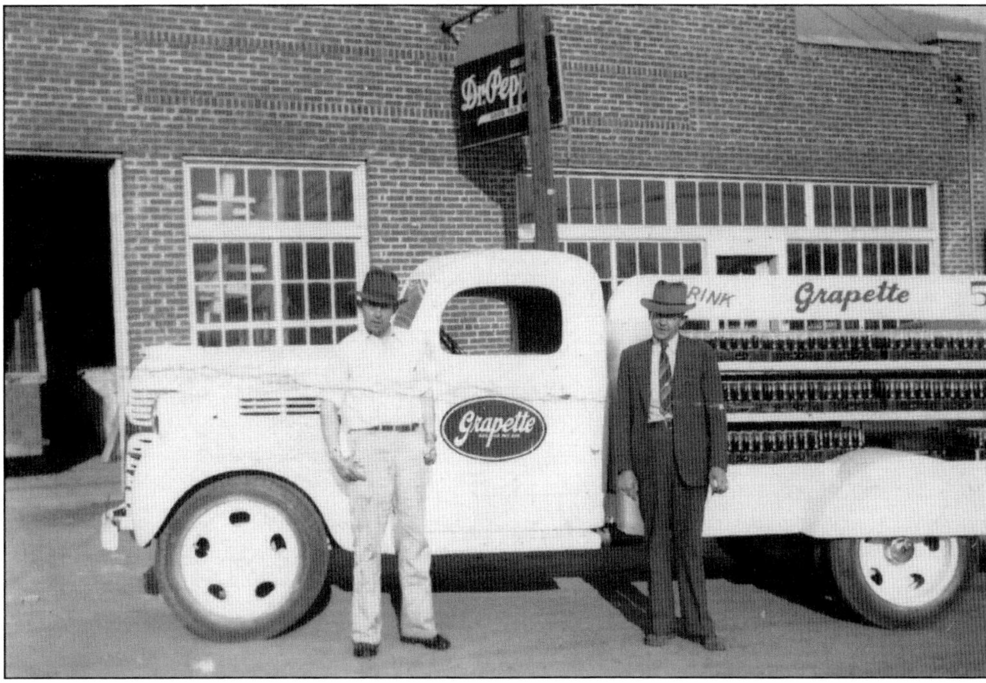

DR. PEPPER PLANT IN WEST JEFFERSON (C. 1940S). Carl F. Colvard and H.R. Vannoy are admiring their new Grapette truck.

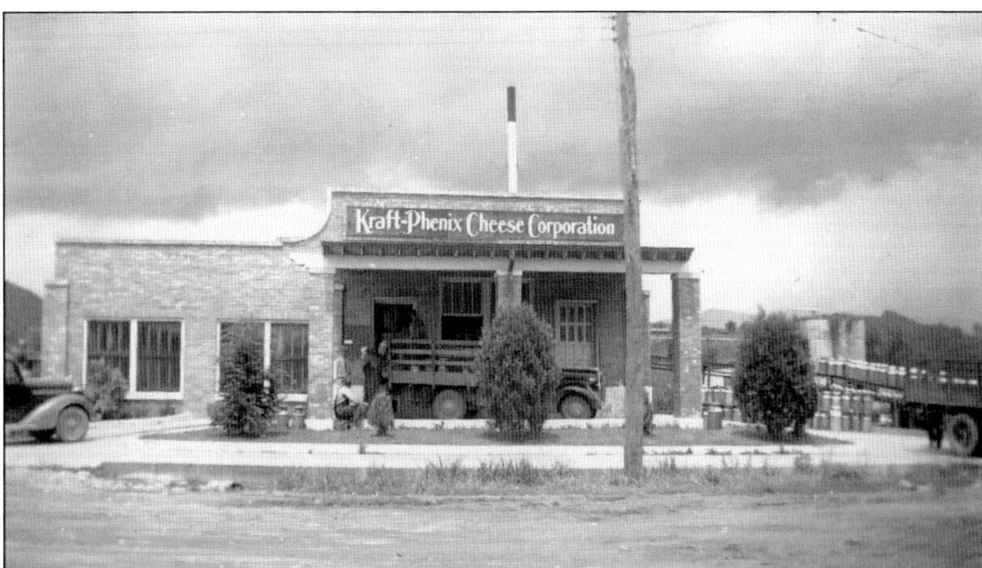

KRAFT-PHENIX CHEESE CORPORATION FACTORY. At this time there was also a creamery factory in Lansing.

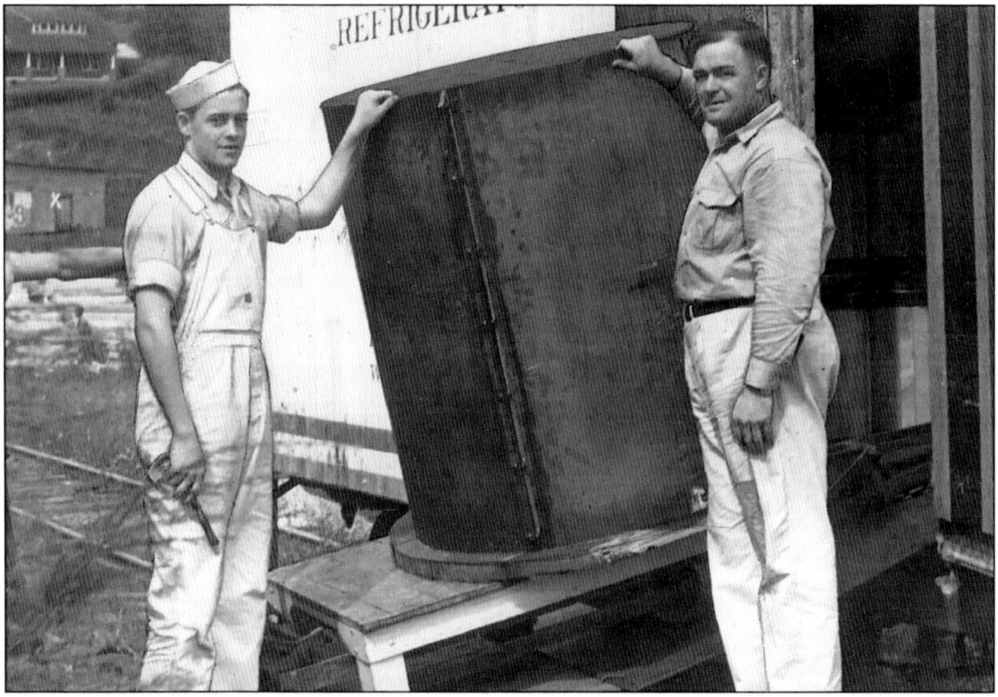

Loading Cheese for Atlanta. Walter Edward Phillips (left) and LaVerne Johnson (right) load a 1-ton cheese hoop on a refrigerated boxcar.

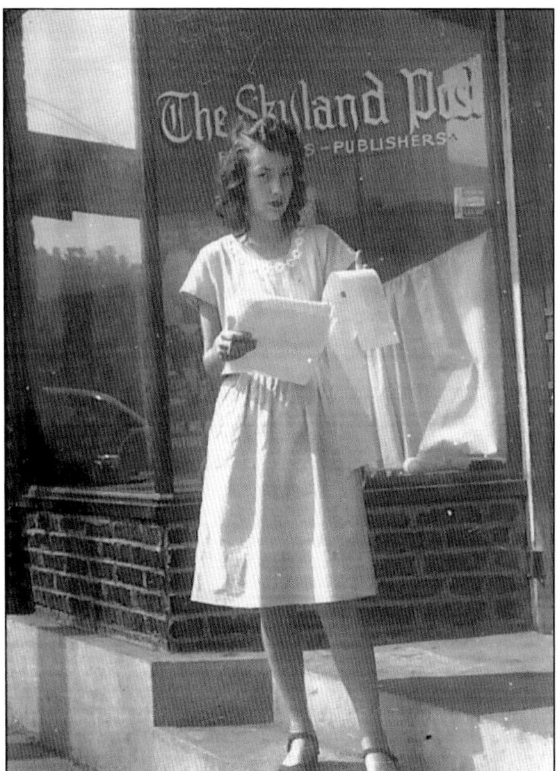

Nancy Johnston in Front of the *Skyland Post*. The *Post* was founded in 1931 by Ruth Reeves. Subsequently the paper was owned and edited by Mrs. Ed M. Anderson. The last owner and editor was also a woman, Patty Wheeler. The newspaper published its last issue on October 12, 1988.

Bank of Ashe in Jefferson. Pictured standing, left to right, are Ed Johnson, Joe C. Worth, Walter H. Worth, and unidentified.

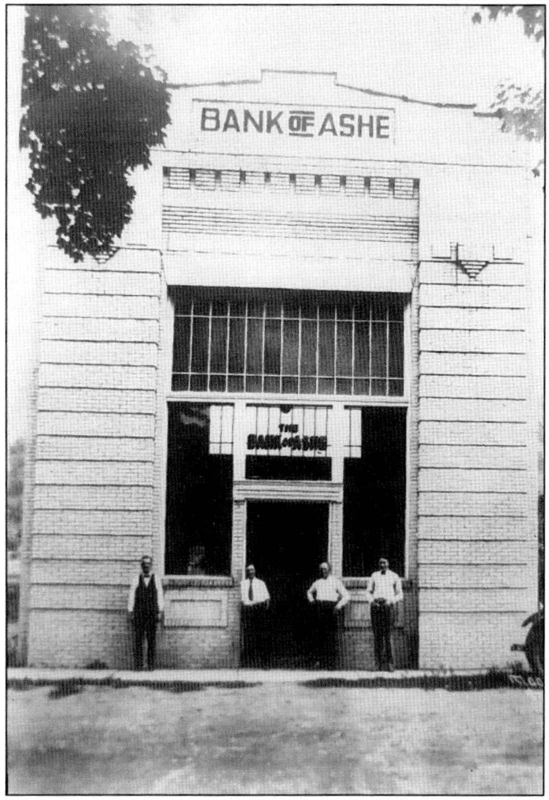

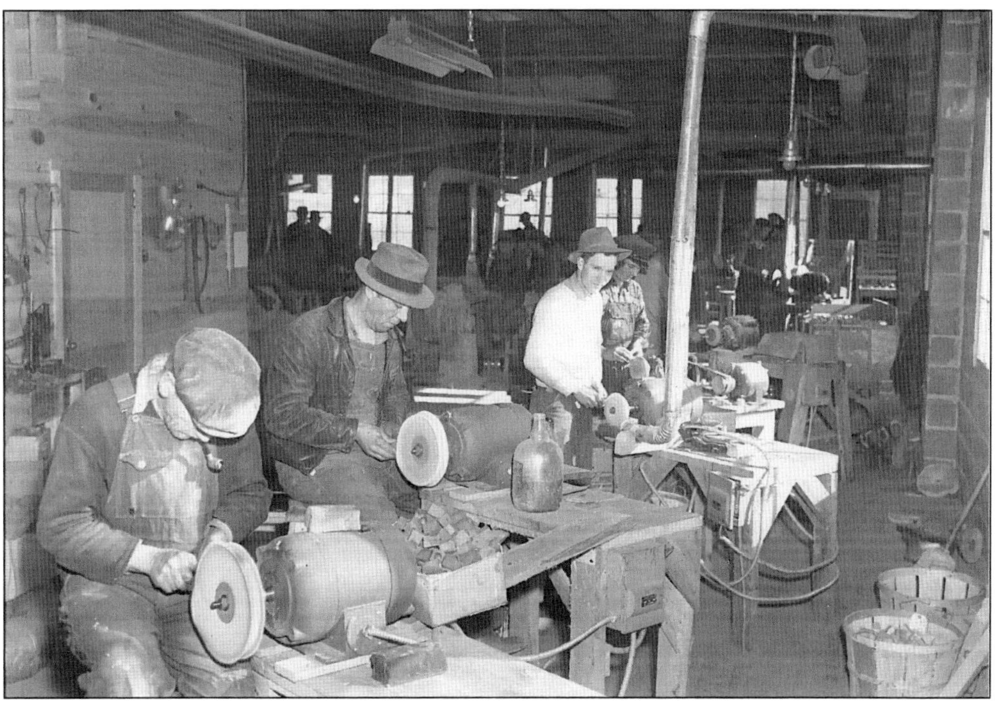

Pipe Factory. This factory in West Jefferson shaped pipe bowls from laurel burls.

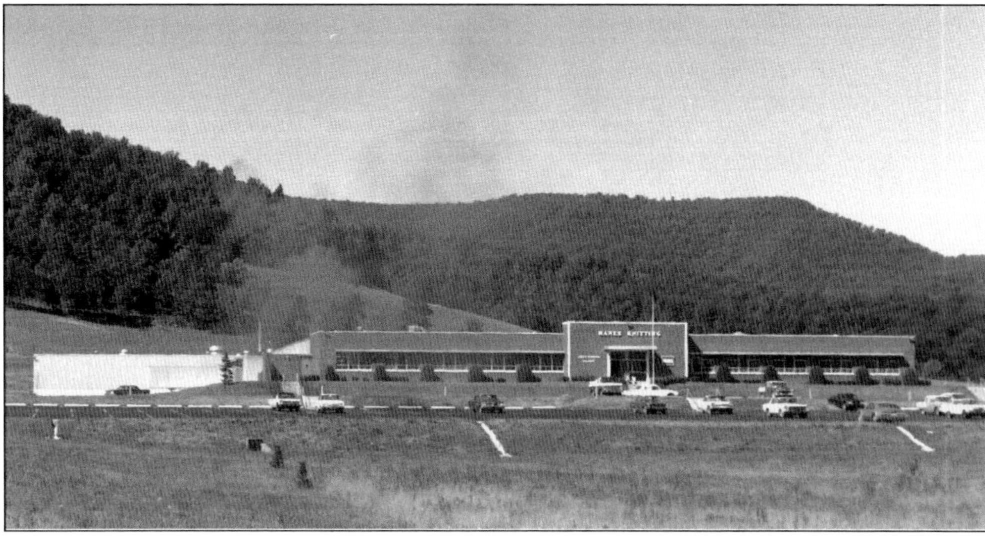

HANES KNITTING PLANT. Beginning its operation in 1957, the plant specialized in making T-shirts. One of Leviton's three plants in the county now occupies this building.

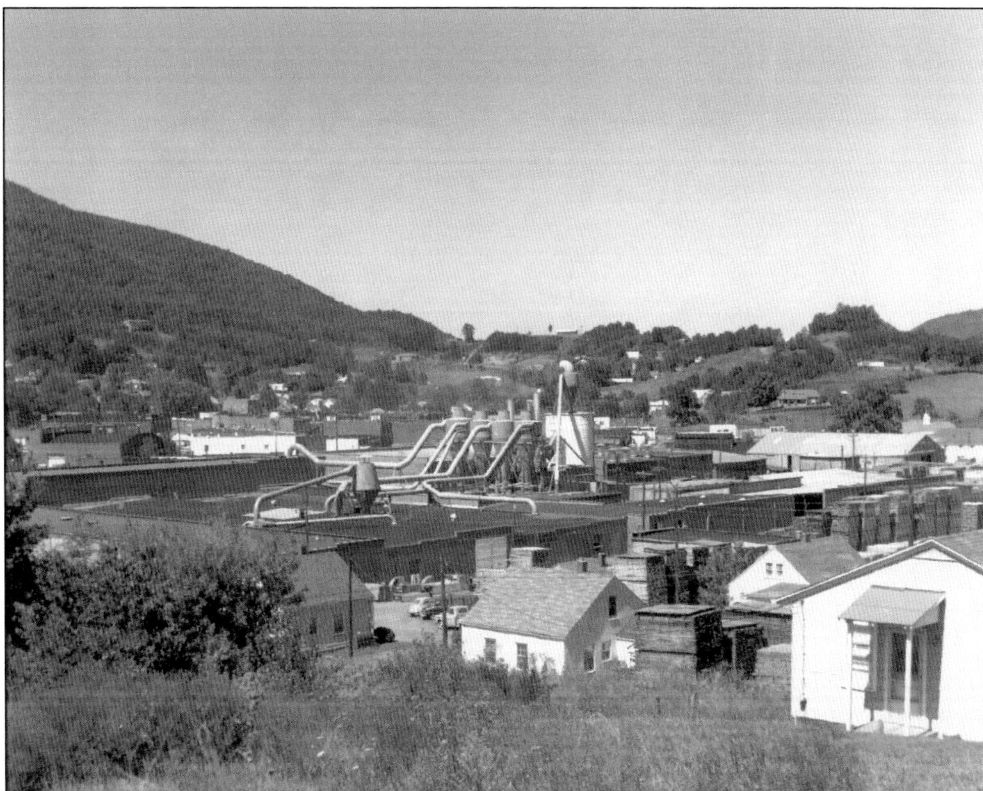

PHENIX CHAIR COMPANY. This is the oldest on-going industry in Ashe County. It was founded and owned for several years by the Barr family.

Five

TRANSPORTATION

Transportation in the formative years of Ashe County was a constant challenge. Sam Shumate recalls stories his grandmother, Claudia Johnson, told him of childhood trips to Wilkesboro with her father in the early 1900s. Great-grandfather Jones, a Warrensville merchant, would take two or three wagons to Wilkesboro for supplies every few months.

It took a whole day to travel down the mountain on the old Jefferson/Wilkesboro Turnpike. They would spend the night, load up the next morning, and drive the wagons to a campground by the Reddies River at the foot of the mountain. The horses were rested for the trek up the mountain and back to Warrensville on the third day.

While transportation in Ashe lags behind much of the nation, our forefathers would consider our present roads, bridges, and modern conveyances a blessing from heaven.

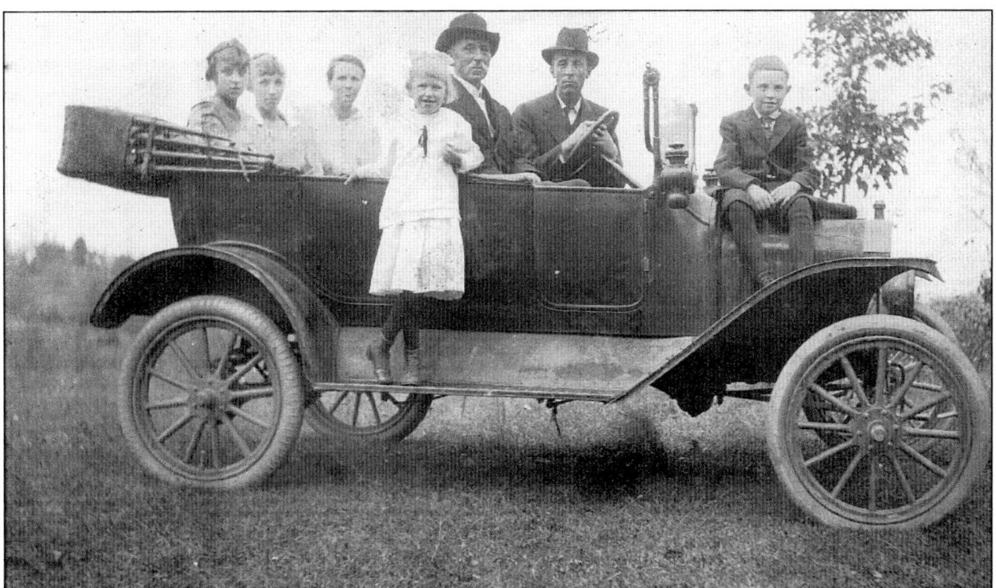

ONE OF THE FIRST AUTOMOBILES IN ASHE COUNTY. This photograph was taken in the early 1920s. Pictured here, from left to right, are Ethel Poplin Watt, Lena Poplin Vannoy, Carrie Kushat Harris Poplin, Betty Poplin Stone, Sam Poplin, Leet Poplin, and Glen Poplin.

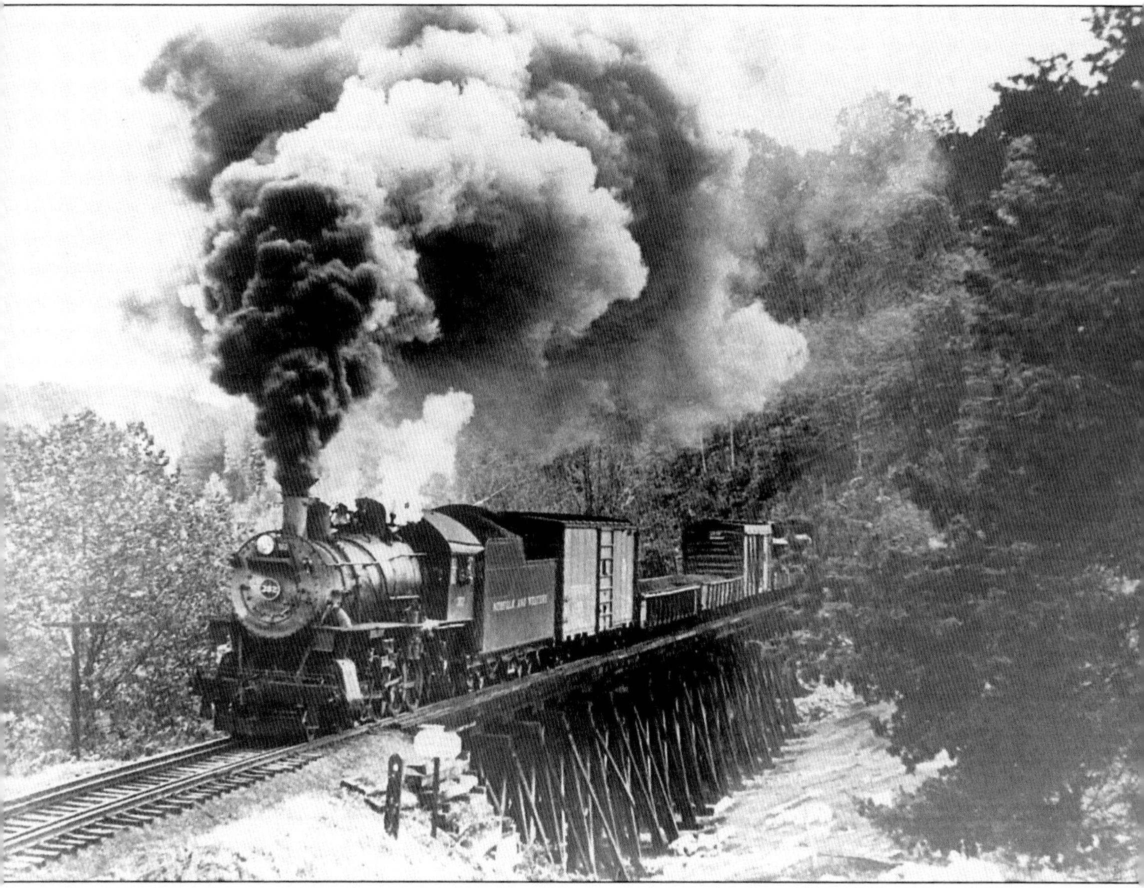

The Norfolk and Western Train Going over Horse Creek. The train crossed Little Horse Creek 17 times before it reached Lansing. Though the speed limit was 18–25 miles per hour, rarely did the train reach such speeds. In fact, the train often slowed to 5 miles per hour.

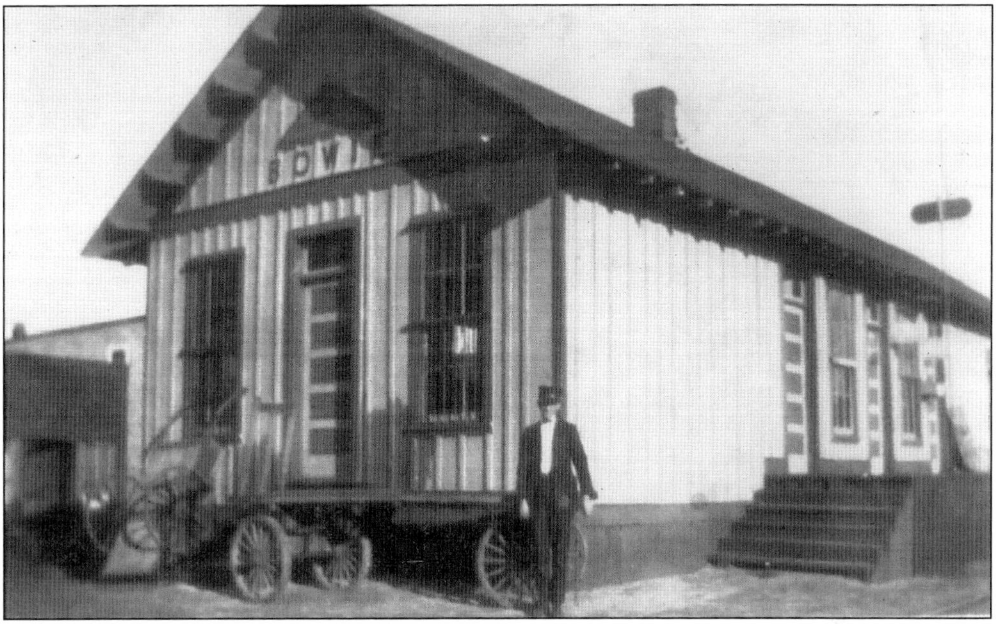

BOWIE (NOW FLEETWOOD) TRAIN DEPOT. Building the extension to Bowie is one example of the railroad's being "penny-wise and pound foolish" because, in its eagerness to build as close to timber resources as possible, the company often followed streams. Frequent flooding repeatedly washed tracks and trestles away.

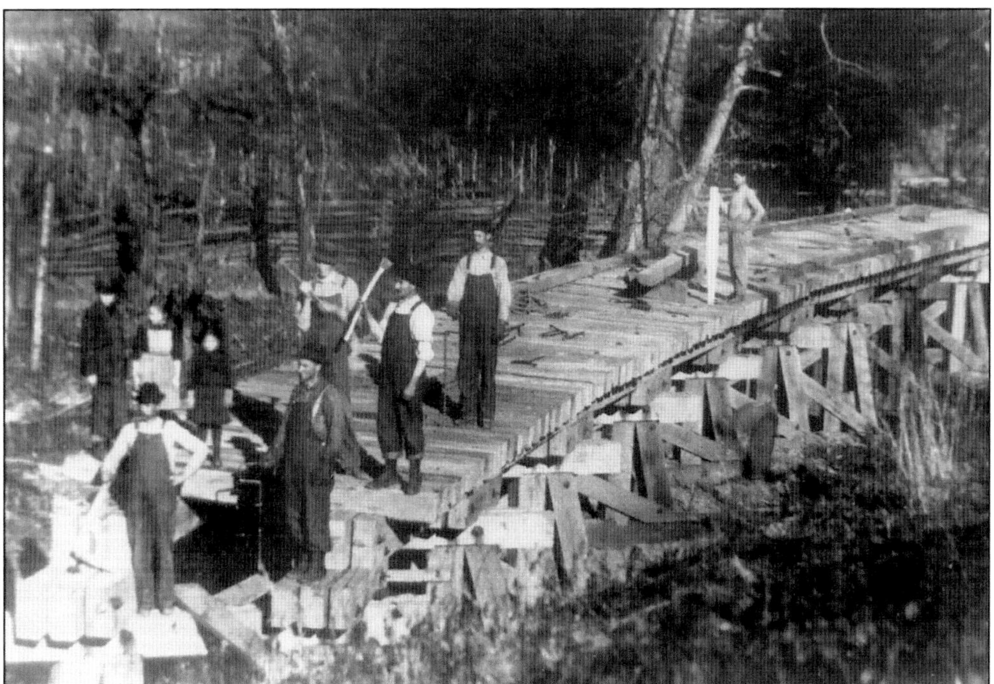

BUILDING A RAILROAD TRESTLE AT TUCKERDALE. The trestle is on a site near Tuckerdale Baptist Church.

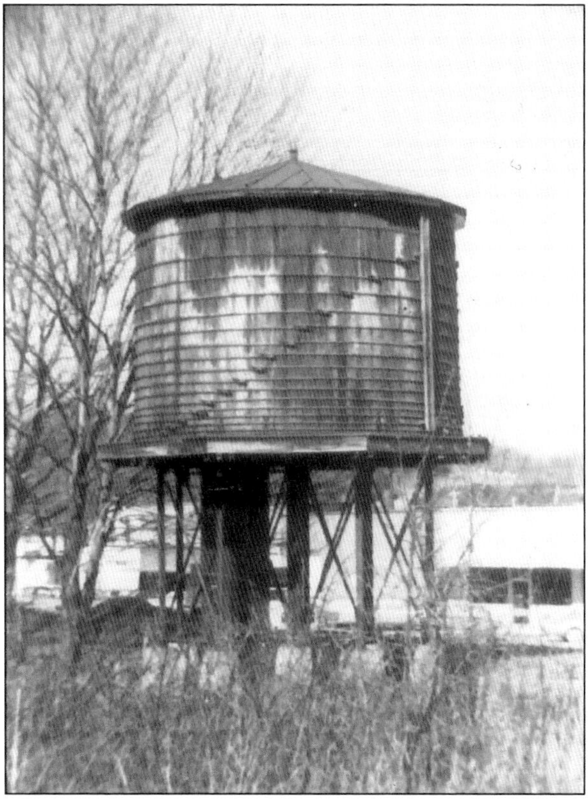

West Jefferson Railroad Water Tank. This is one of a few stations at which the train could fill its boiler with water.

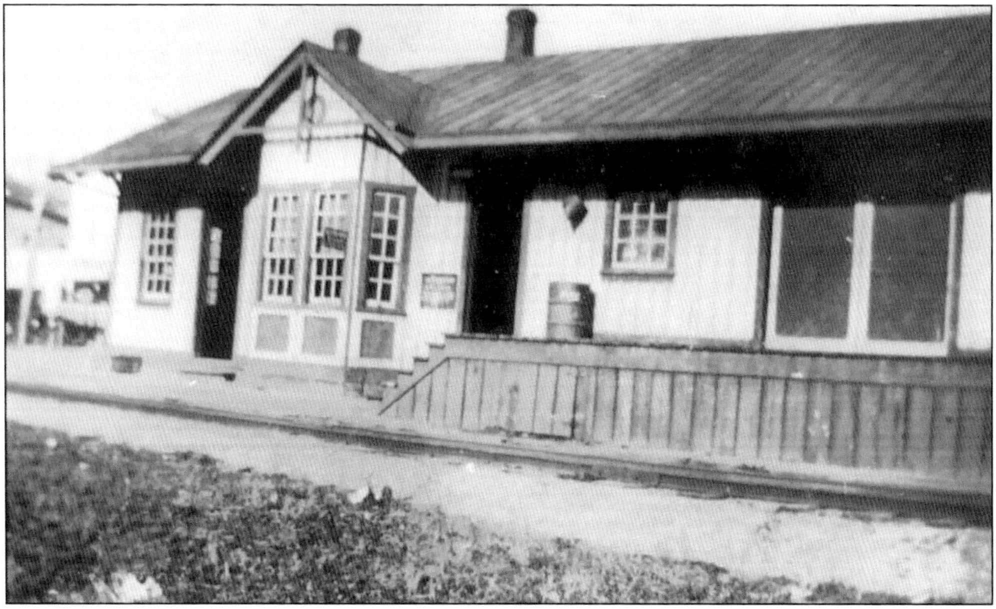

Lansing Depot. This is a view of the depot as incoming passengers would have seen it.

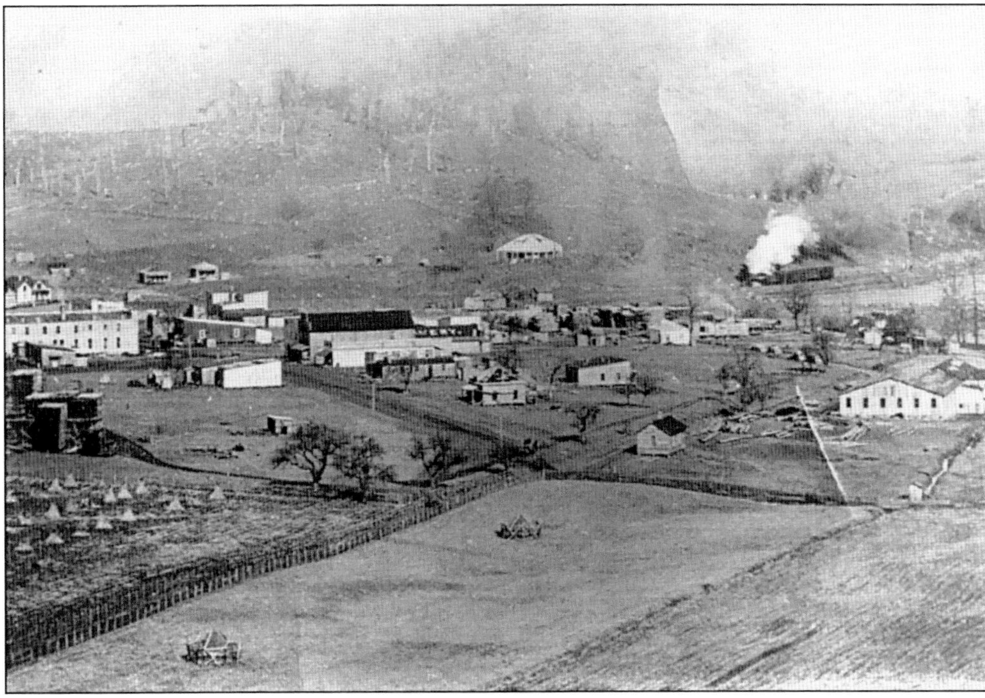

THE VIRGINIA CREEPER'S MAIDEN RUN. The train can be seen coming around Paddy Mountain into West Jefferson.

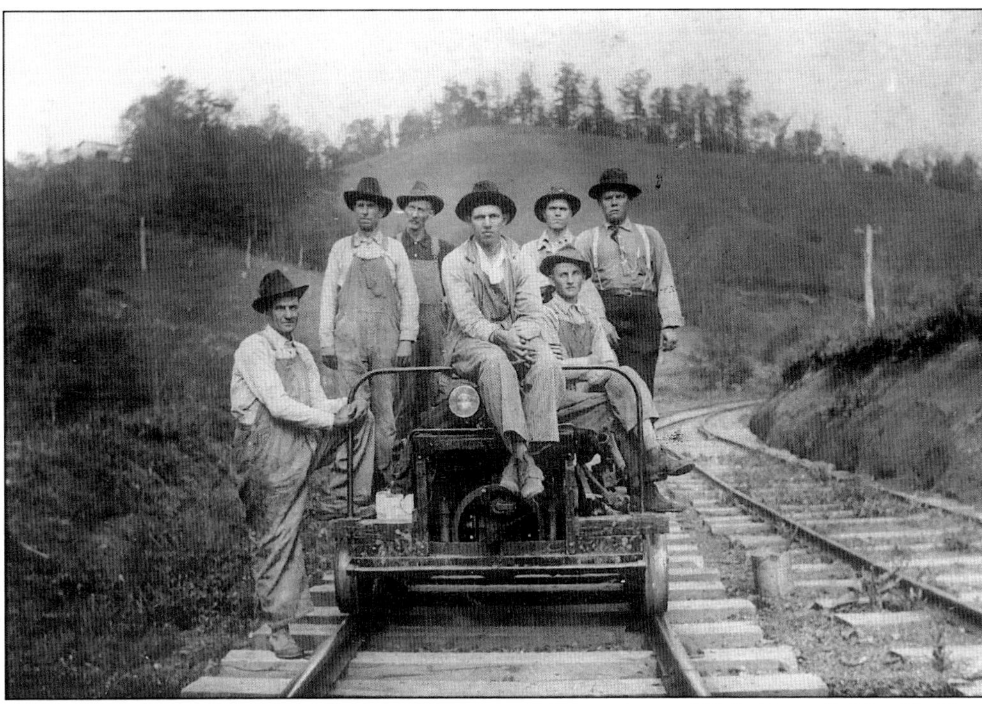

TUCKERDALE SECTION CREW. Pictured here, from left to right, are Wade Darnell, Jake Childers, Roby Blevins, James Rush, Sam Broomfield, Mr. Rush (foreman), and Ira Powers.

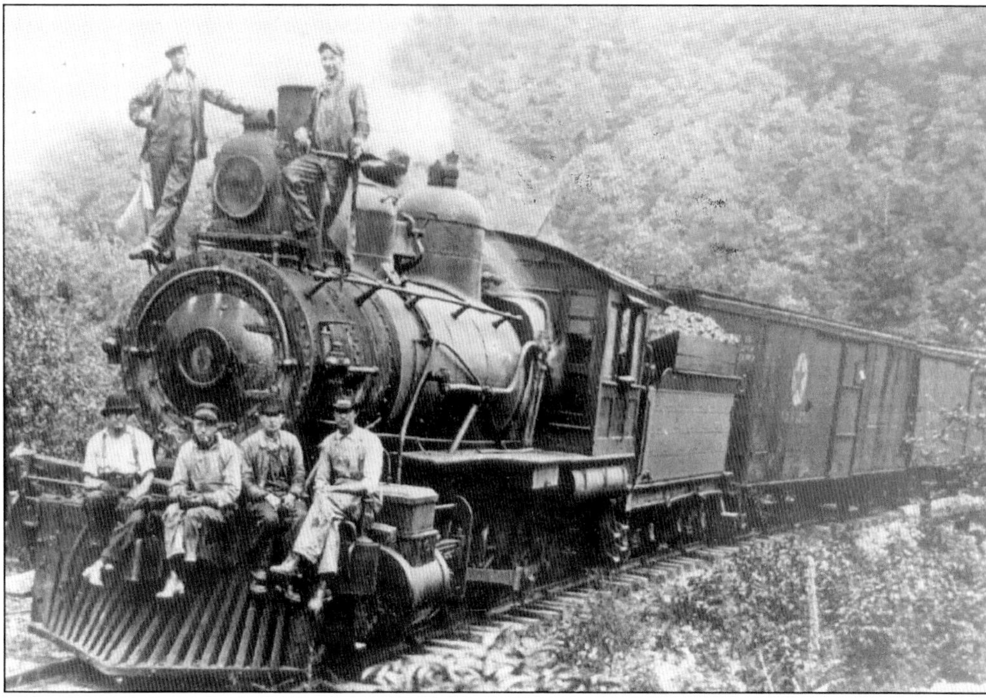

LAST TRAIN OUT OF TODD. Engine Number 6 and its crew are shown here, from left to right, as follows: (seated) Charles Wright, Edgar Pennington, John Minix, and Shadie Estep; (standing) R.H. Sneed and H.S. Steelman.

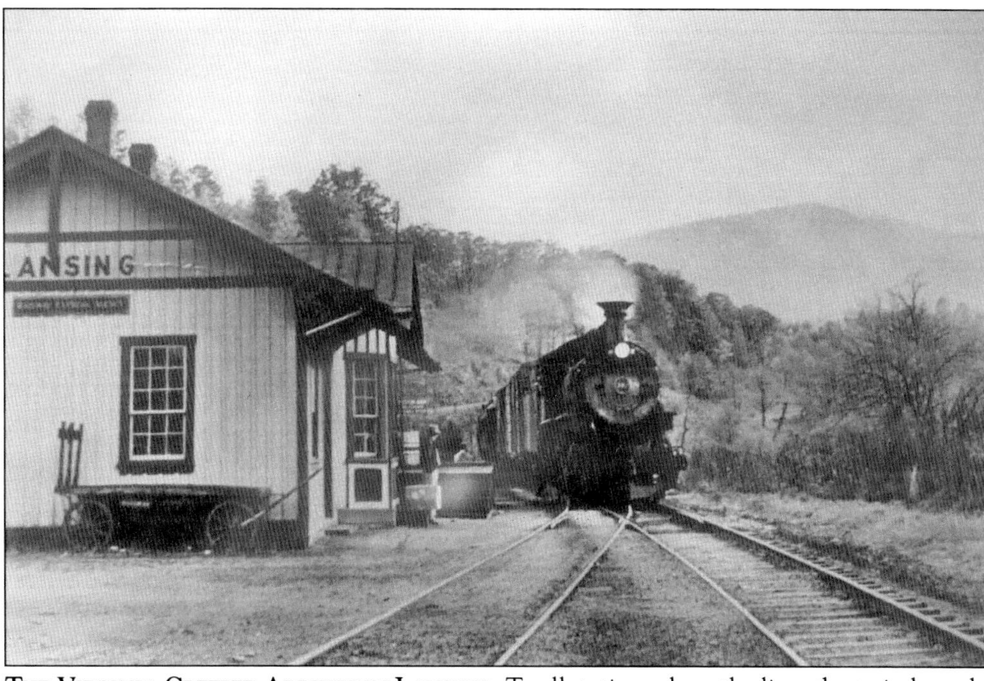

THE VIRGINIA CREEPER ARRIVES IN LANSING. To all stations along the line, the train brought the mail and unloaded mail-order merchandise. Because of the train, even in these early days, visitors and tourists from neighboring areas found Ashe County.

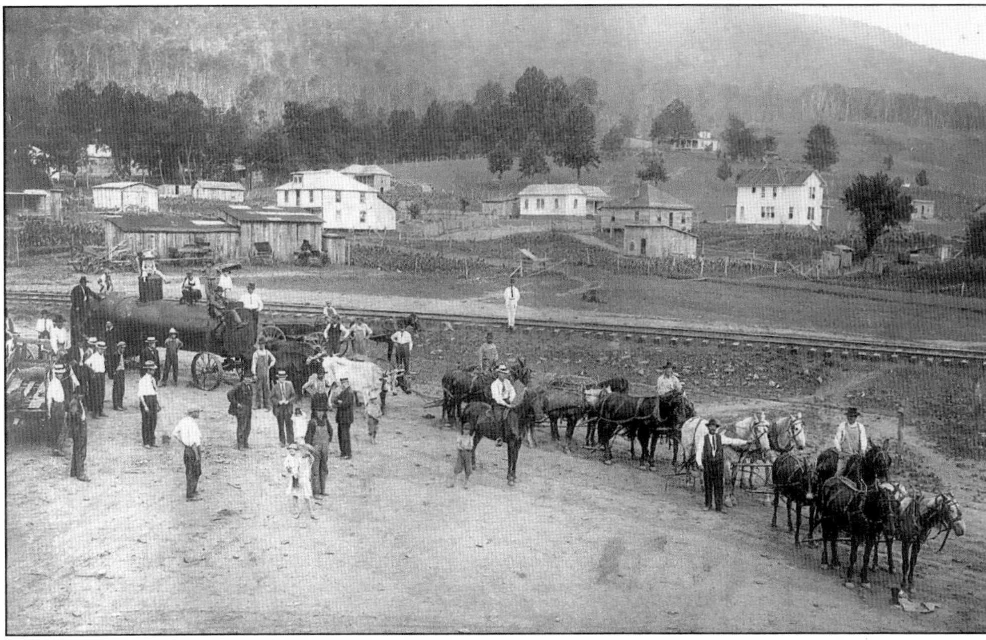

NORFOLK AND WESTERN TRACKS IN WEST JEFFERSON (C. 1917). A team of horses pulls the steam boiler. This picture was taken on the site of the present Dollar Tire Store.

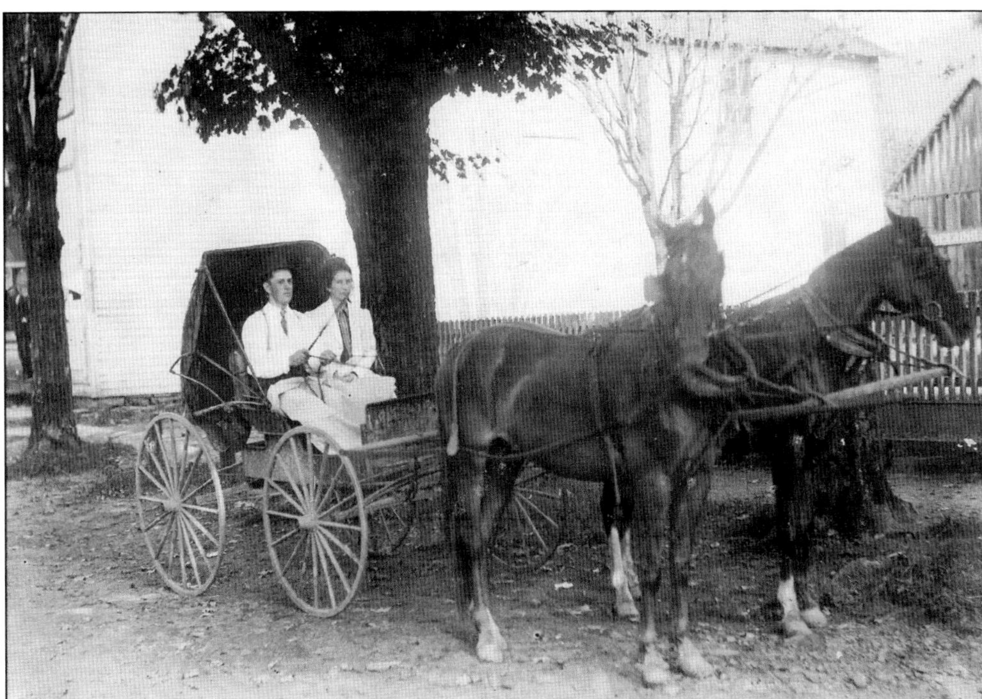

TRANSPORTATION IN 1906. Walter H. and Maude Allen Worth are out for a ride.

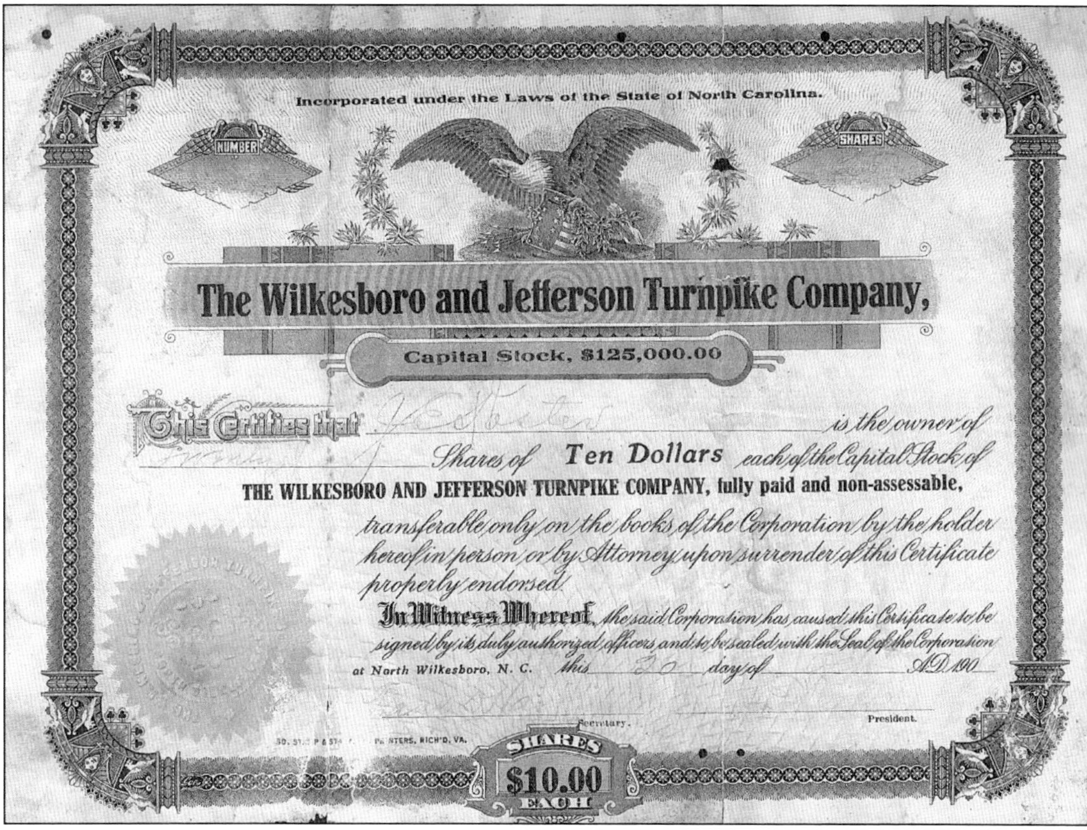
Incorporated under the Laws of the State of North Carolina.

NUMBER

SHARES

The Wilkesboro and Jefferson Turnpike Company,

Capital Stock, $125,000.00

This Certifies that ________ is the owner of ________ Shares of **Ten Dollars** each of the Capital Stock of THE WILKESBORO AND JEFFERSON TURNPIKE COMPANY, fully paid and non-assessable, transferable only on the books of the Corporation by the holder hereof in person or by Attorney upon surrender of this Certificate properly endorsed.

In Witness Whereof, the said Corporation has caused this Certificate to be signed by its duly authorized officers and to be sealed with the Seal of the Corporation at North Wilkesboro, N. C. this ____ day of ________ A.D. 190__

Secretary. President.

SHARES $10.00 EACH

STOCK CERTIFICATE. In the early 1900s the Wilkesboro and Jefferson Turnpike Company sold stock to construct the first major road into Ashe County.

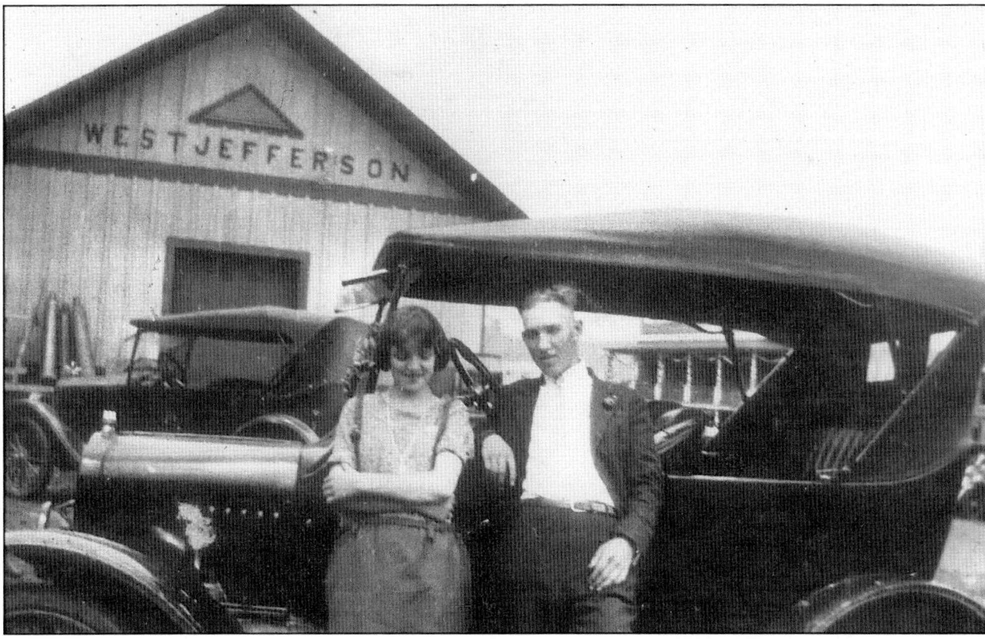

West Jefferson Depot in the Early 1920s. From 1914 to 1977, West Jefferson was one of the major stations for the train. It was one of the last stations to be closed.

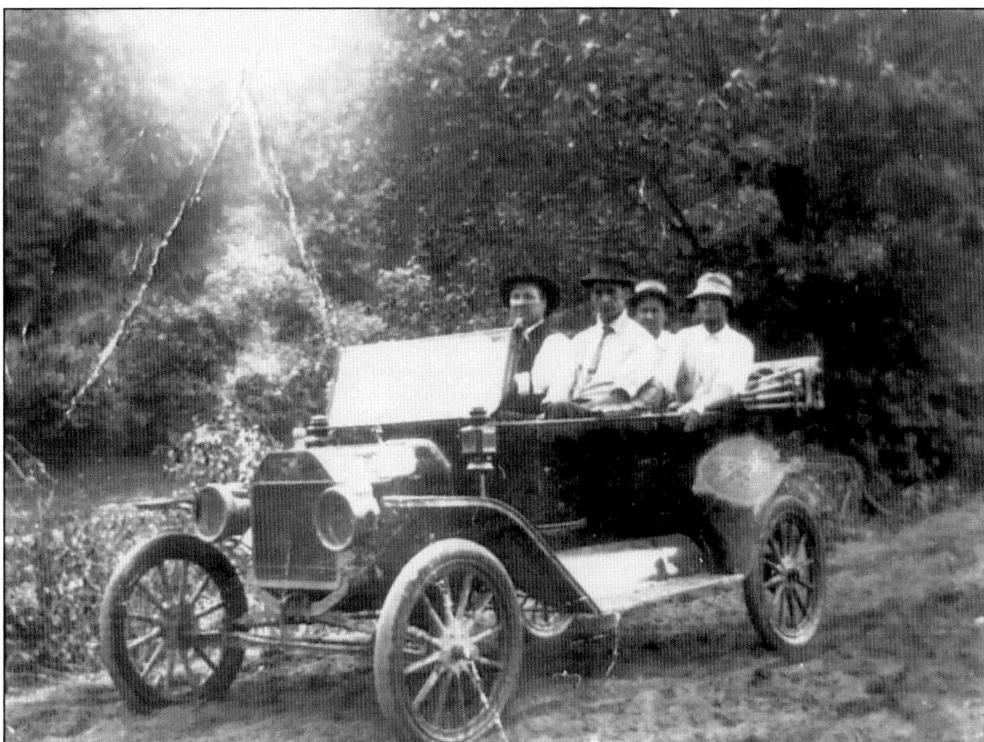

First Car Driven from West Jefferson to Whitetop Mountain. Harrison Tucker is the passenger in the front seat and James Allen Sr. is the driver.

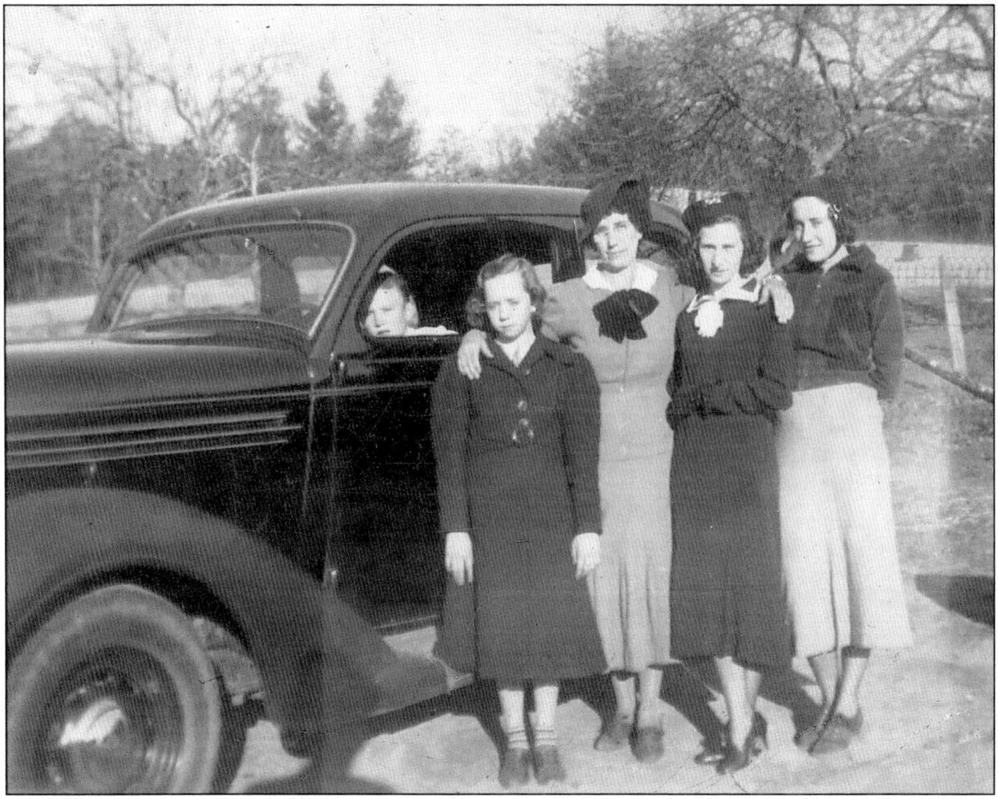

ARVILLA JONES FAMILY IN THEIR 1930S AUTOMOBILE. Pictured here, from left to right, on Lower Nettle Knob Road are Ryland Jones, Ada Jones Harliss, Arvilla Jones, Sadie Jones Waugh, and Zella Jones Williams.

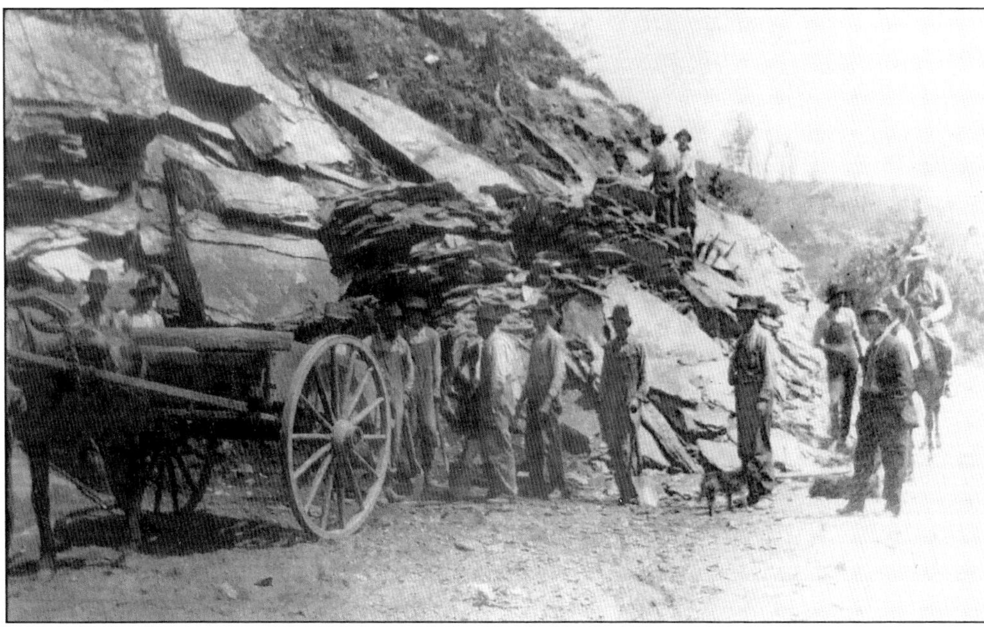

ROAD BUILDING USING HORSES. Booger Rock near Fleetwood is being removed.

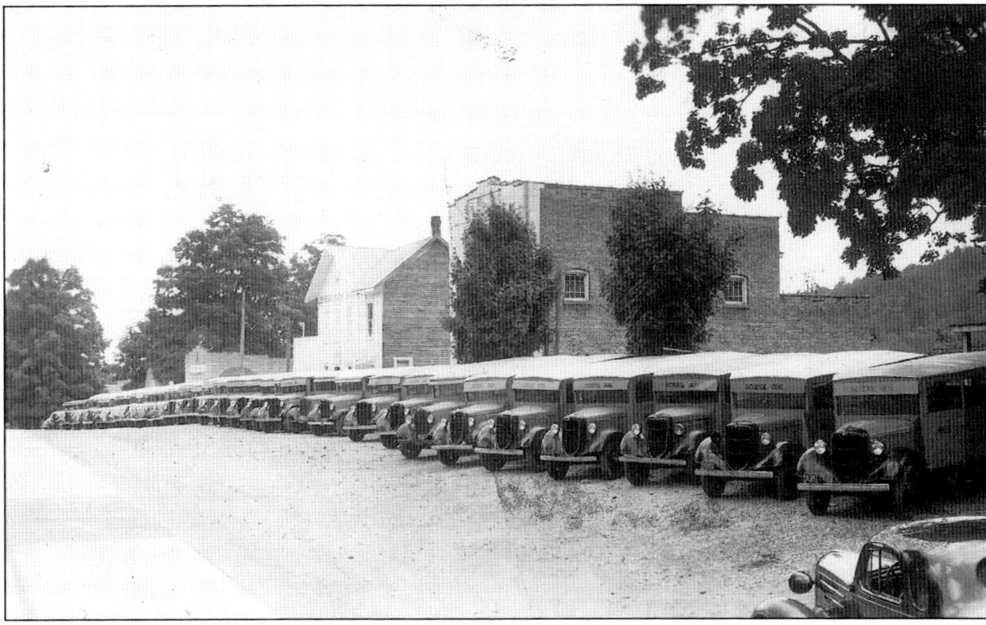

First Ashe County School Buses. The buildings in the background, from left to right, are the fire station, post office, Odd Fellows Hall, and Northwestern Bank in Jefferson.

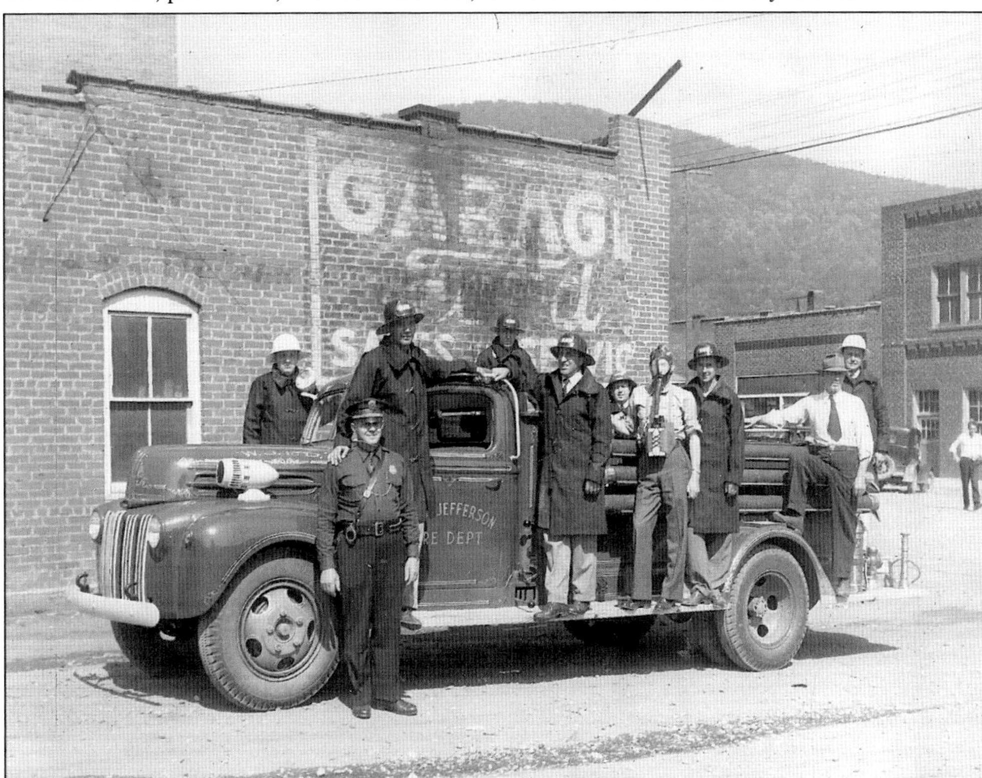

West Jefferson Volunteer Fire Department in 1940. This volunteer fire department was the first one organized in Ashe County.

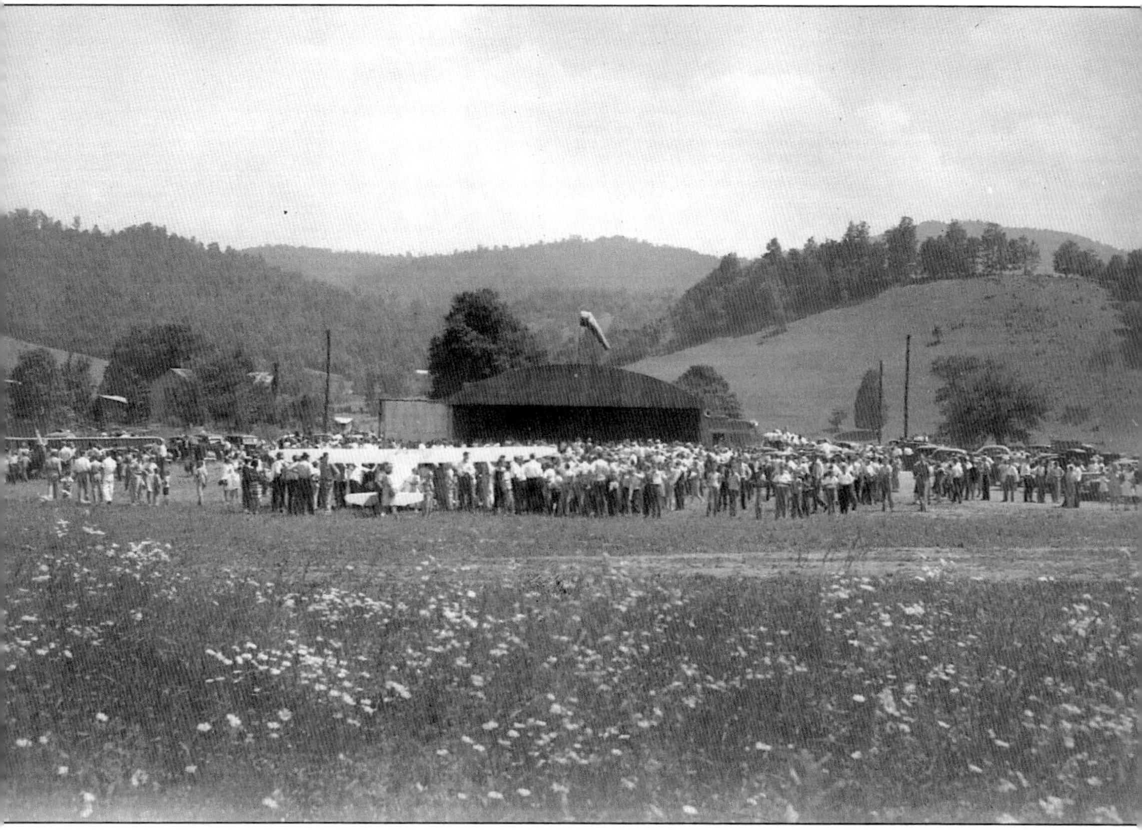

Dedication of the Ashe County Airport. The dedication ceremony was held in 1940 at the Beaver Creek community facility.

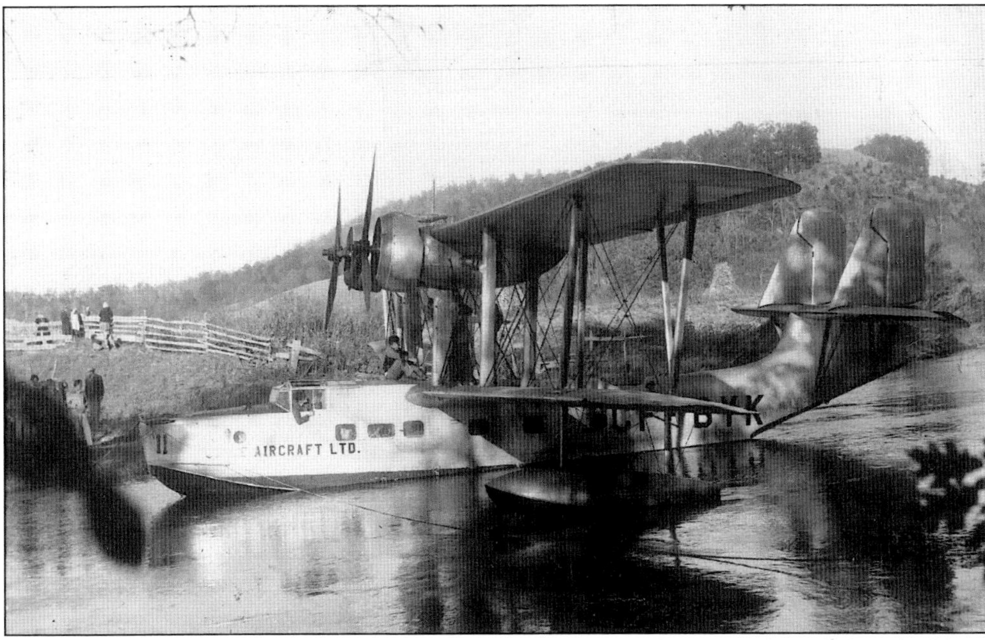

SEAPLANE LANDING ON THE NEW RIVER IN 1935. In November 1935, this seaplane had been lost in the fog and made an emergency landing in the New River on the Lew Reeves Farm in Nathan's Creek.

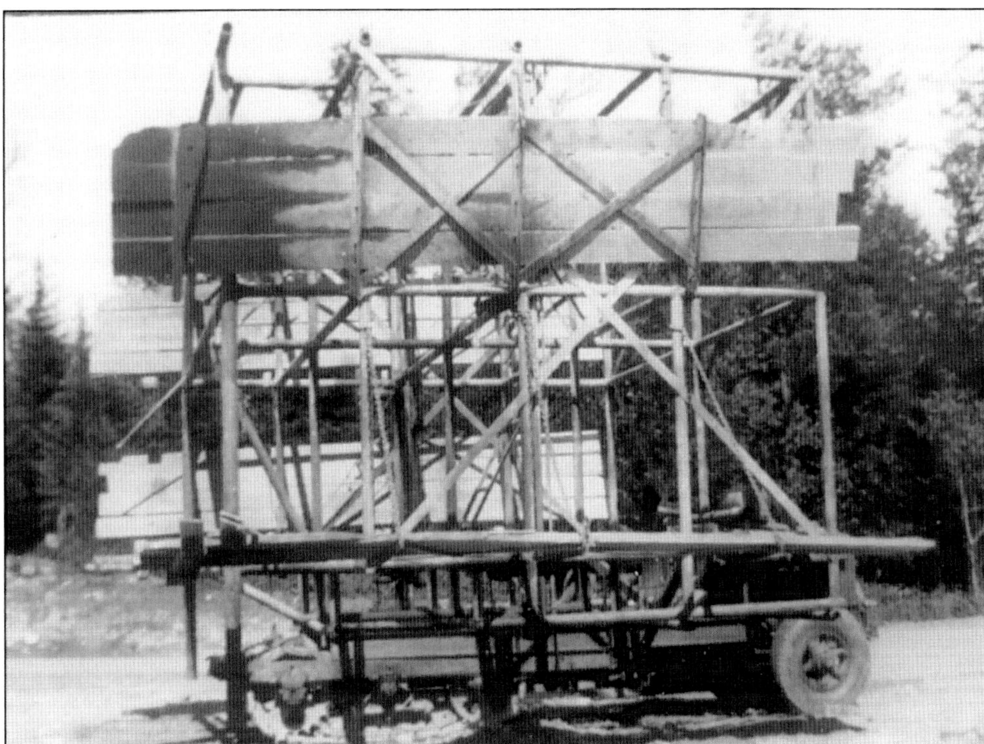

BLUE RIDGE PARKWAY CONSTRUCTION. A scaffold was used to build the Blue Ridge Parkway overpasses above Ashe County roads.

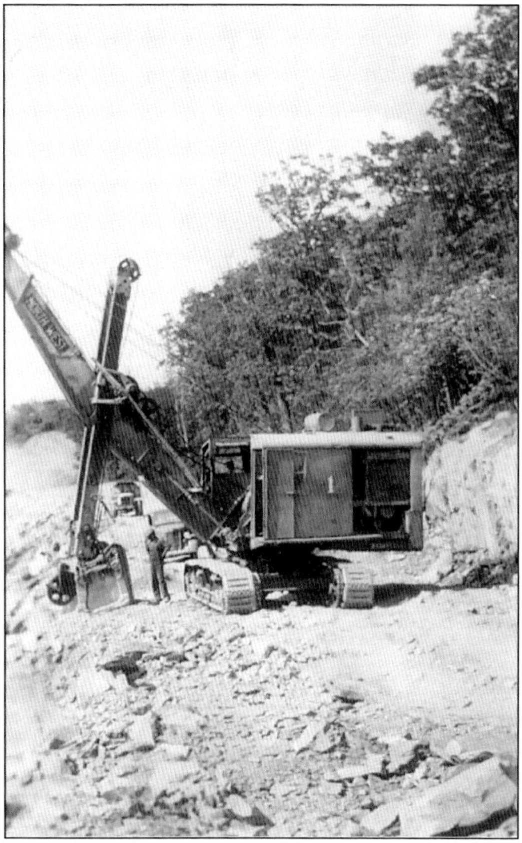

CONSTRUCTION ON THE BLUE RIDGE PARKWAY. An ambitious WPA road project, the 470-mile parkway, which was begun in the mid-1930s, was finally completed in 1987.

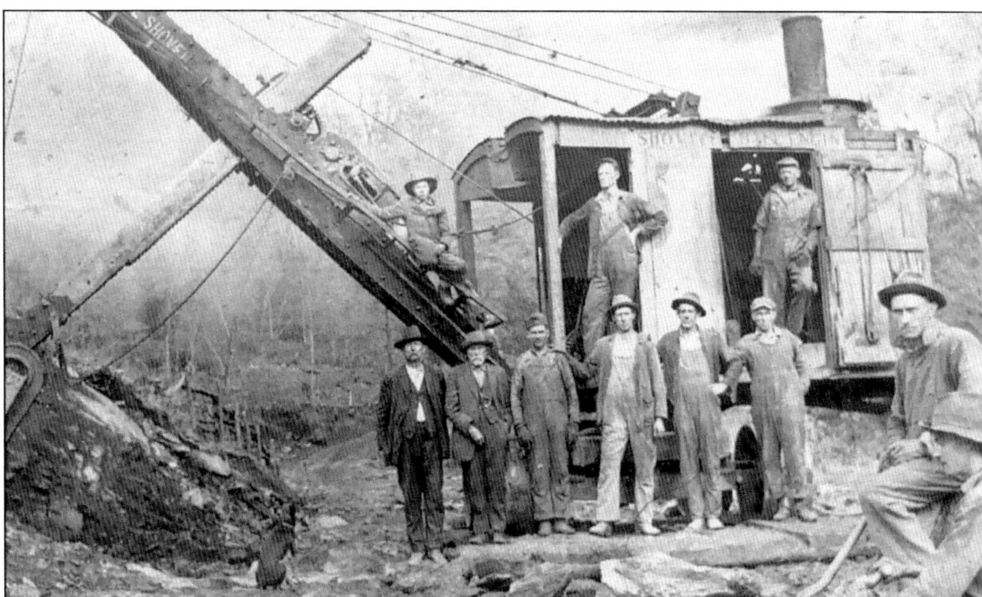

ROAD BUILDING IN ASHE COUNTY. This is the first road in Ashe County built with a steam shovel instead of horses. This picture was taken near the Judd Blevins store on Phoenix Creek Road.

Six

Churches and Schools

The many churches that seem to rest at every crossroads in Ashe County, mostly Baptist and Methodist in the early days of the county, reflect the deeply religious nature of the original settlers in the mountains. These early settlers first put a shelter over themselves, but they also built a place to worship very quickly. These well-kept structures, often the best building in a community, allow us to understand how communities were formed.

The early schools of Ashe County could be called community schools, one-room structures with one teacher and accessible on foot. Students had only one textbook, known as the *Blue Back Speller*. Education was always a priority; in fact, records show that Ashe County had more students in 1900 than 1960. As roads were built and transportation became easier, schools began consolidating, and today's facilities are modern in every respect.

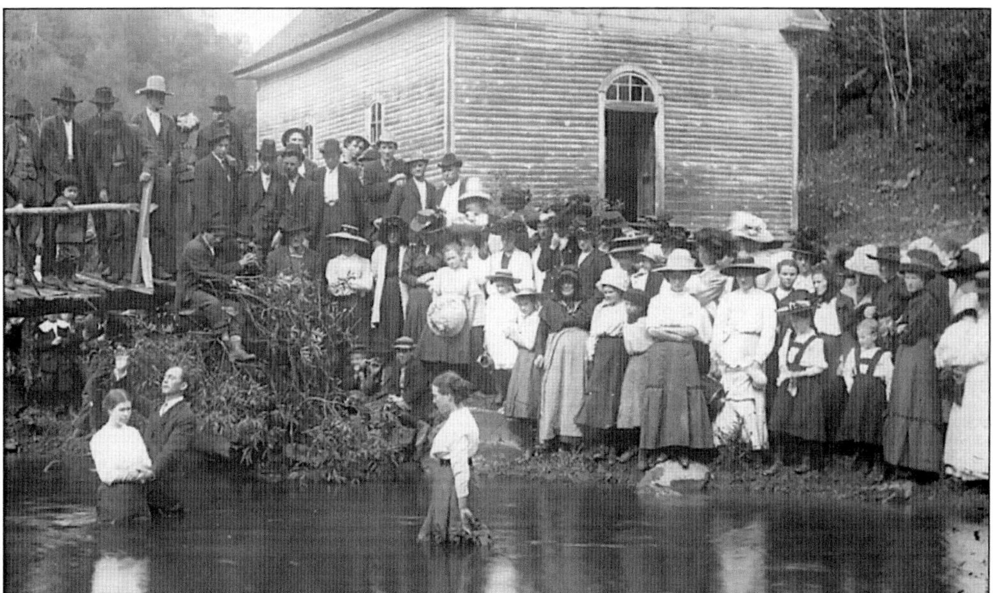

Baptism at Tuckerdale Baptist Church. The church building, which housed its first service in 1917, was constructed on land donated by James and Laura Wagoner.

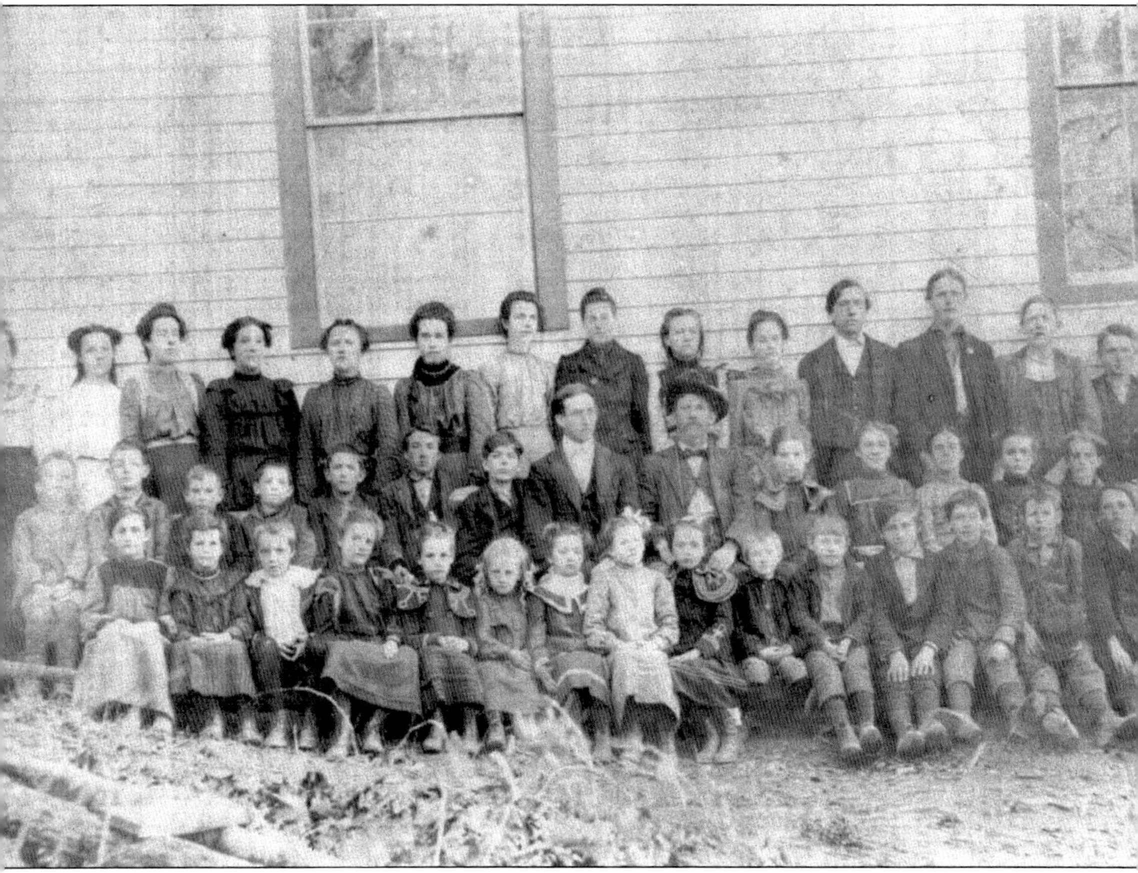

OAKVIEW SCHOOL, A TWO-ROOM SCHOOL IN WEAVERSFORD, 1905. The 45 students and their teachers in this photograph represent the following family names: Hill, Stump, DeBoard, Phipps, Smithy, Dancy, Young, Davis, Sawyer, and Livesay.

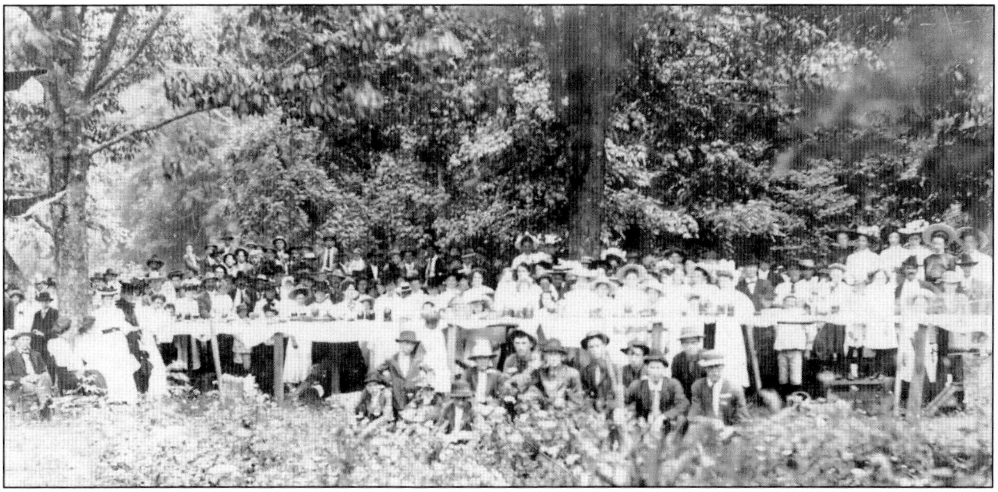

PICNIC AT CRESTON UNITED METHODIST CHURCH IN THE LATE 1800S. Creston United Methodist Church, originally known as Worth's Chapel, was organized before the Civil War. Church picnics such as this one were common social events for early Ashe Countians.

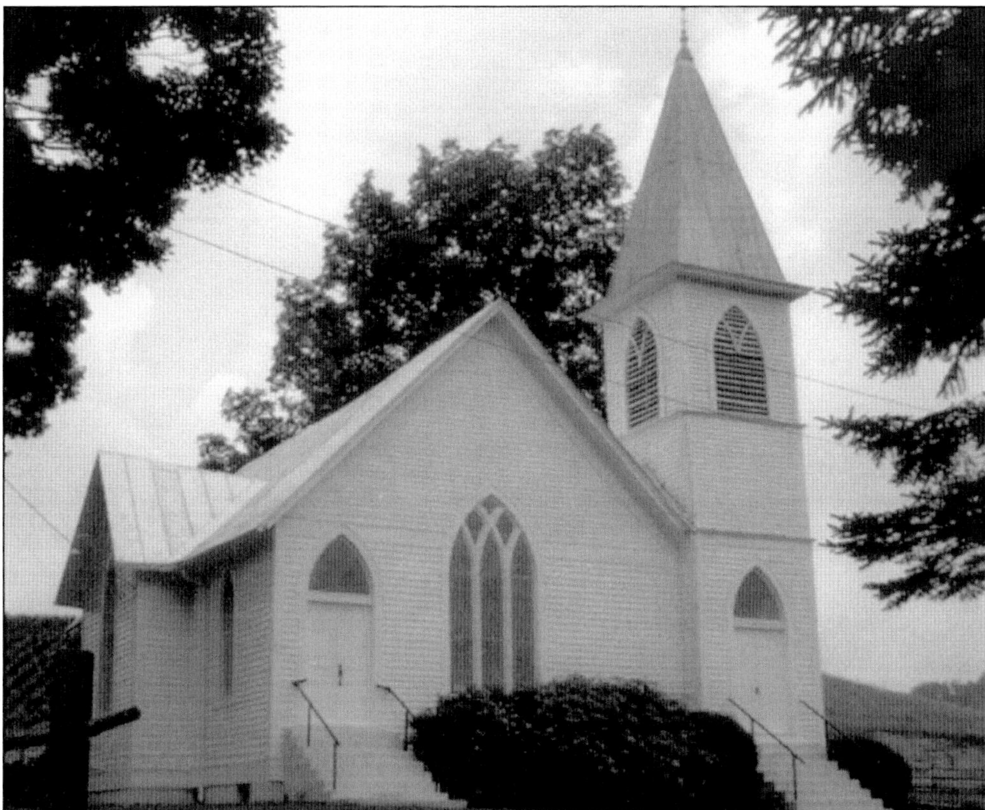

GRASSY CREEK METHODIST CHURCH. The congregation was organized in the late 1800s. The membership continues to worship in this sanctuary, which was built in 1904. The building, with its original stained-glass windows, was placed on the National Register of Historic Places in 1977.

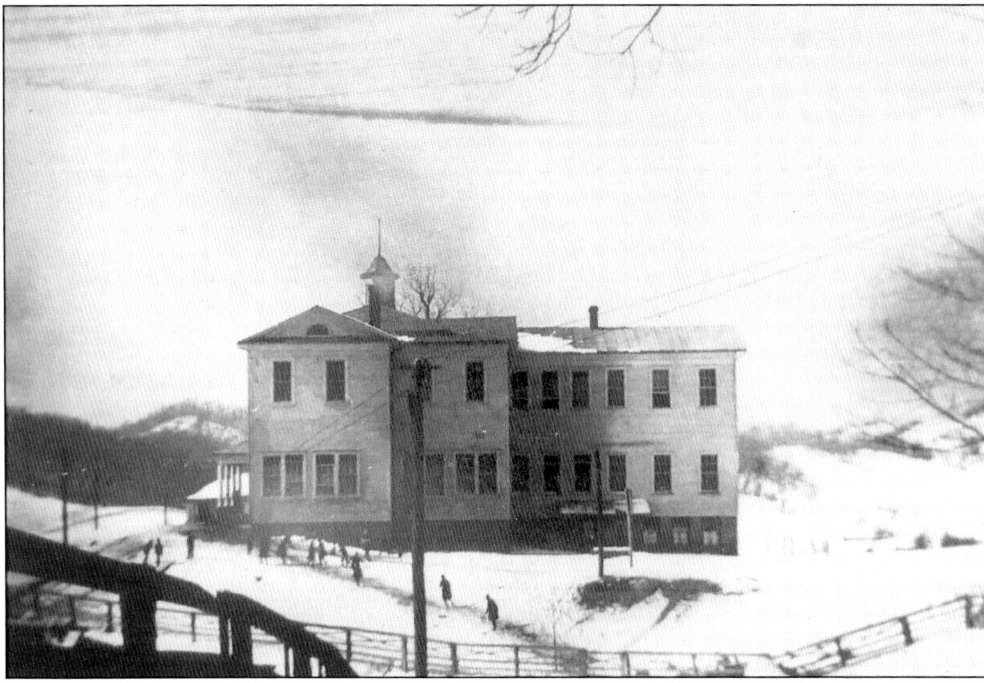

OLD VIRGINIA-CAROLINA SCHOOL. Built in 1913, the school straddled the Virginia–North Carolina state line. It was replaced in 1940 by a brick structure that was later destroyed by fire in 1967.

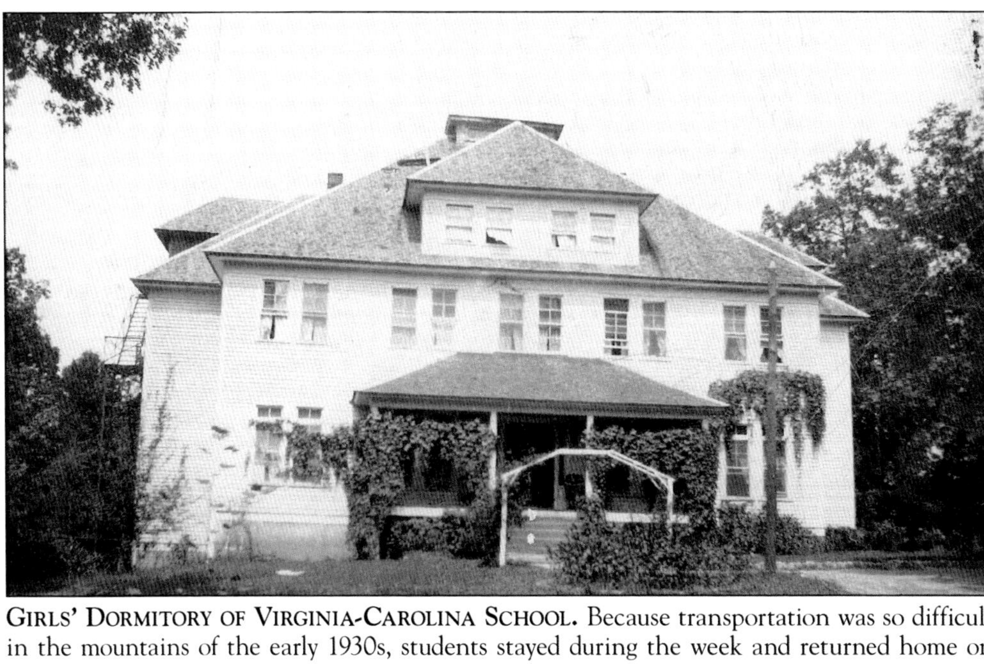

GIRLS' DORMITORY OF VIRGINIA-CAROLINA SCHOOL. Because transportation was so difficult in the mountains of the early 1930s, students stayed during the week and returned home on the weekends.

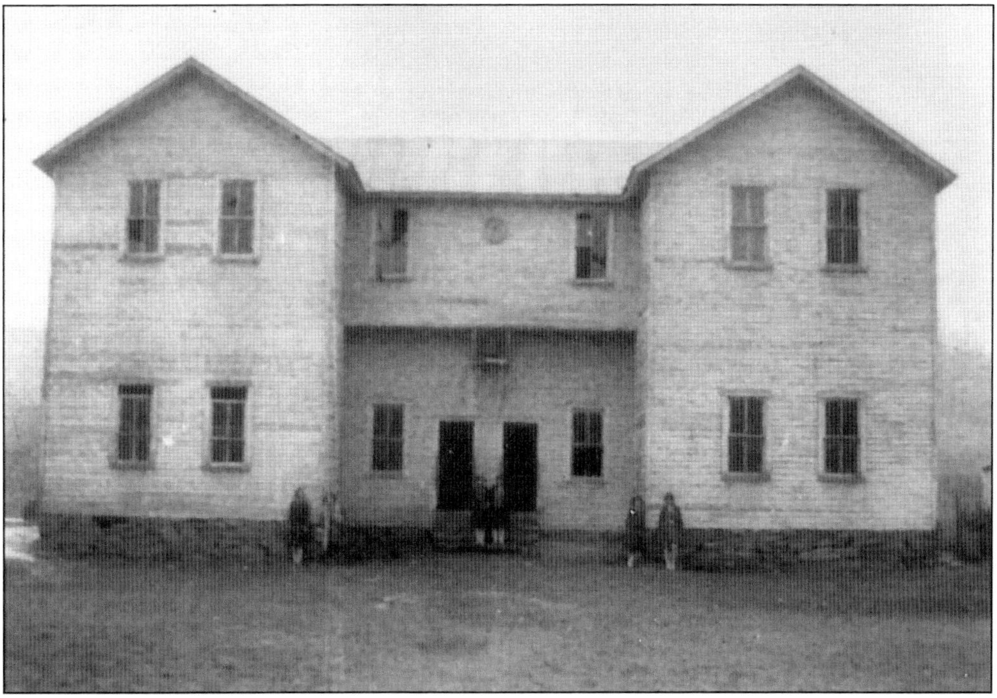

HELTON ACADEMY. This was the first high school in Ashe County to hold classes through the 11th grade.

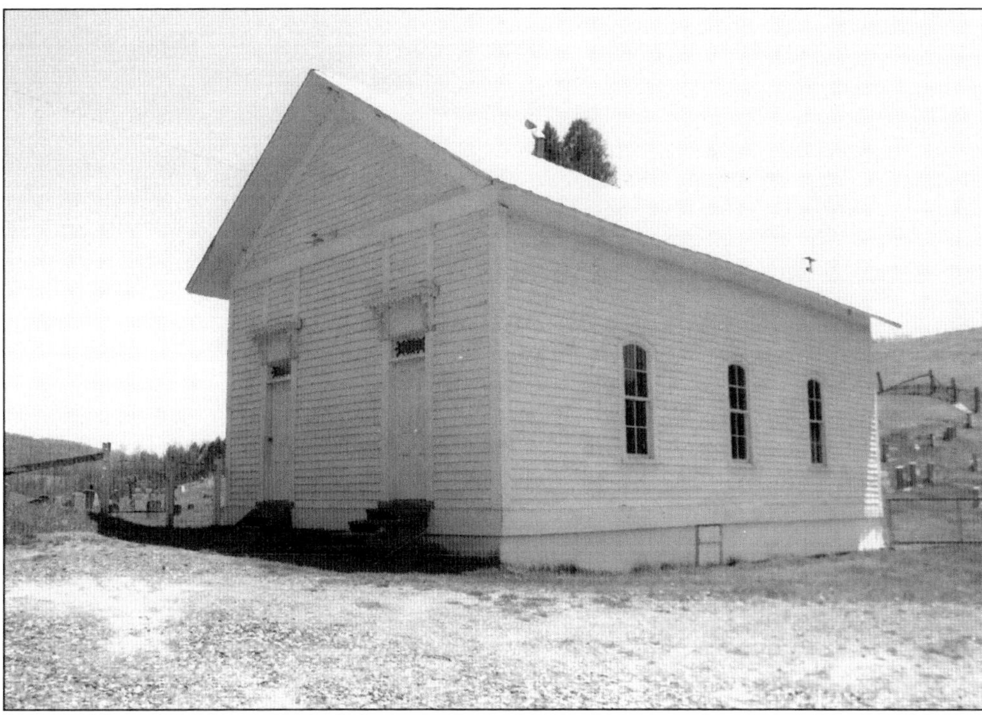

CHAPEL CHURCH, BIG HELTON CREEK. The church has two front doors, one for men and the other for women to enter.

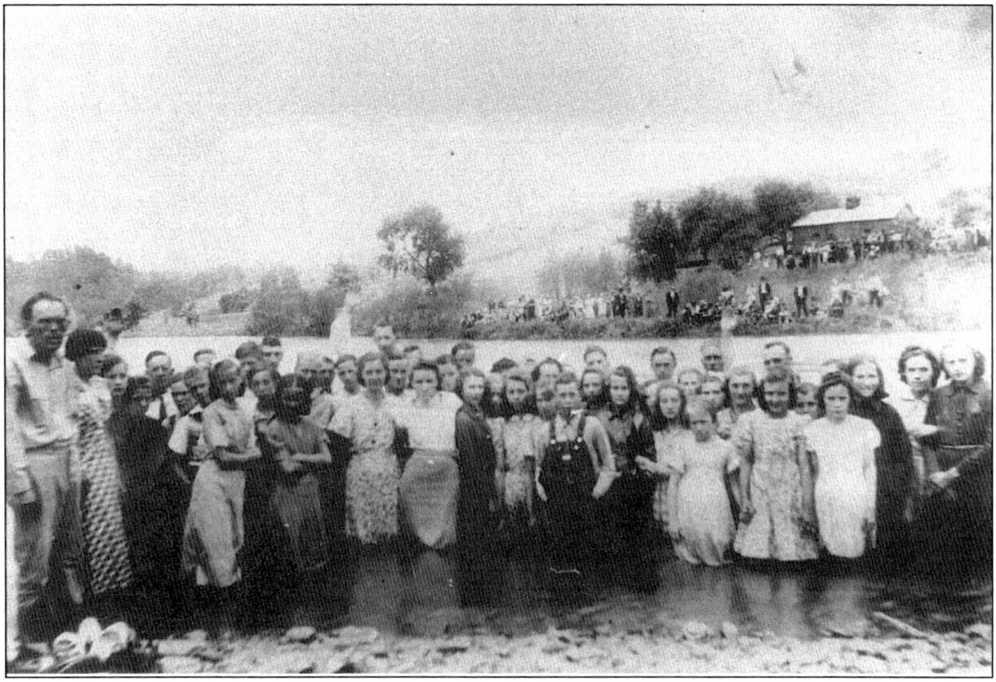

Baptism at Green's Chapel in Crumpler. This group of candidates was baptized together in the North Fork of the New River.

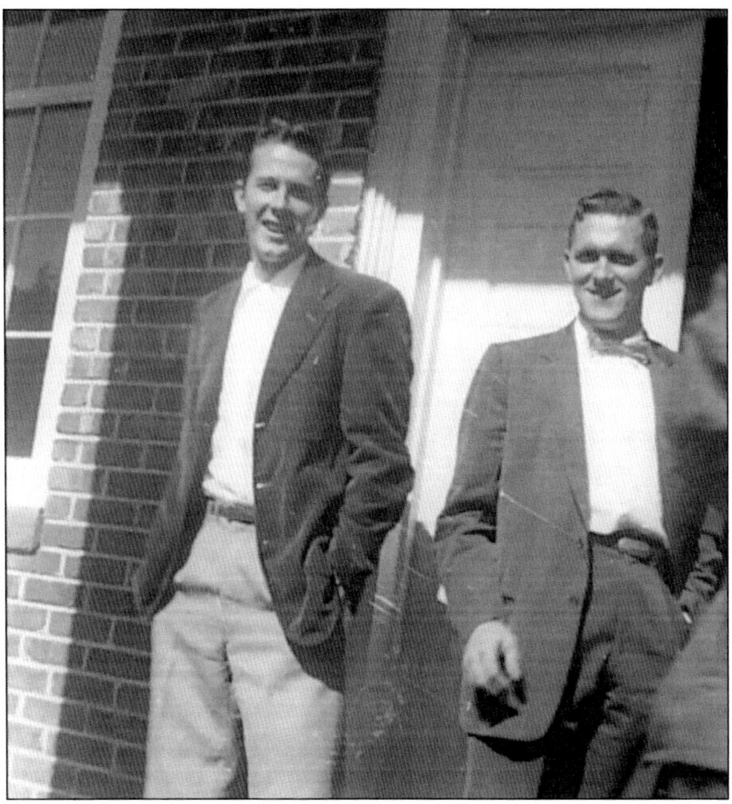

Healing Springs School Teachers. The two teachers are Burl Fowler and Jody Robinson.

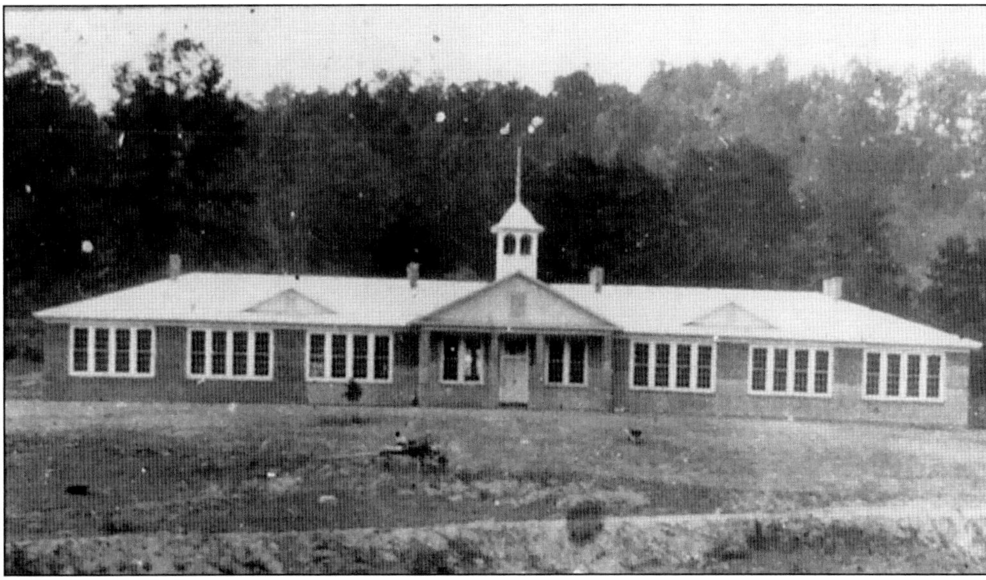

Healing Springs School. The Playwright's Project has recently brought this building back to life after it was closed following consolidation of the county high schools.

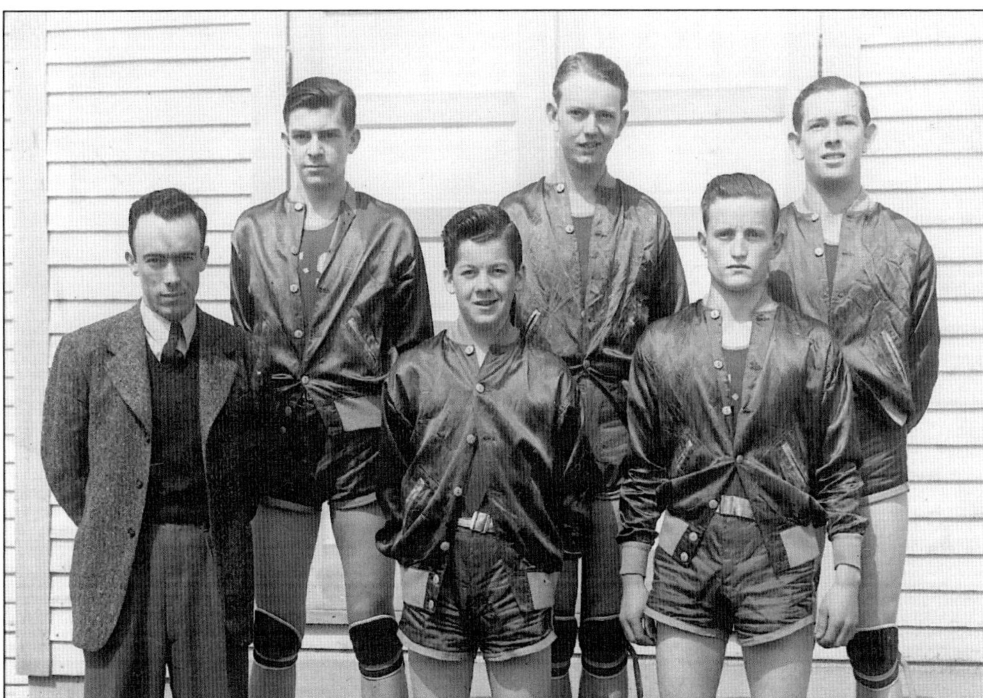

Healing Springs School Boys' Basketball Team. This photograph was taken prior to 1957, when the school became an elementary school.

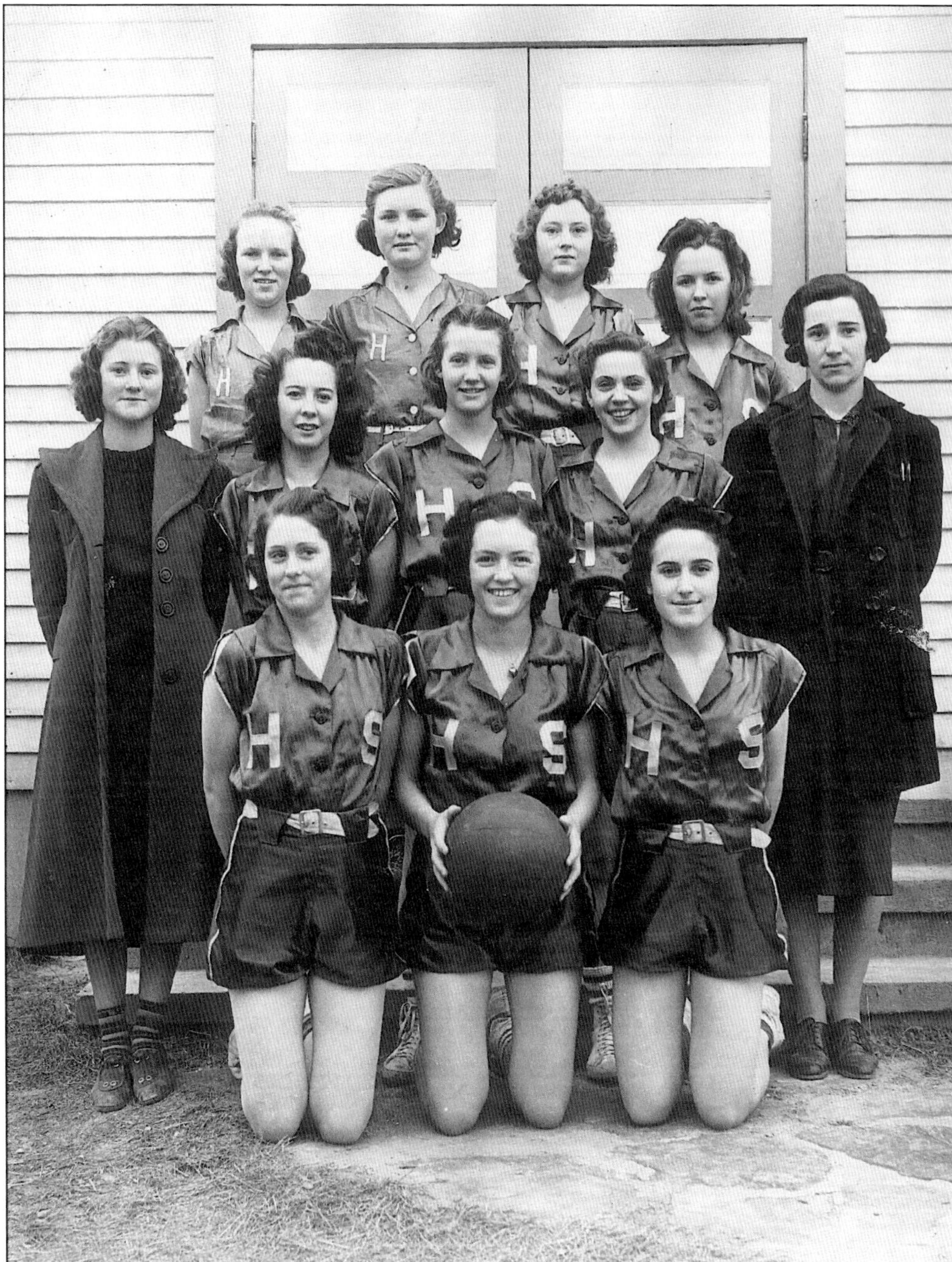

HEALING SPRINGS SCHOOL GIRLS' BASKETBALL TEAM. When the gym was built in 1934, it became possible to have competitive sports such as basketball.

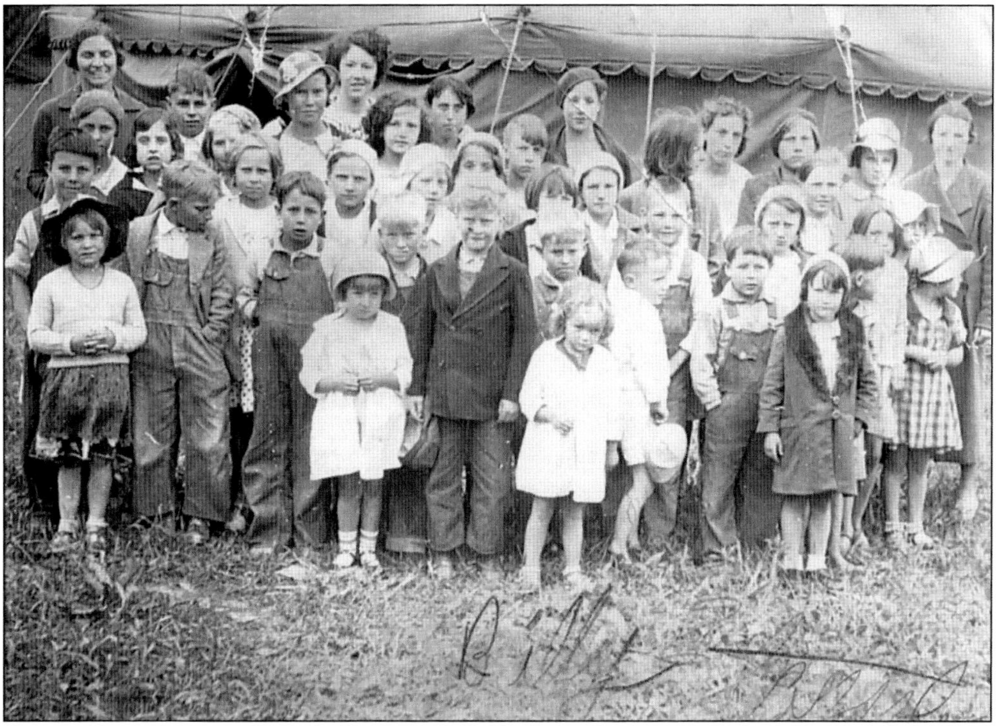

GILLESPIE PRESBYTERIAN CHURCH CHAUTAUQUA. This summer Bible school was held at Little Horse Creek in 1934.

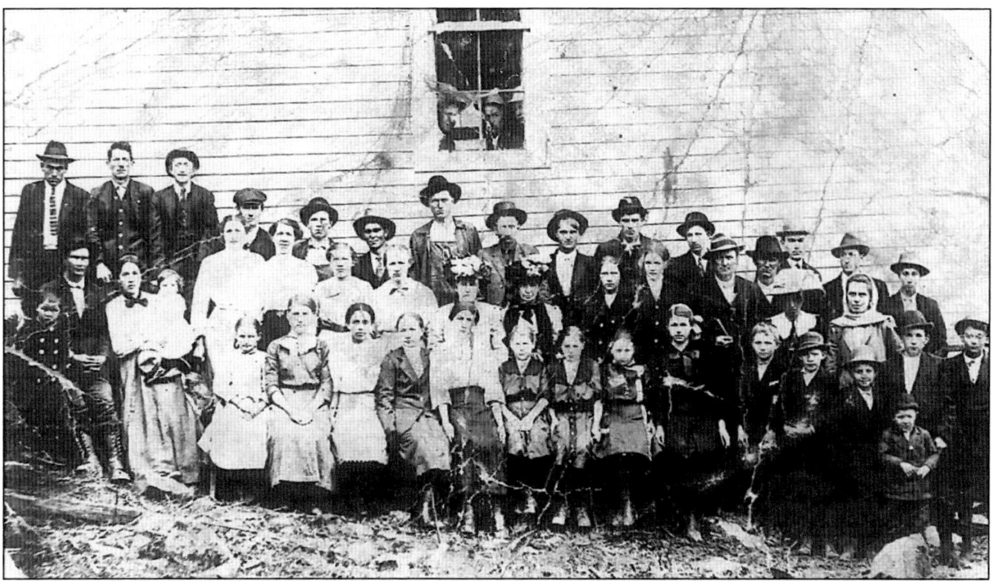

OLD SABBATH HOME CHURCH AT LITTLE HORSE CREEK. This church was built around 1912.

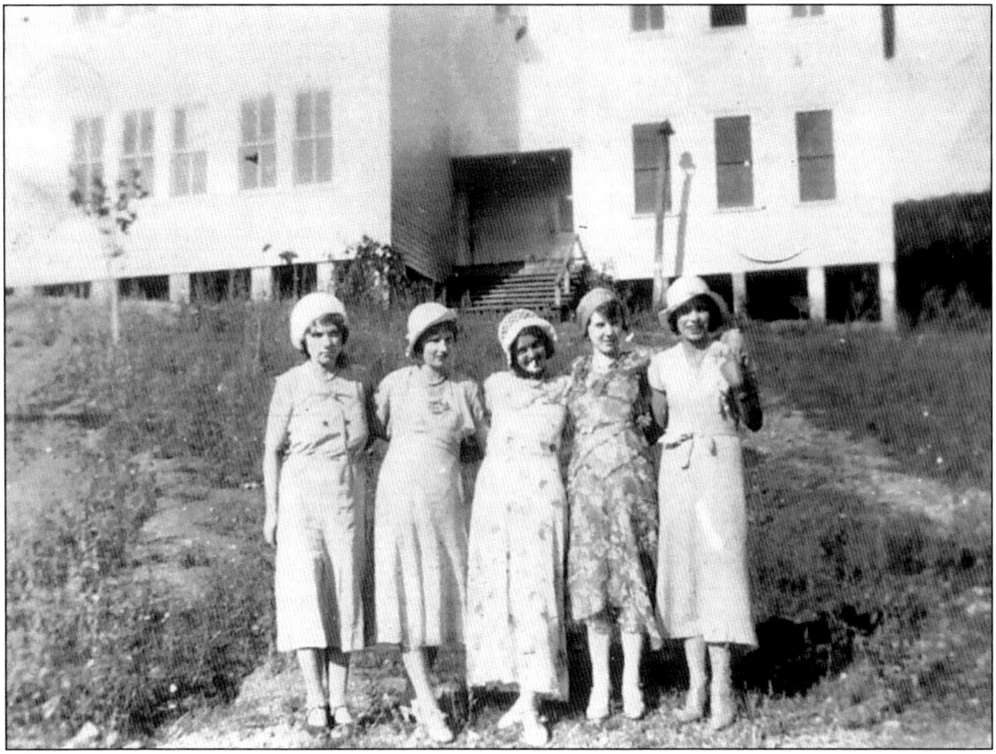

OLD LANSING SCHOOL. This original wooden structure was used prior to the WPA's construction of a new stone building.

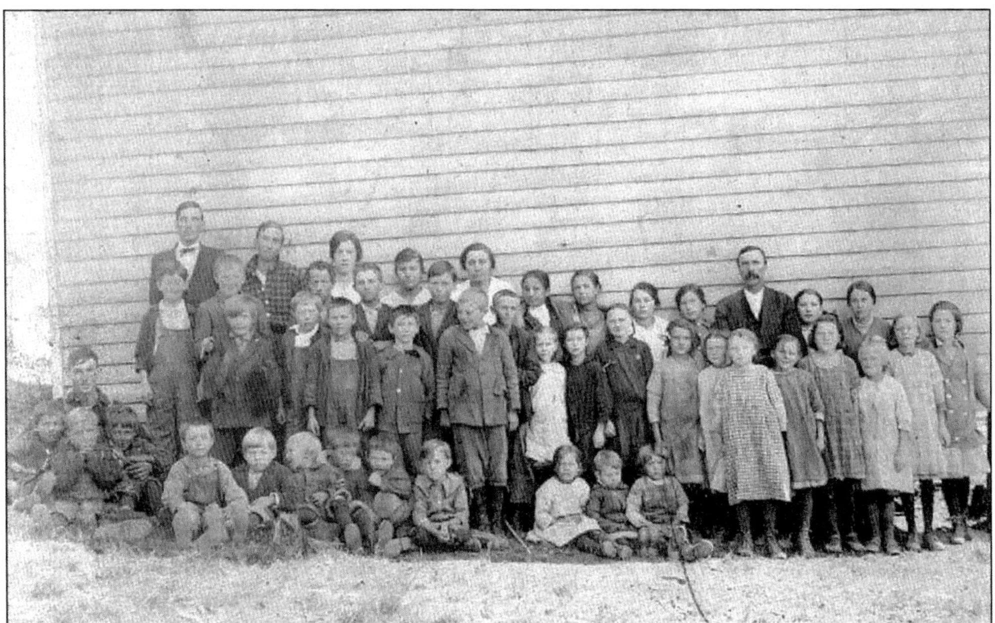

OLD FAIRVIEW SCHOOL IN THE LANSING AREA. This school picture was taken around 1912. The Fairview School served as a Horse Creek community school until the late 1940s.

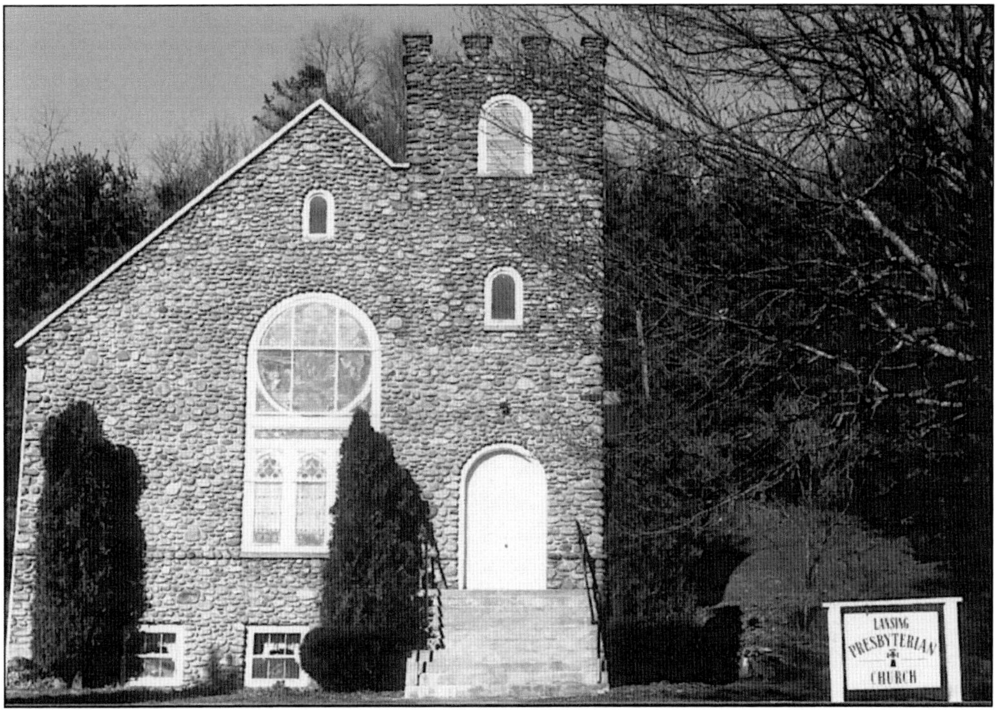

LANSING PRESBYTERIAN CHURCH. Built in 1928, the church is made of native stone.

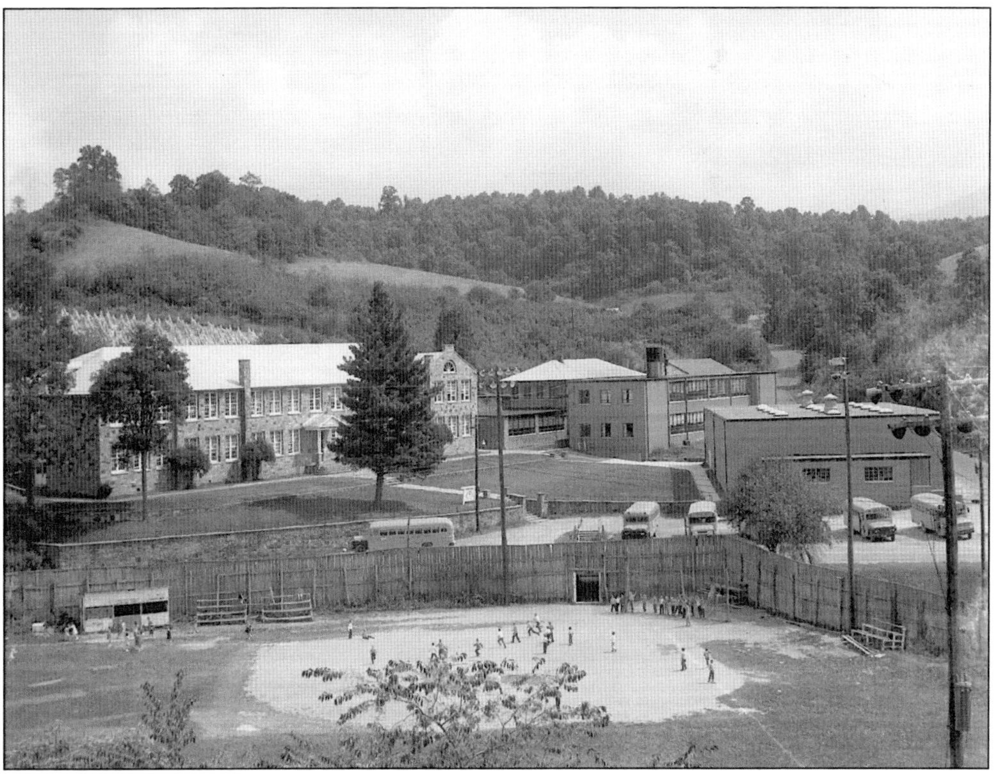
LANSING SCHOOL. This building was constructed by the WPA in the late 1930s.

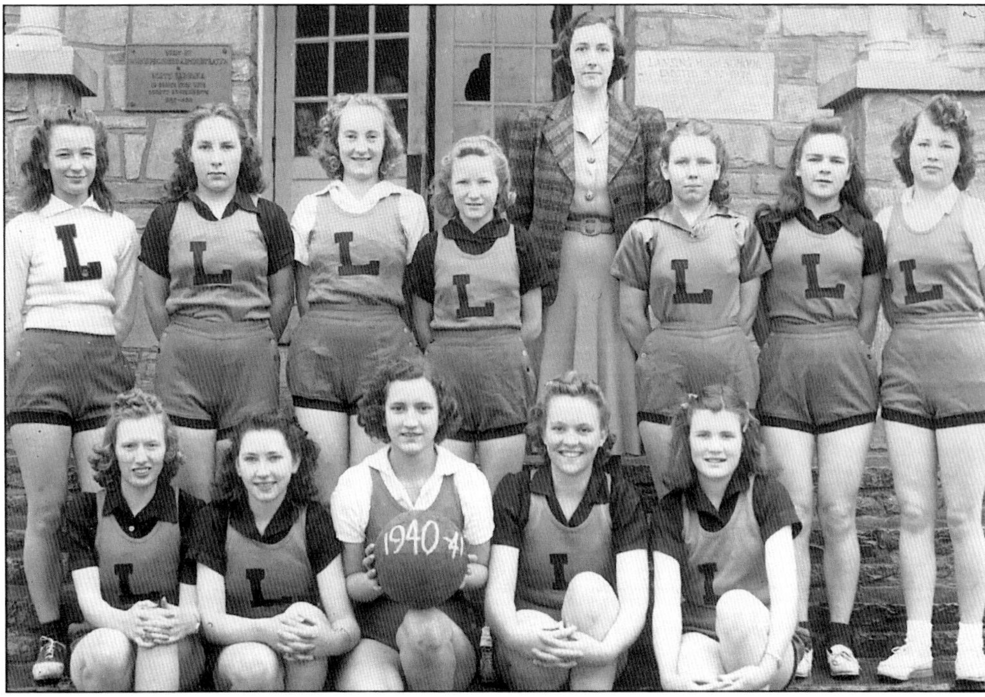

LANSING HIGH SCHOOL GIRLS' BASKETBALL TEAM. Pictured here, from left to right, are the following: (front row) Iris Young, Estella Blevins, Madge Kilby, Ruby Sullivan, and Mildred Farmer; (back row) Glenna Baldwin, Kathleen King, unidentified, Irene Baldwin, Frances Tucker (teacher and coach), Daphne Eller, Lillian Weaver, and Bonnie Baldwin.

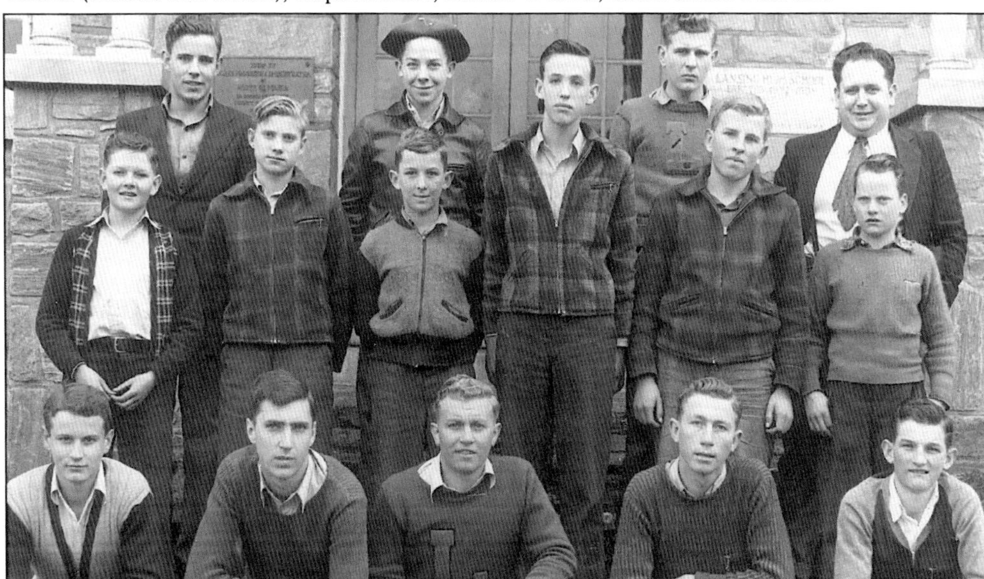

LANSING HIGH SCHOOL BOYS' BASKETBALL TEAM. Pictured here, from left to right, are the following: (front row) Harry Patton, Wells Hart, Robert Faw, Joe Hart, and Warren Hartsog; (second row) Dawes Hartsog, William Stansberry, Paul J. Barr, Ancil Dolinger, Dent Dolinger, and Bill Poe; (back row) Howard Graham, John Barr, Earl King, and Coach Robert Morphus.

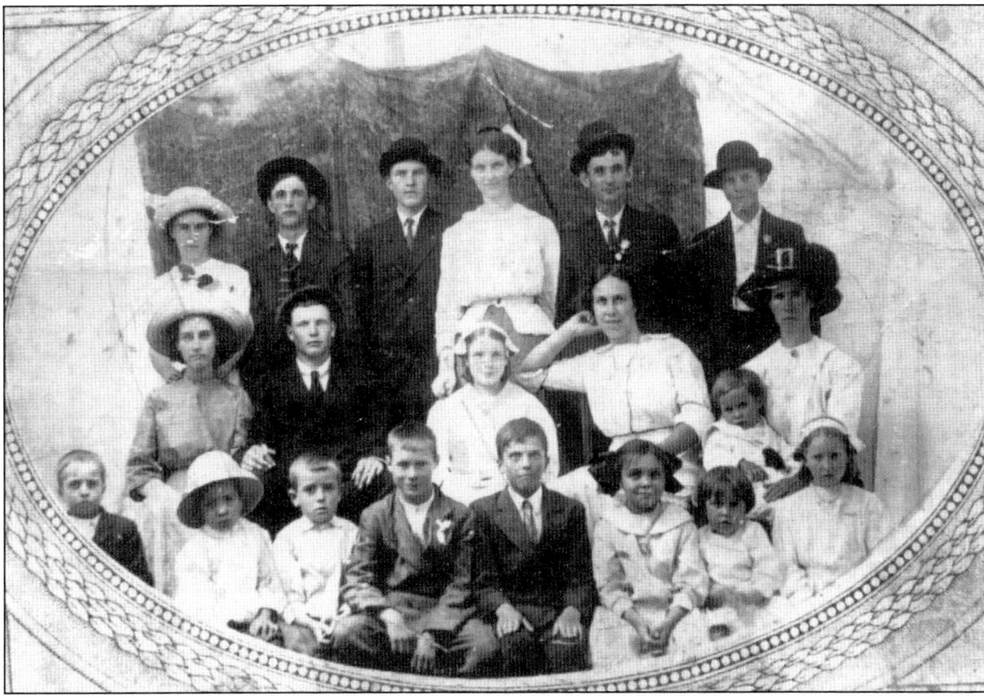

MOUNTAIN UNION BAPTIST CHURCH AT SILAS CREEK. This group was photographed in the late 1920s. Pictured here, from left to right, are the following: (front row) Everett Powers, Miles Reed, Edward Roberts, Carless Roberts, Blanche Powers, Willie Reed, Lucille Reed, and Goldie Roberts; (middle row) Rosa Sexton, Emory Roberts, Bonnie Roberts, Mary Reed, Ramsy Roberts, and Worth Roberts; (back row) Ida Roberts, Dennis Wallace, Austin Roberts, Cordie Roberts, Claude Wallace, and Conard Roberts.

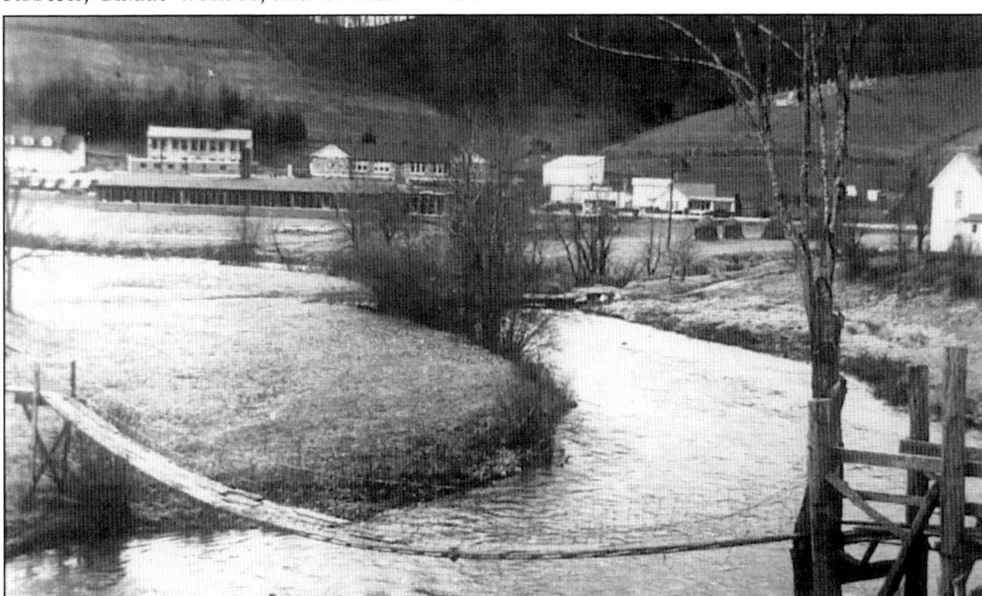

RIVERVIEW COMMUNITY. Pictured behind the school building is the school gym, which later burned. The school is now the Riverview Community Center.

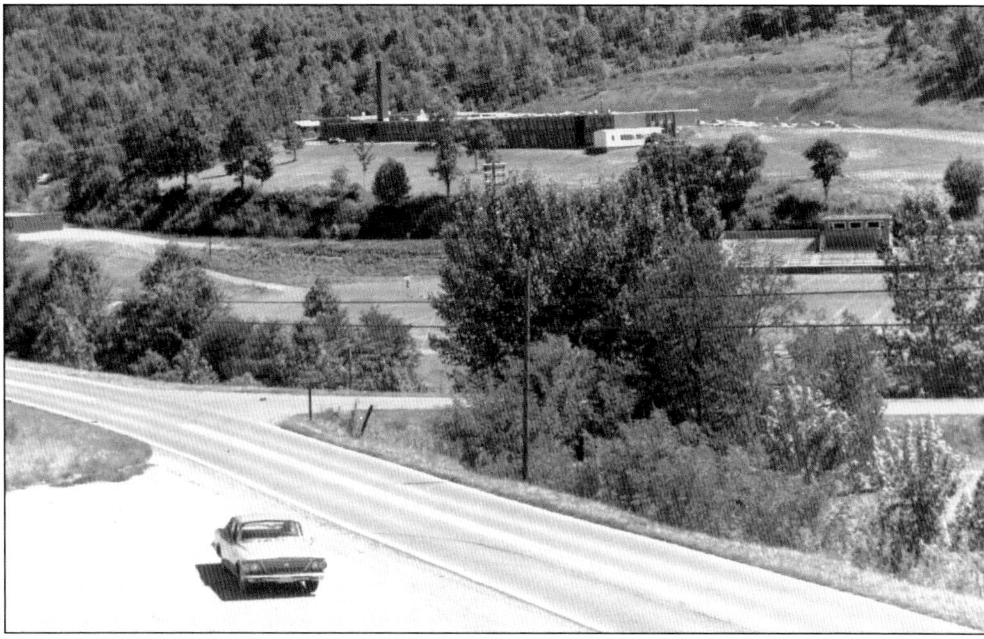

NORTHWEST HIGH SCHOOL BETWEEN WARRENSVILLE AND LANSING. The school population from this area was consolidated into a new high school in 1998. Northwest became the consolidated middle school for Ashe County.

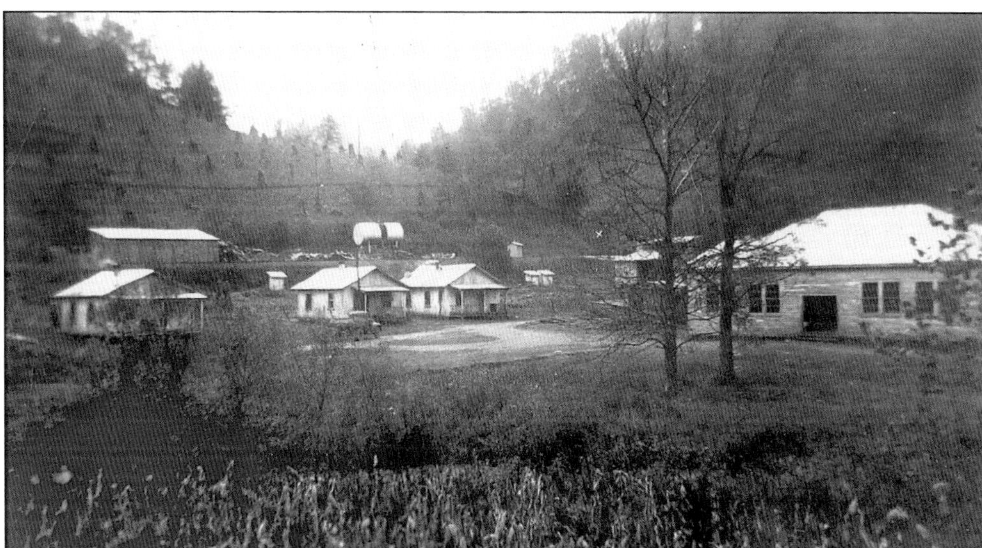

WARRENSVILLE SCHOOL. The school is now the home of the Blue Ridge Opportunity Commission.

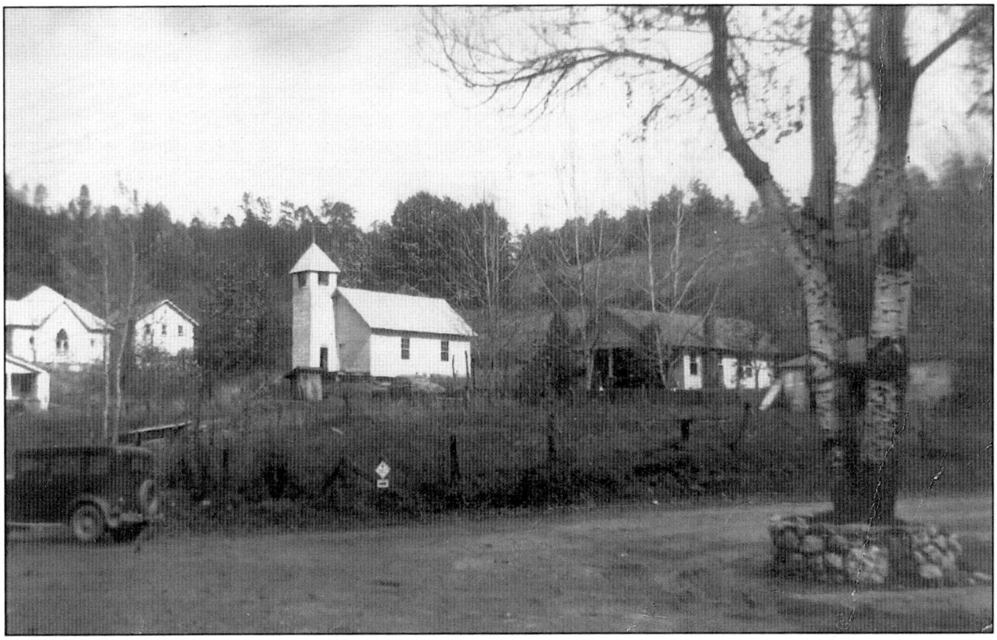

TWO WARRENSVILLE CHURCHES. Pictured on the left is the Warrensville Methodist Episcopal Church and educational building. The early Baptist church is pictured in the center of the photograph

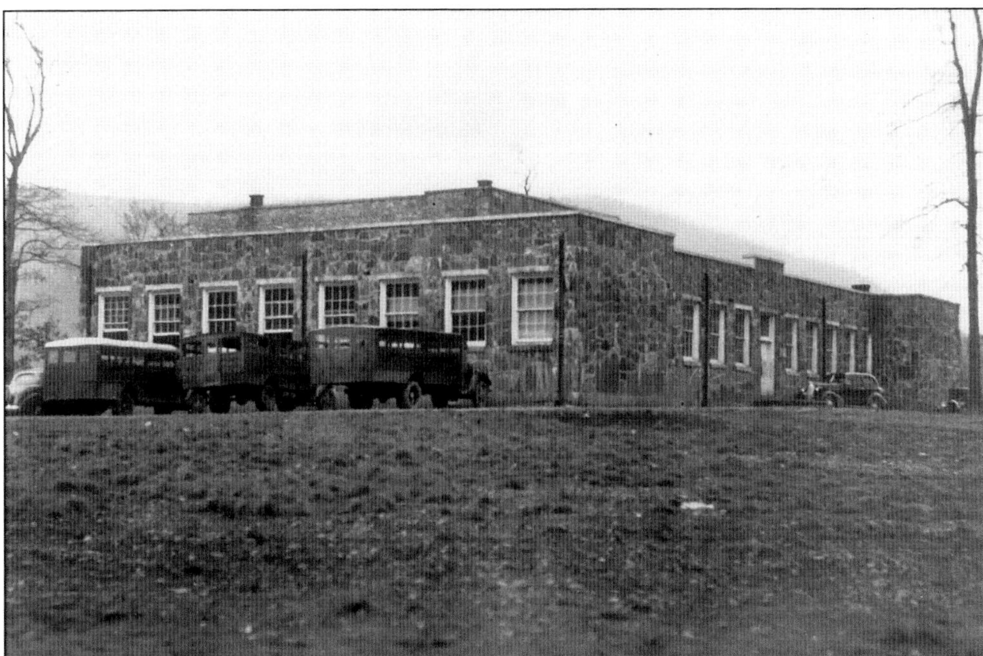

JEFFERSON SCHOOL. This school is one of several structures in Ashe County built in the 1930s as a WPA project.

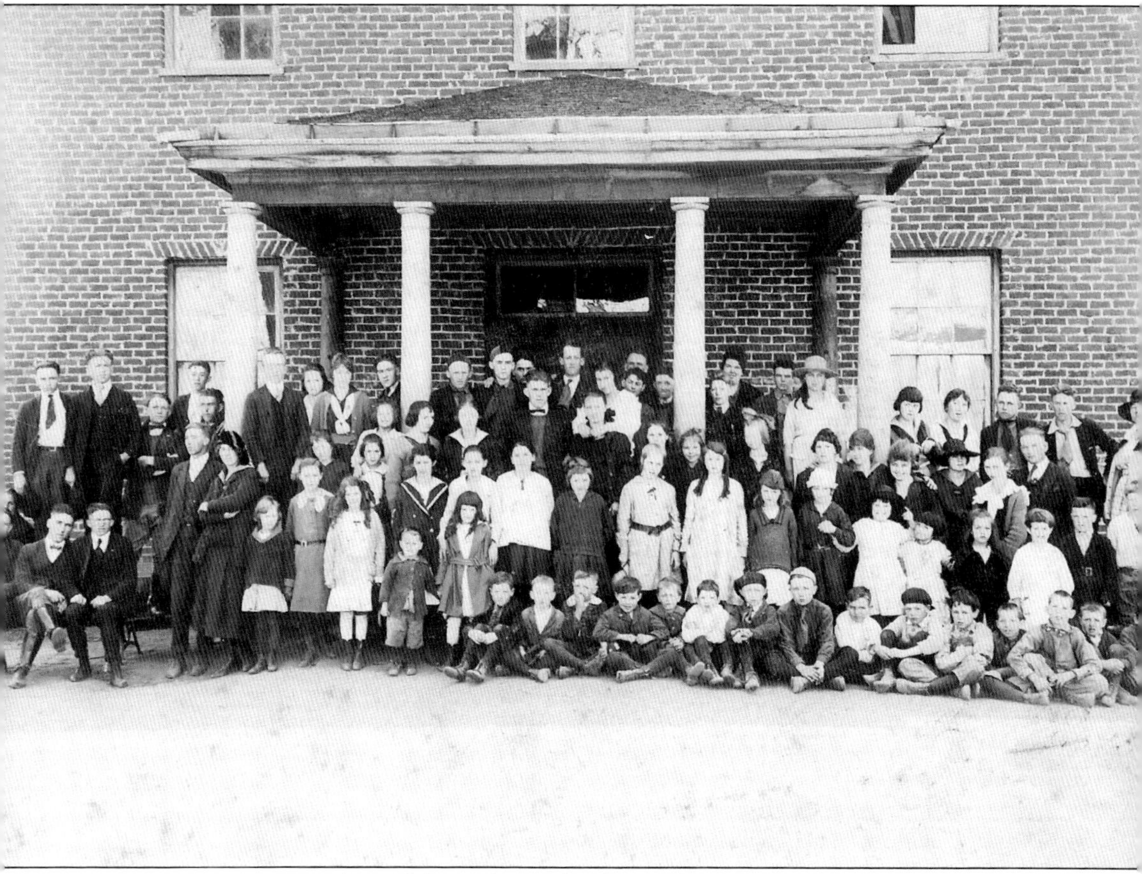

JEFFERSON ACADEMY. One of the earliest schools in Ashe County, the Jefferson Academy was sponsored and operated by the Jefferson Methodist Church. This photograph was taken in the early 1920s.

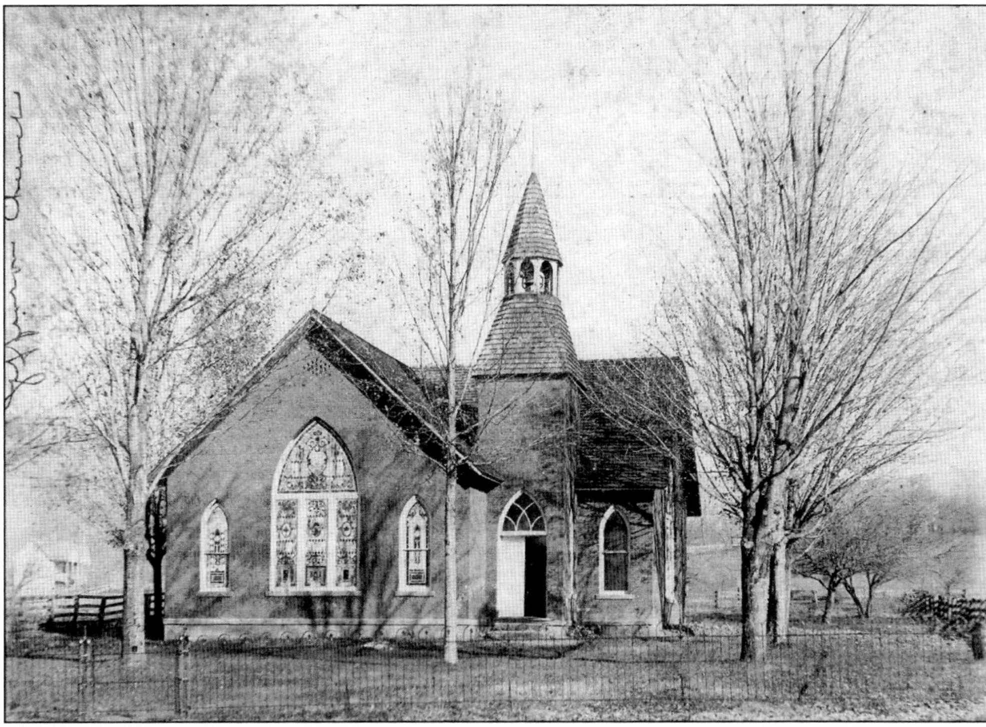

JEFFERSON UNITED METHODIST CHURCH. This church has always been a community social, religious, and civic center.

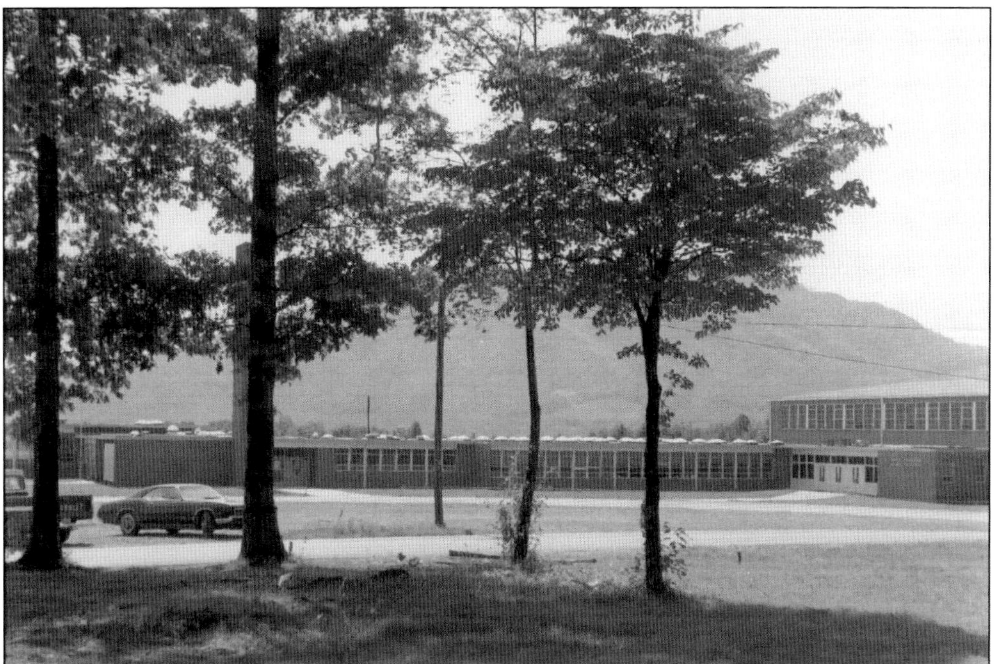

ASHE CENTRAL HIGH SCHOOL. This photograph was taken before the school was absorbed by the new consolidated high school in 1998.

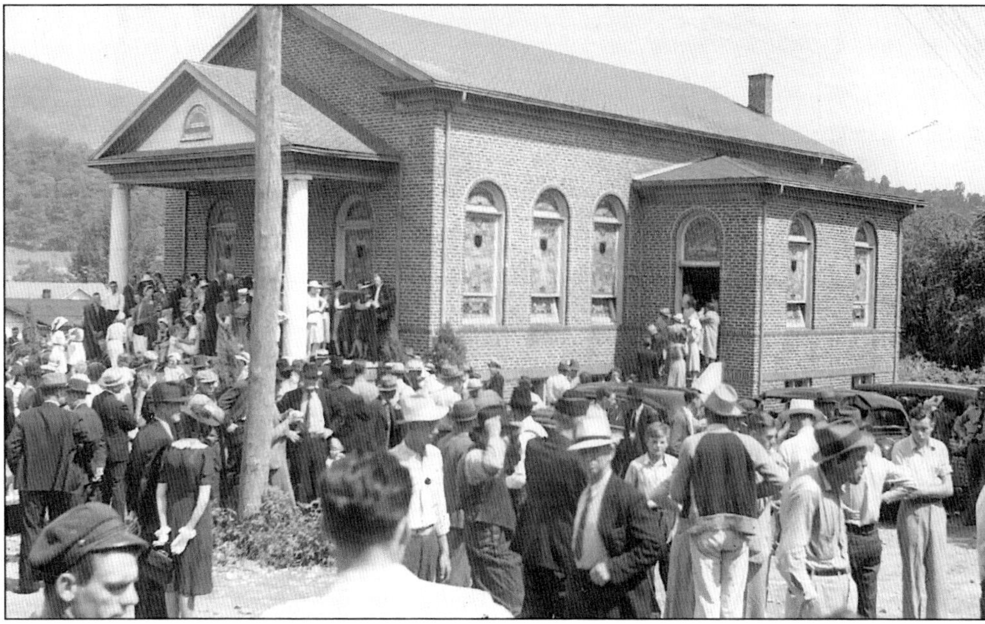

WEST JEFFERSON UNITED METHODIST CHURCH IN THE 1940S. The congregation is seen socializing after services.

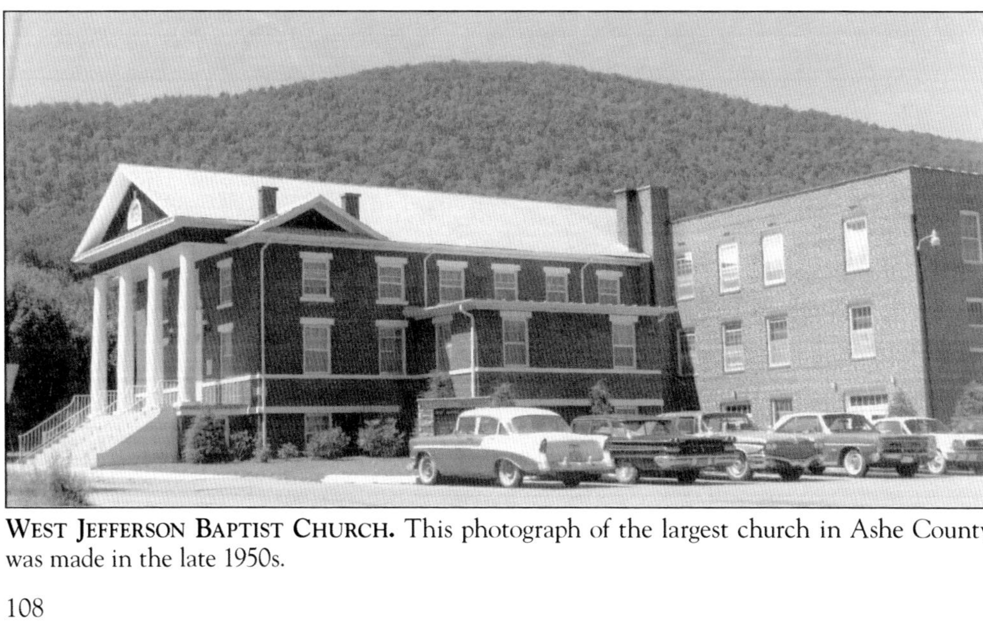

WEST JEFFERSON BAPTIST CHURCH. This photograph of the largest church in Ashe County was made in the late 1950s.

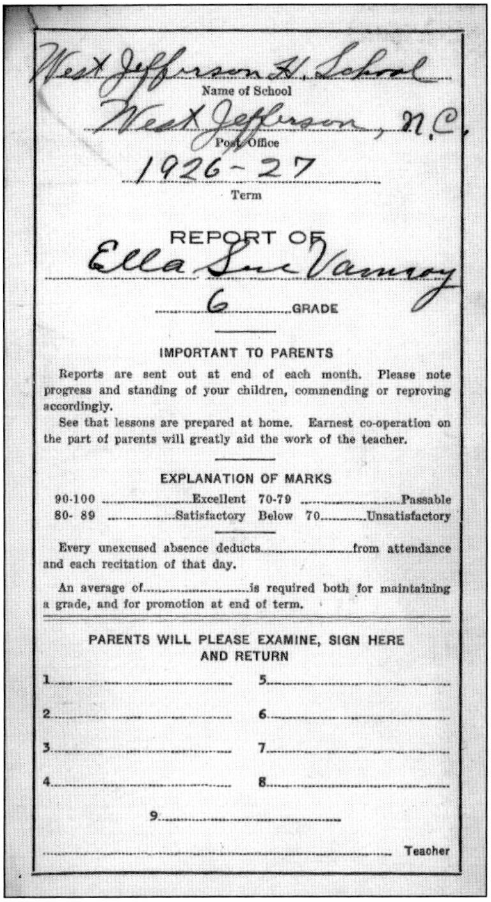

West Jefferson H. School
Name of School
West Jefferson, N.C.
Post Office
1926-27
Term

REPORT OF
Ella Sue Vannoy
6 GRADE

IMPORTANT TO PARENTS

Reports are sent out at end of each month. Please note progress and standing of your children, commending or reproving accordingly.

See that lessons are prepared at home. Earnest co-operation on the part of parents will greatly aid the work of the teacher.

EXPLANATION OF MARKS

90-100 .... Excellent 70-79 .... Passable
80- 89 .... Satisfactory Below 70........ Unsatisfactory

Every unexcused absence deducts........from attendance and each recitation of that day.

An average of........is required both for maintaining a grade, and for promotion at end of term.

PARENTS WILL PLEASE EXAMINE, SIGN HERE AND RETURN

1. .... 5. ....
2. .... 6. ....
3. .... 7. ....
4. .... 8. ....
9. ....

.... Teacher

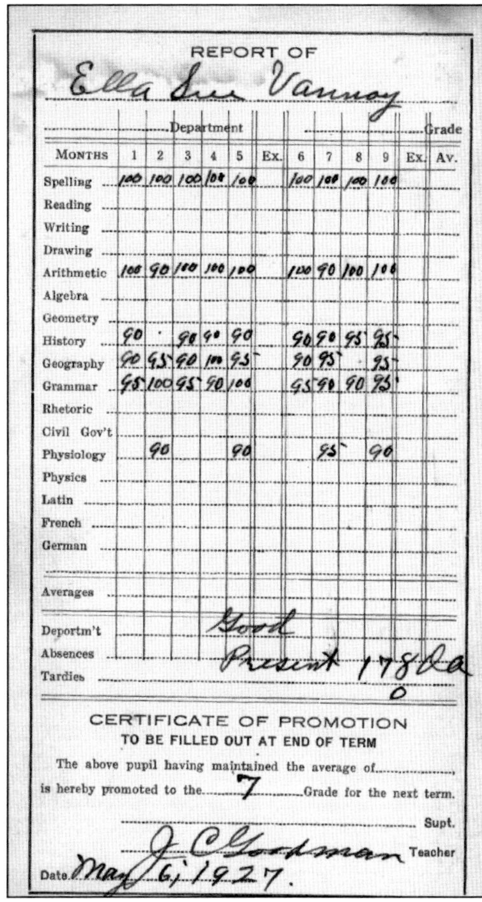

REPORT OF
Ella Sue Vannoy
.... Department .... Grade

Months	1	2	3	4	5	Ex.	6	7	8	9	Ex.	Av.
Spelling	100	100	100	100	100		100	100	100	100		
Reading												
Writing												
Drawing												
Arithmetic	100	90	100	100	100		100	90	100	100		
Algebra												
Geometry												
History	90		90	90	90		90	90	95	95		
Geography	90	95	90	100	95		90	95		95		
Grammar	95	100	95	90	100		95	90	90	95		
Rhetoric												
Civil Gov't												
Physiology		90			90			95		90		
Physics												
Latin												
French												
German												
Averages												
Deportm't	Good											
Absences	Present 178 Da											
Tardies	0											

CERTIFICATE OF PROMOTION
TO BE FILLED OUT AT END OF TERM

The above pupil having maintained the average of........, is hereby promoted to the 7 Grade for the next term.

.... Supt.
J C Goodman Teacher
Date May 6, 1927.

A 1927 Report Card from West Jefferson High School. This shows Ella Sue Vannoy Colvard's end-of-year report.

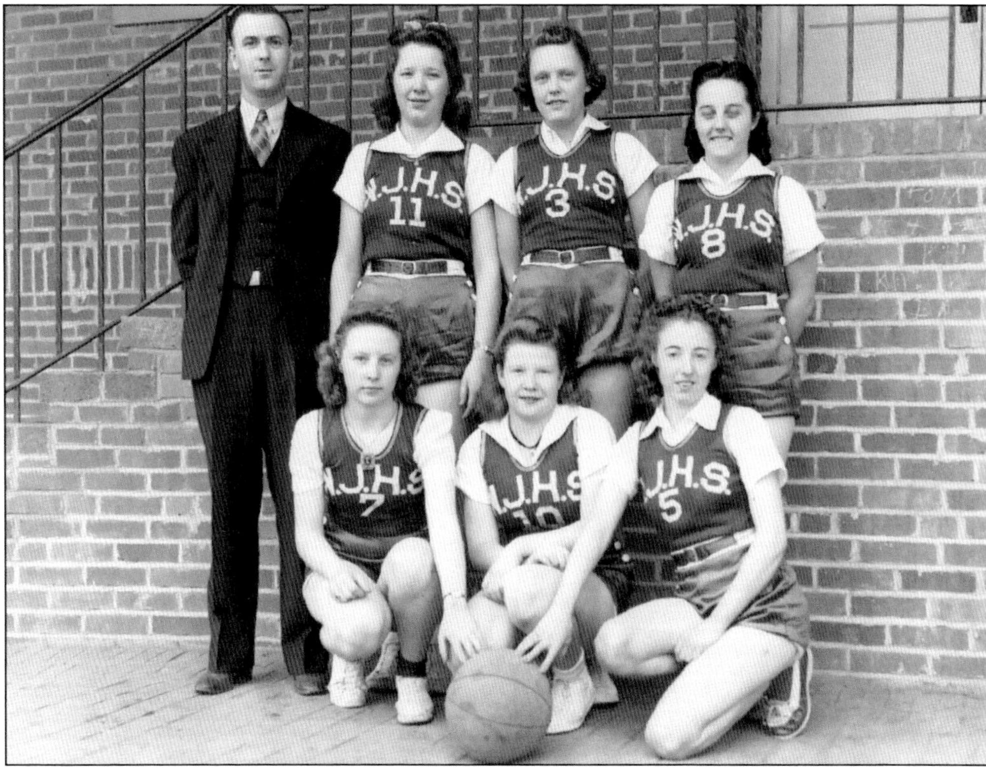

WEST JEFFERSON HIGH SCHOOL GIRLS' BASKETBALL TEAM. Pictured from left to right are the following: (front row) Marie Woodie McMillan, Helen Sells, and Doris Stevens; (back row) Coach Oscar Houck, Mary Brown Allen, Vivian Johnston (Garvery), and Kathrine Woodie Hege.

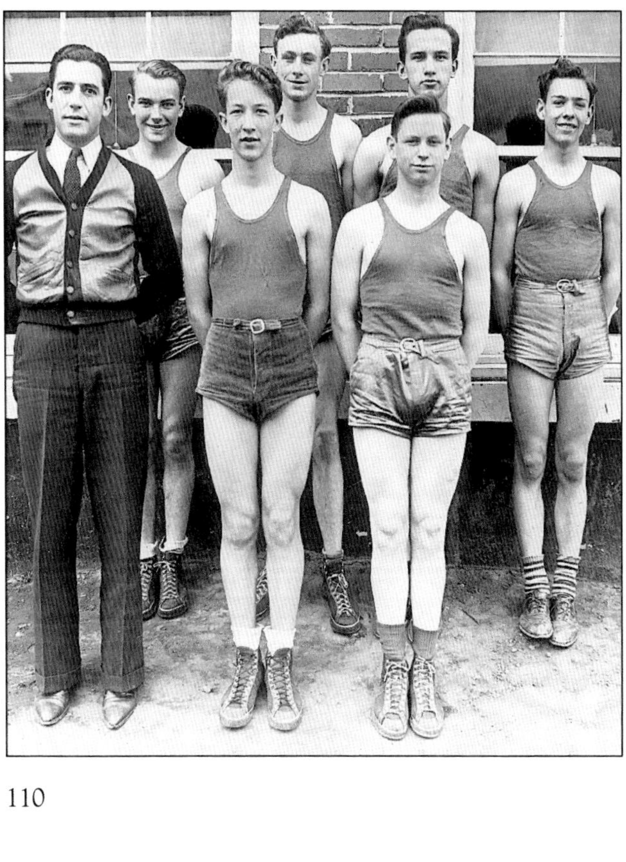

WEST JEFFERSON HIGH SCHOOL BOYS' BASKETBALL TEAM. Pictured here, from left to right, are the following: (front row) Principal Paul Perkins, Jack Miller, and R.C. Miller; (back row) unidentified, Jim Allen, Edwin Weaver, and unidentified.

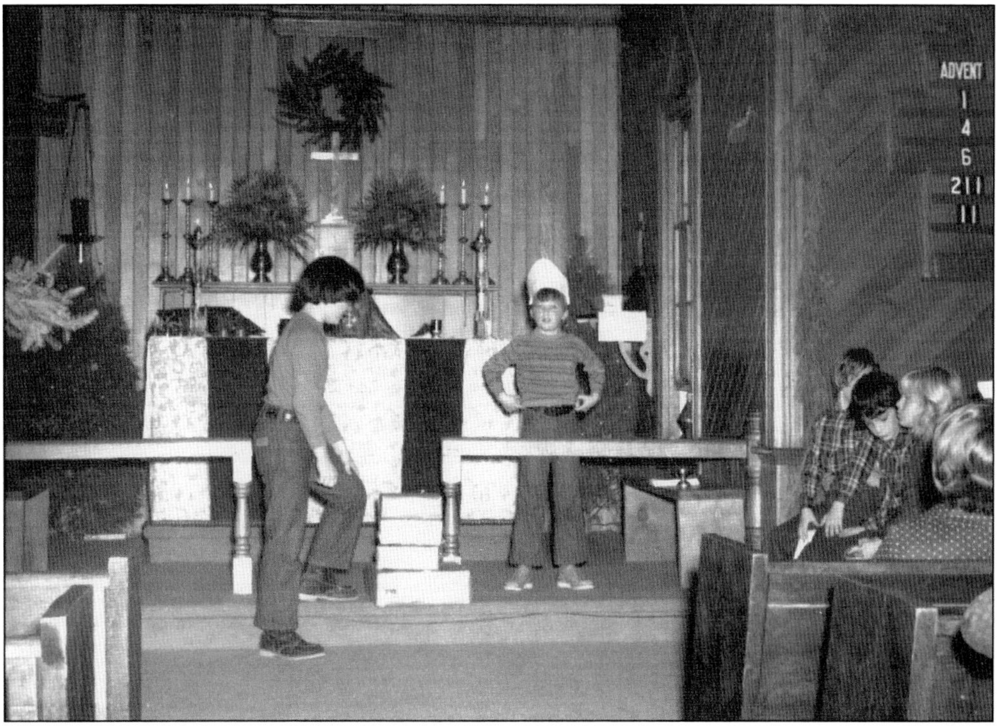

St. Mary's Church in Beaver Creek. This photograph was made in the early 1970s, before the famous Ben Long frescoes were painted. The children participating in the program are Richard Faulkenberry (left) and John Mills (right).

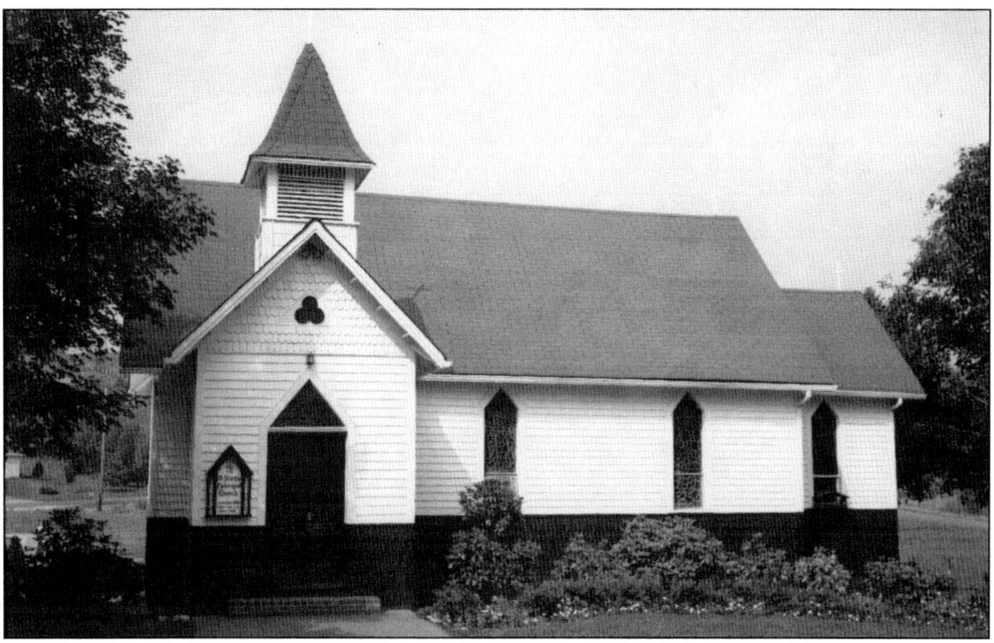

Exterior of St. Mary's Church, Beaver Creek (c. 1978). At the time this photograph was taken, the three frescoes by Ben Long had been completed, but a handicapped ramp and additional planting had not been completed.

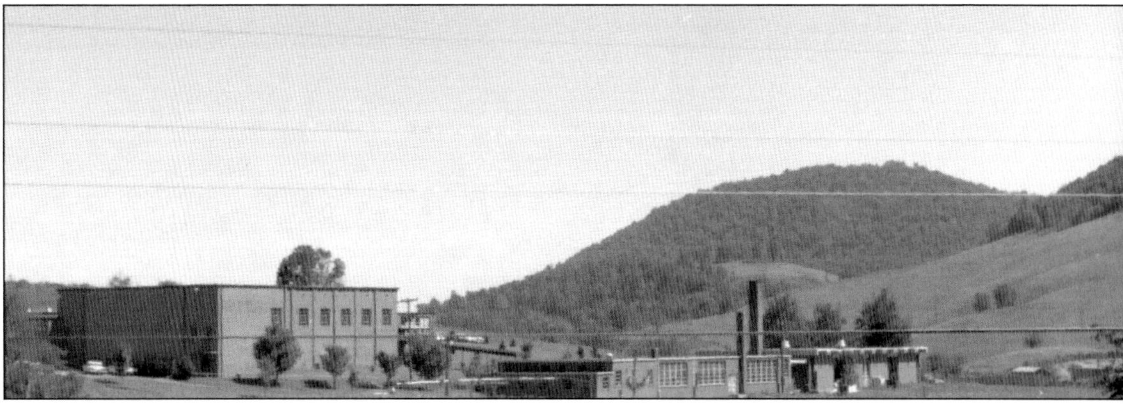

Beaver Creek High School. The population of this school was absorbed into the new consolidated high school in 1998.

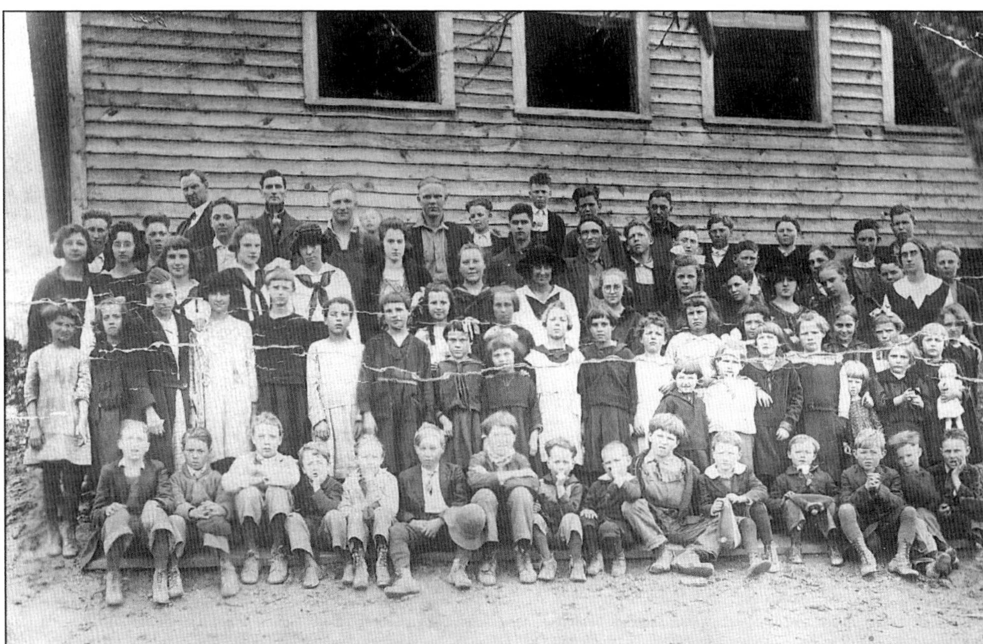

Fleetwood School. The school opened its doors to students in 1921.

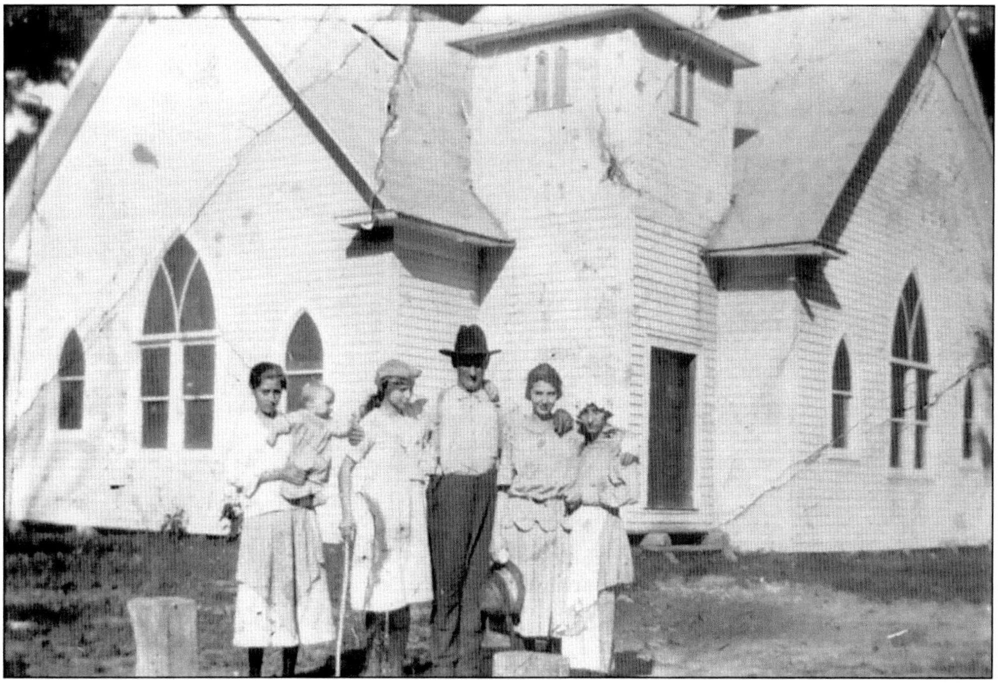

OLD BETHANY METHODIST CHURCH. A modern stone church was erected on this site in 1952.

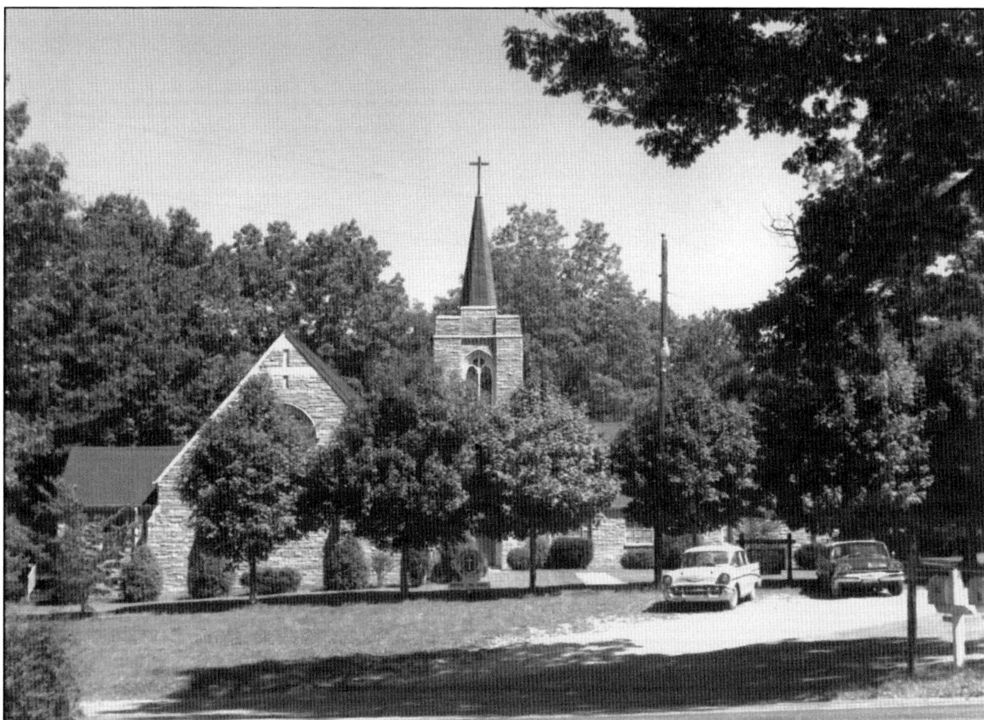

NEW BETHANY METHODIST CHURCH. This church in Baldwin, built in 1952, was featured in the May 19, 1956 issue of the *Saturday Evening Post* in an article about its architect, Howard Haines.

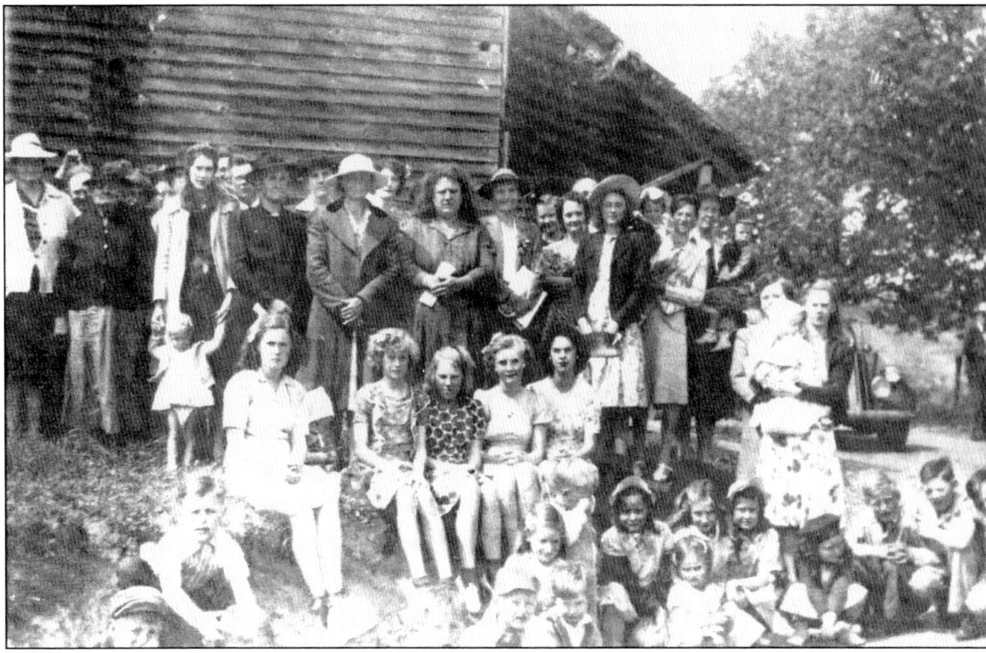

CHERRY LANE CHURCH IN IDLEWILD. This church changed its name to Stephen's Memorial Methodist Church in the early 1950s.

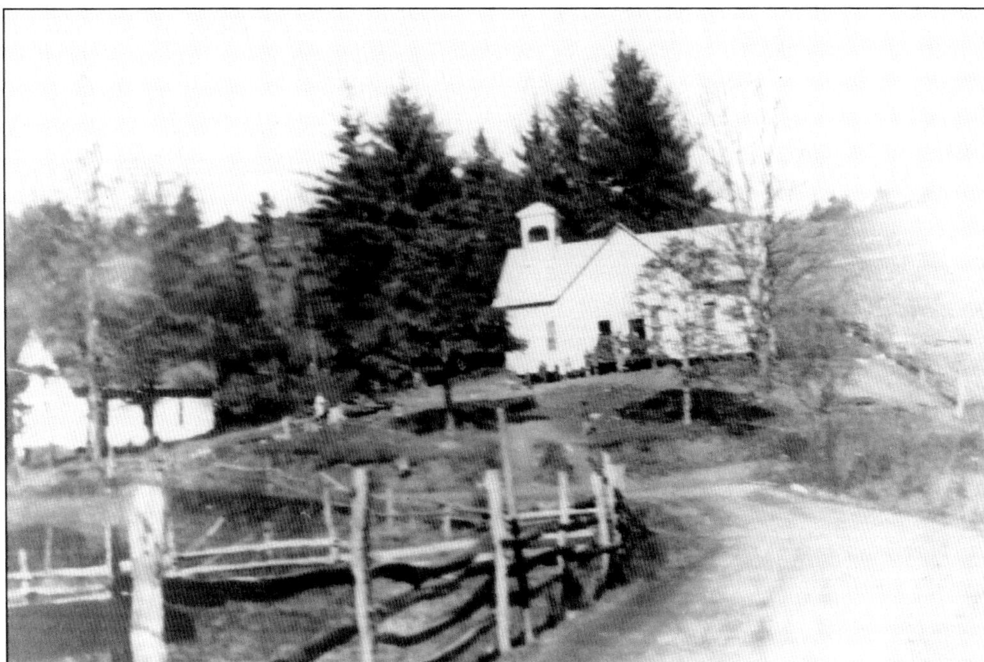

PINE SWAMP CHURCH IN THE IDLEWILD SECTION. When Idlewild School was closed in the 1950s, its bell was moved to this churchyard.

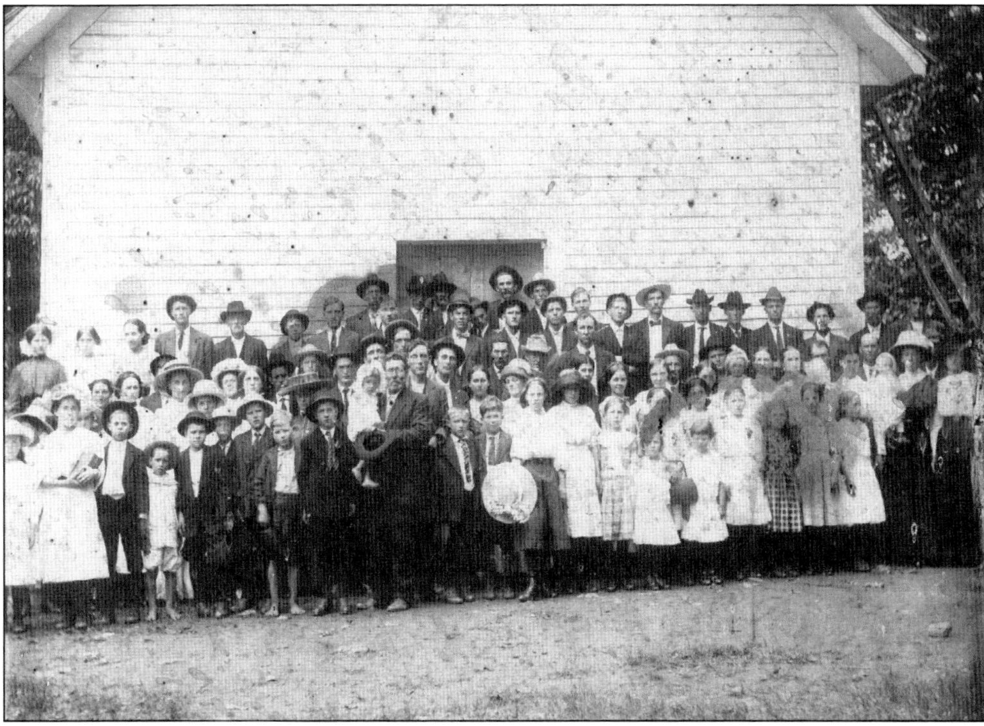

IDLEWILD METHODIST CHURCH. This picture was taken in 1912. Notice that the children are barefoot, although they are otherwise dressed in their Sunday best.

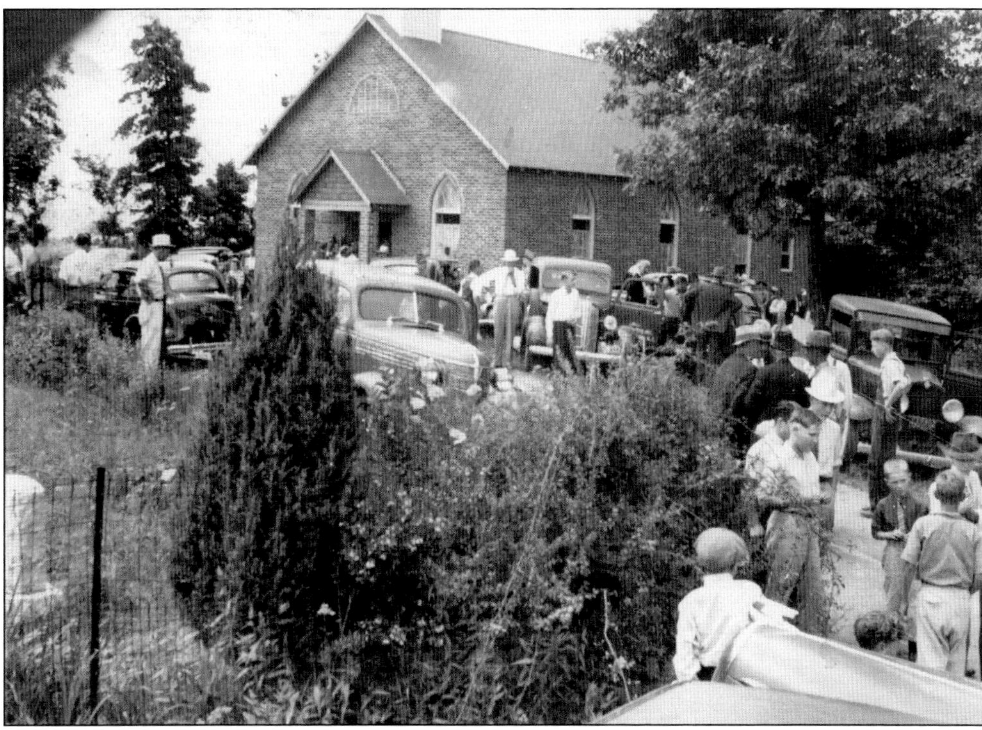

PARKWAY BAPTIST CHURCH. Pictured in 1937, this church is located in Glendale Springs.

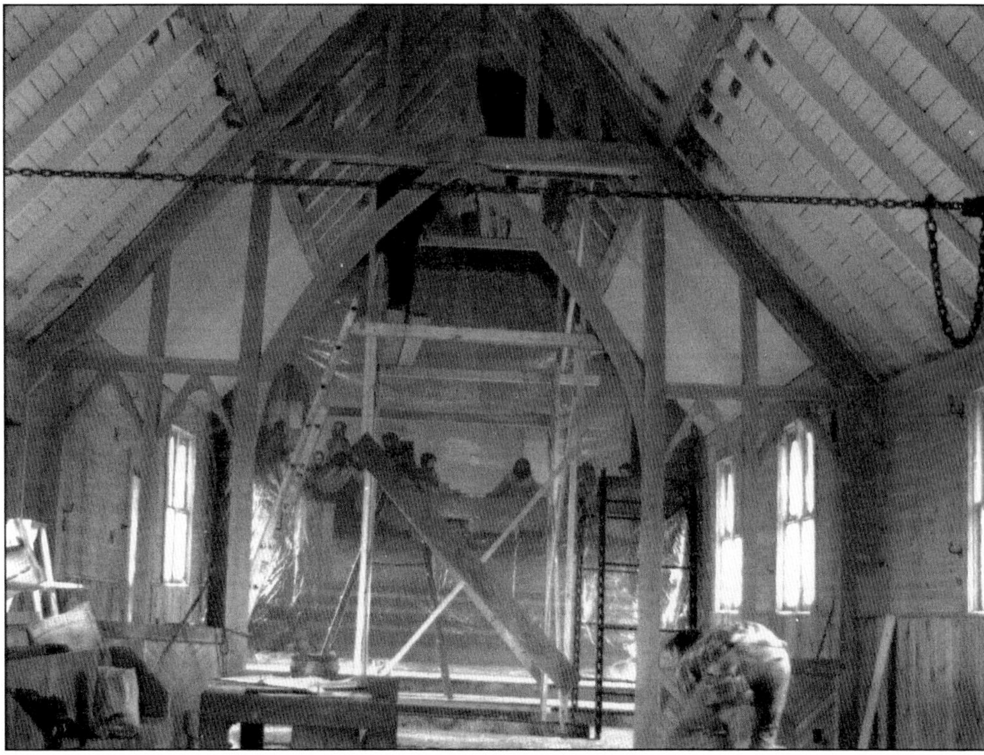

INTERIOR OF HOLY TRINITY CHURCH, GLENDALE SPRINGS (C. 1980). After Ben Long painted his fresco, *The Last Supper*, extensive reconstruction of the church, which had fallen into total disrepair, was necessary.

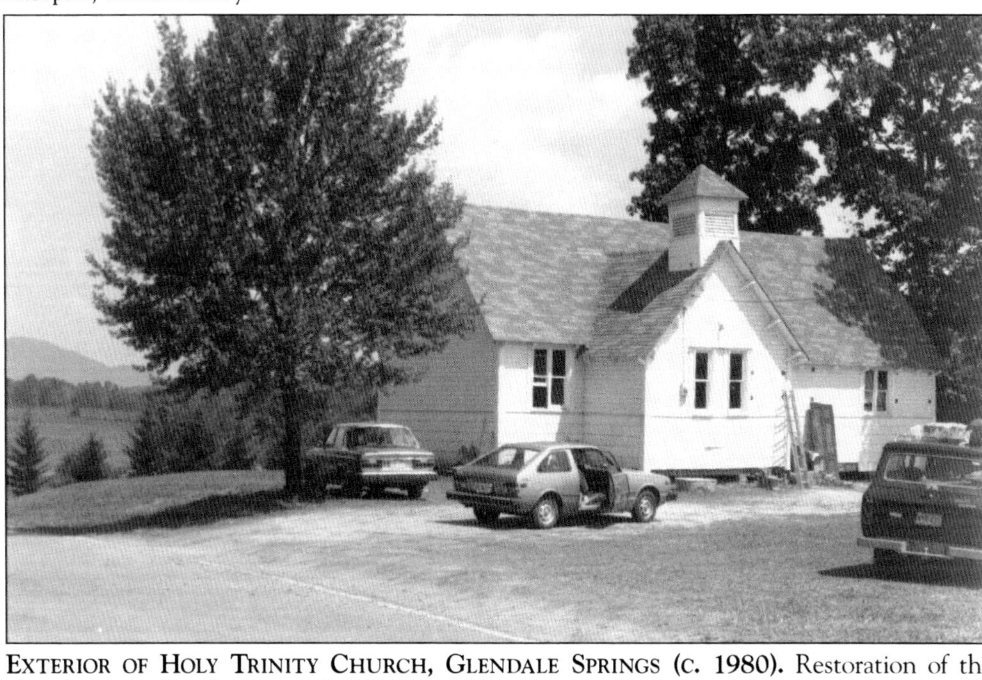

EXTERIOR OF HOLY TRINITY CHURCH, GLENDALE SPRINGS (C. 1980). Restoration of the church exterior has been completed, but new windows are not yet in place.

Seven

Recreation and Socializing

In early Ashe County, social life revolved largely around the church, which often served as a school. The big social events were the annual dinners and spring and fall revivals. A young man hoped to win his gal's heart by "bidding off" her box at the box supper. To keep the revival running as long as possible, each night different young people would volunteer to go up to the altar.

Men and women had various social activities often associated with their work. These varied from quilting and making apple butter to corn shucking and barn raising.

In many family gatherings, the men ate first, the children, second, and the women, last. For more formal meals, they would kill a fat hen. Back then children ate last or were admonished to "take an old cold tater and wait."

Everyone looked forward to having company. Relatives would come from a distance and sometimes stay for weeks or months. Even total strangers passing through would stop for meals and a night's rest. This was Southern hospitality at its finest.

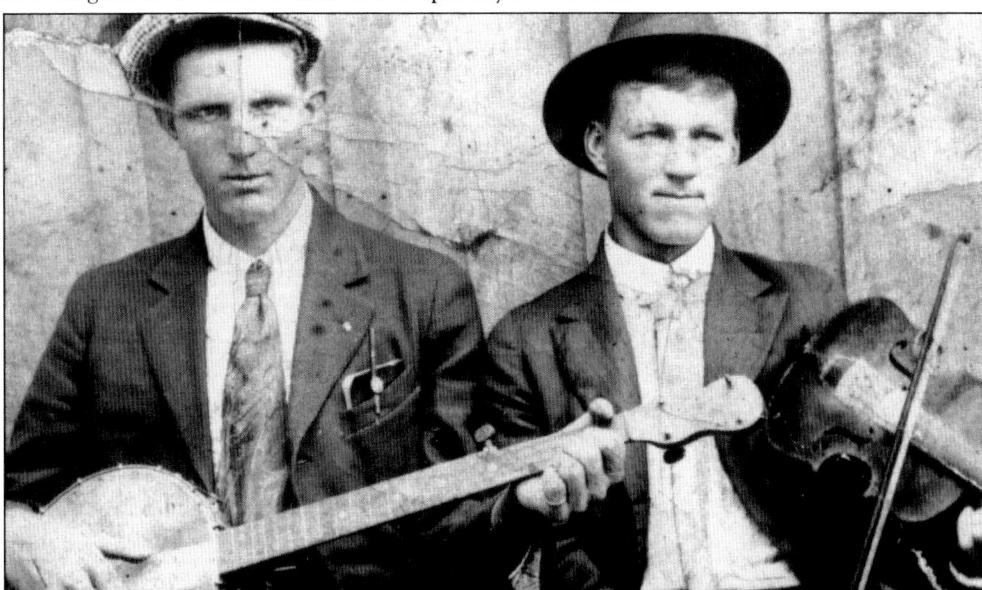

CONARA ROBERTS AND CHARLIE FRANCIS, EARLY MUSICIANS. This front porch pastime allowed early citizens to preserve the ballads of the old country while creating music which continues to grow in popularity.

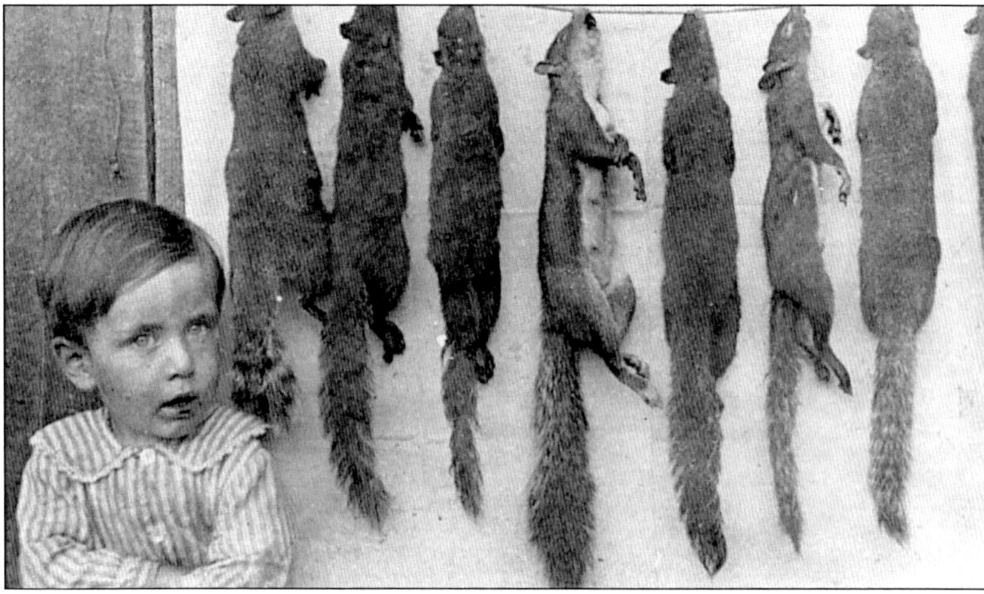

FRED SPENCER. This Helton youth admires the results of a good hunt for gray squirrels.

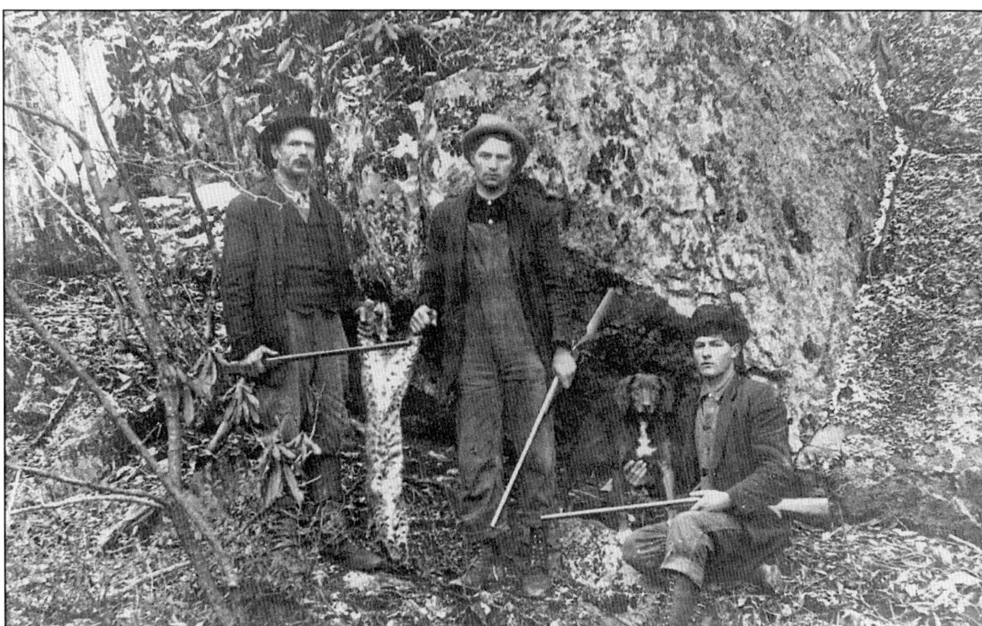

THE RESULTS OF ONE HUNTING TRIP. Eck Perry, Victor Spencer, and Greely Spencer killed this cougar at Feese Branch in 1930.

CLYDE NYE AND DEMMA WOODIE. Clyde (left) and Demma (right) are making spending money from a bounty offered for capturing rats.

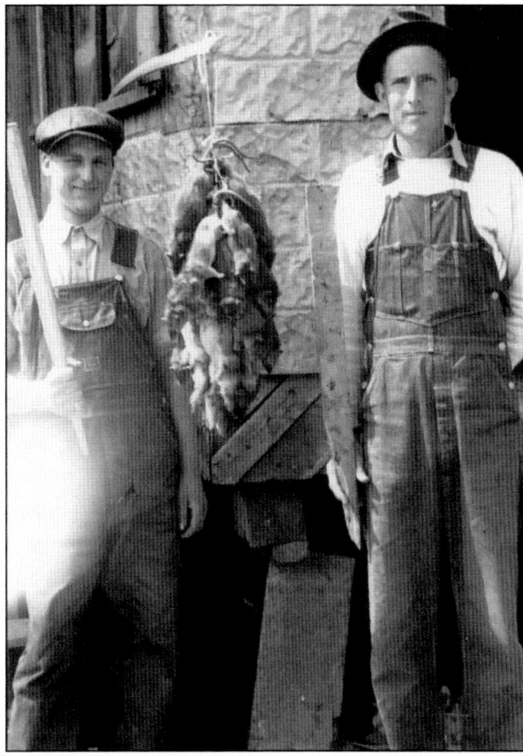

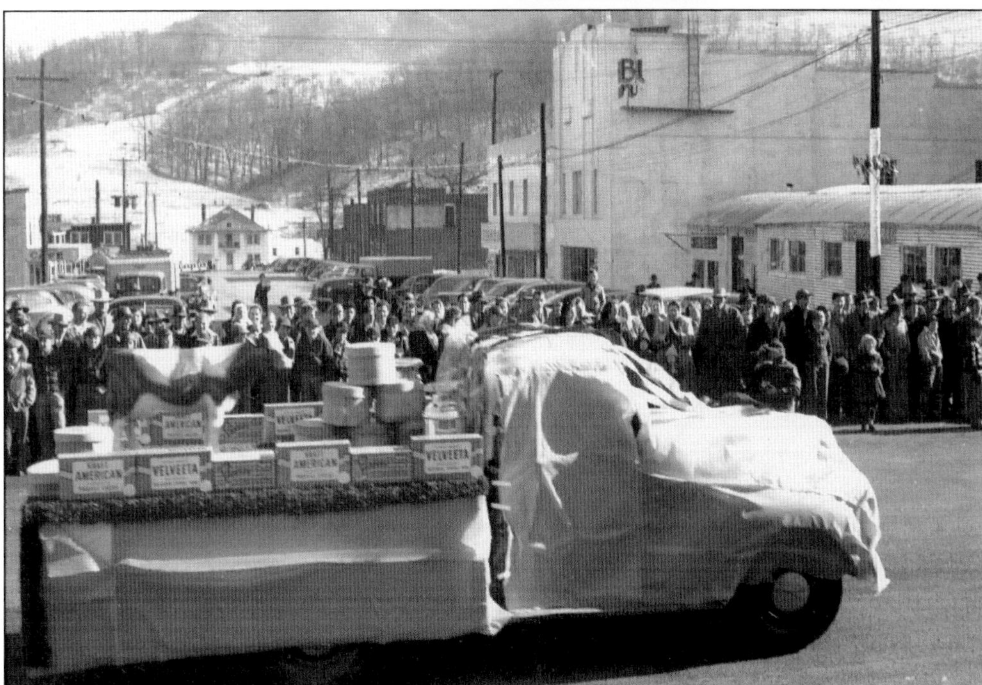

CHRISTMAS PARADE IN WEST JEFFERSON. The Academy can be seen at the end of Main Street, where Badger Funeral Home is now located. Old Burgess Furniture store is on the right, and a fruit stand occupies the old Quonset hut on the right.

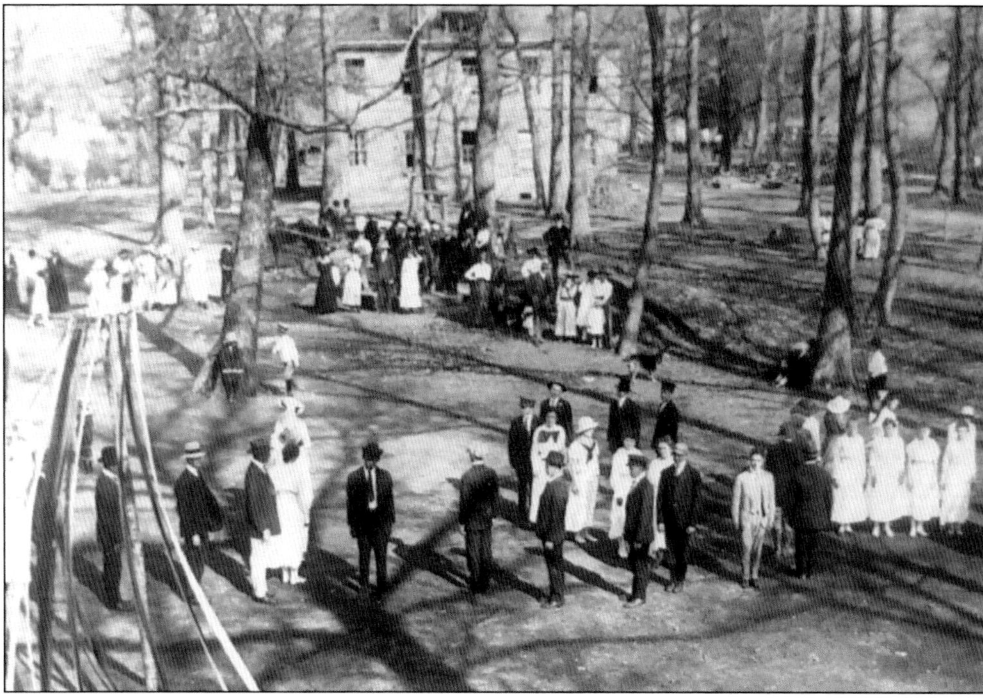

MAYPOLE CELEBRATION. This annual activity was held on the grounds of the old Jefferson School.

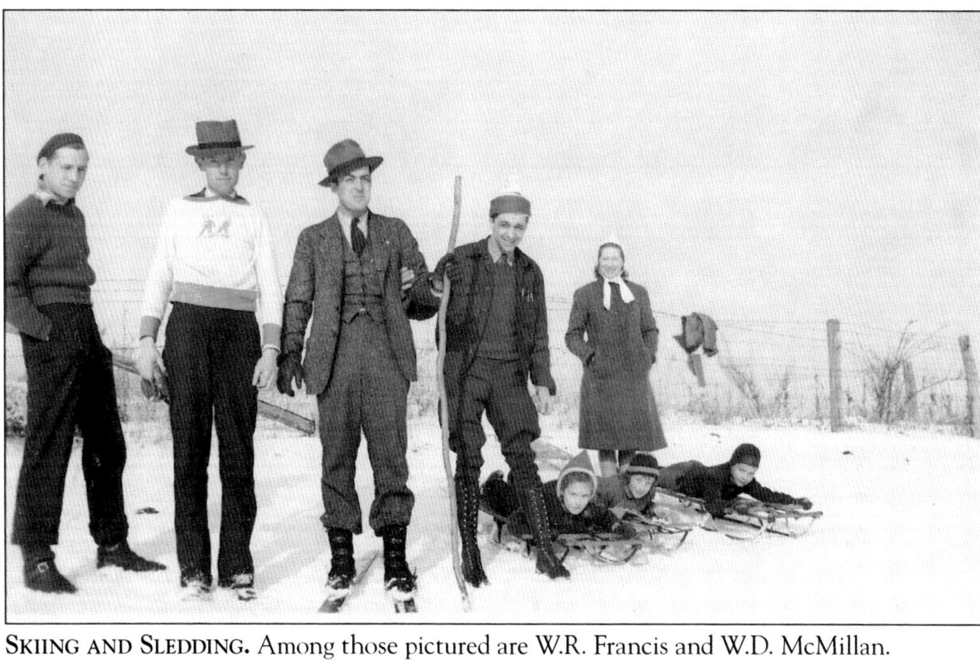

SKIING AND SLEDDING. Among those pictured are W.R. Francis and W.D. McMillan.

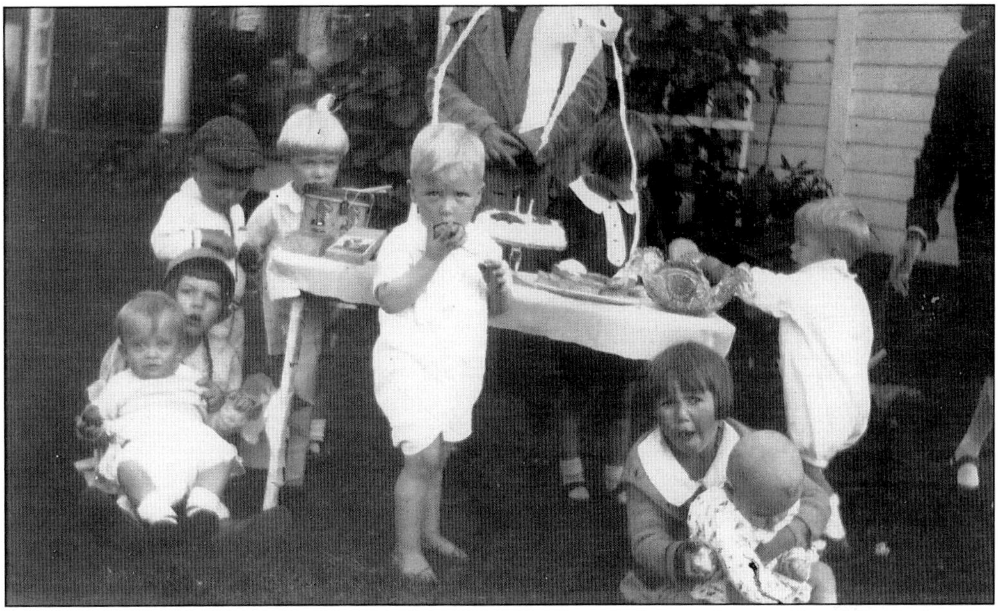

LEET VANNOY'S SECOND BIRTHDAY. Pictured here, from left to right, are Basil Duke Barr Jr., Nina Bell Barr Shepherd, Carol Jackson, Winfred Barr, Leet Vannoy, unidentified, Elizabeth McNeill, Kyle Vannoy, and unidentified.

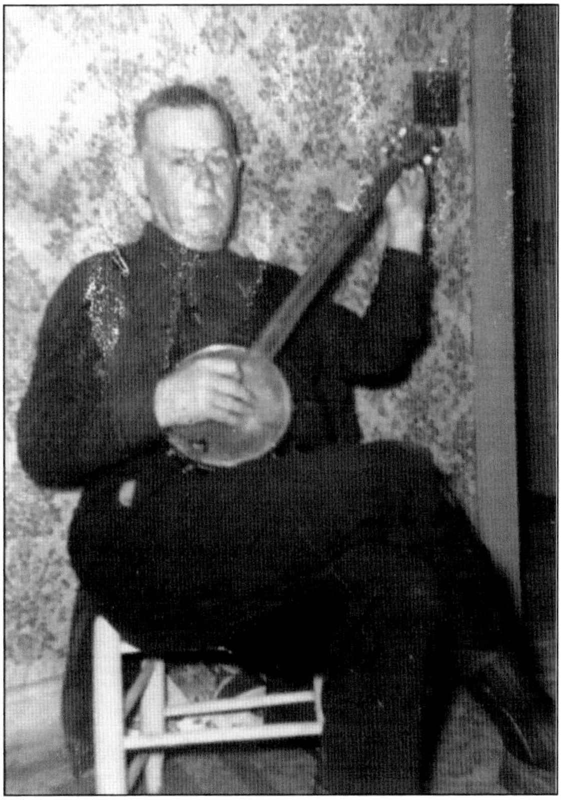

MACK KILLEN WITH BANJO. Mack lived in the Buffalo community and music was his hobby. The banjo was made by Bill Lewis.

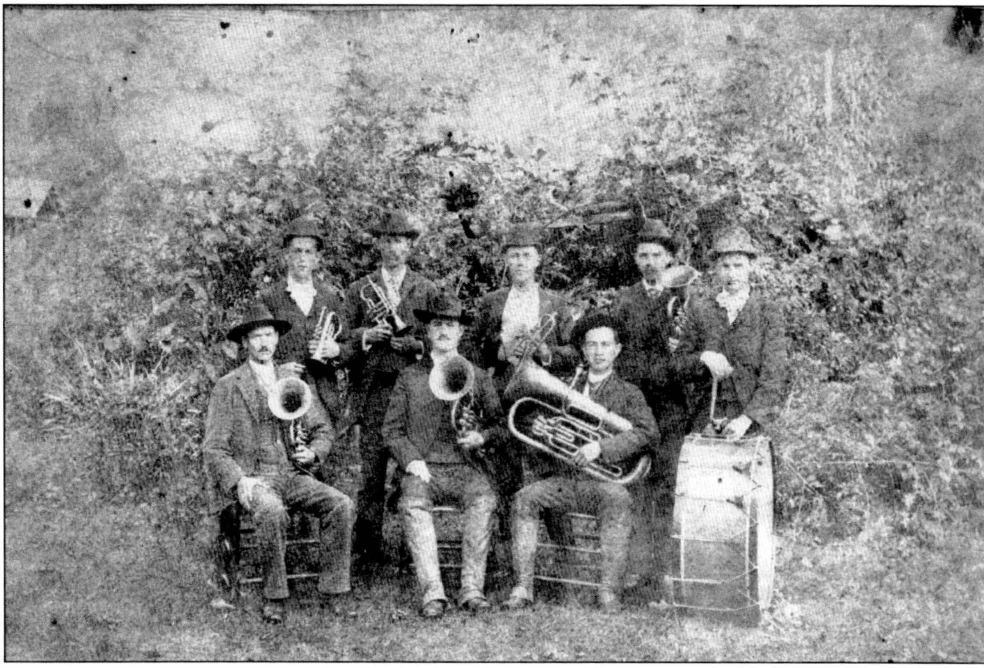

AN EARLY BAND IN ASHE COUNTY. This picture was taken around the late 1800s or early 1900s.

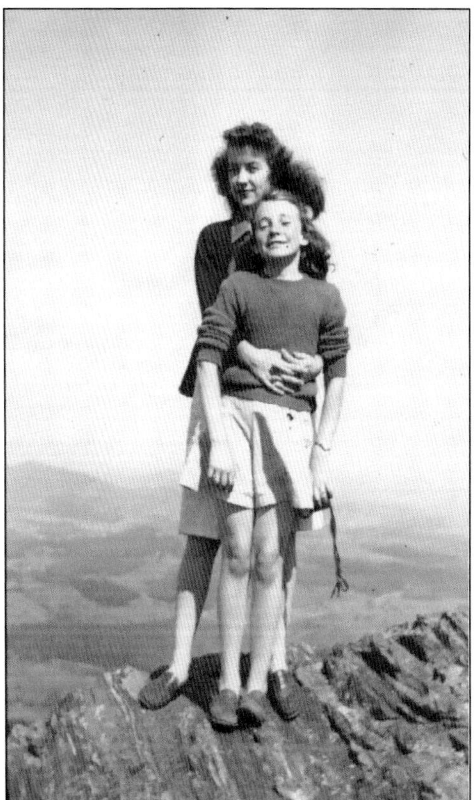

NANCY KENNICHELL JOHNSTON AND COUSIN STELLA W. ANDERSON TRAPP. The two reporters for the *Skyland Post* are enjoying the view from atop Mount Jefferson.

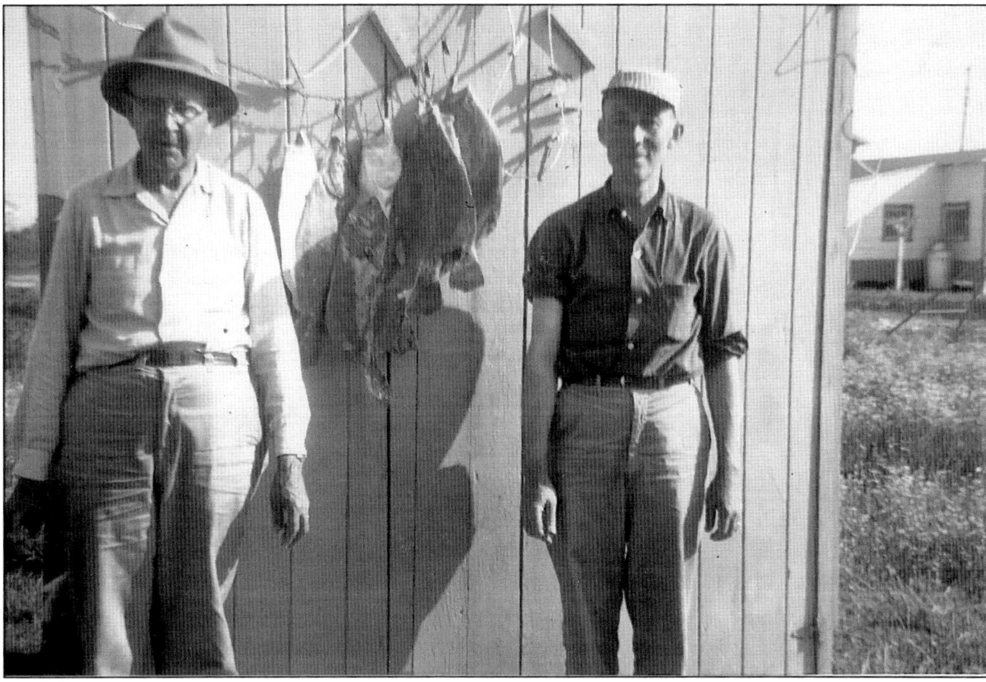

H.R. VANNOY AND DWIGHT MCGRADY ON A FISHING TRIP. The two friends often fished on the South Carolina coast. This photograph was taken in 1958.

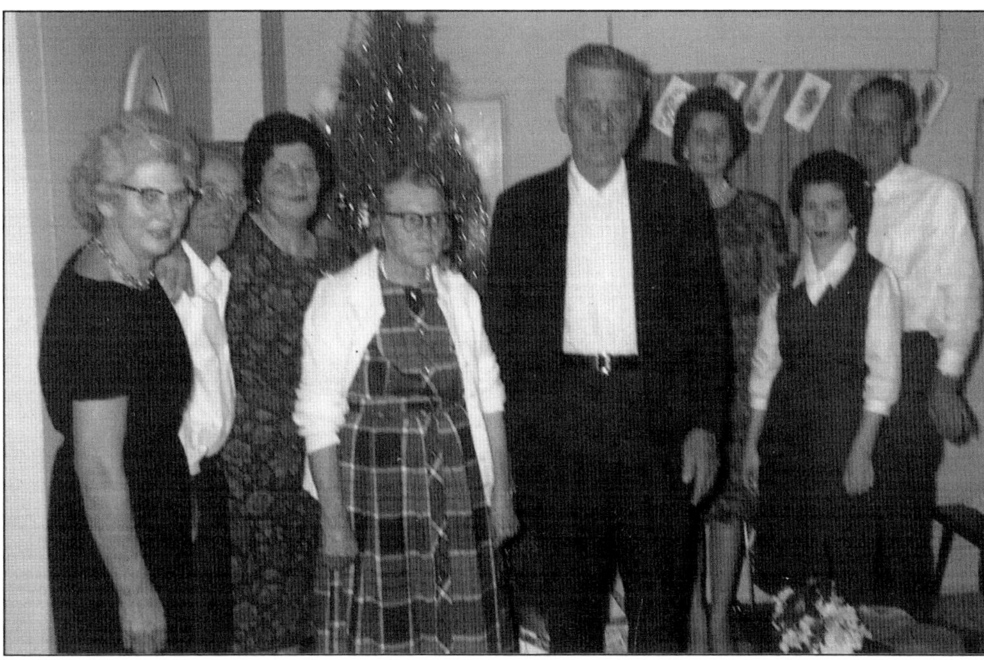

CHARLIE ASHLEY FAMILY. Several of Lula and Charlie Ashley's children returned to their Clifton home to celebrate Christmas in 1965.

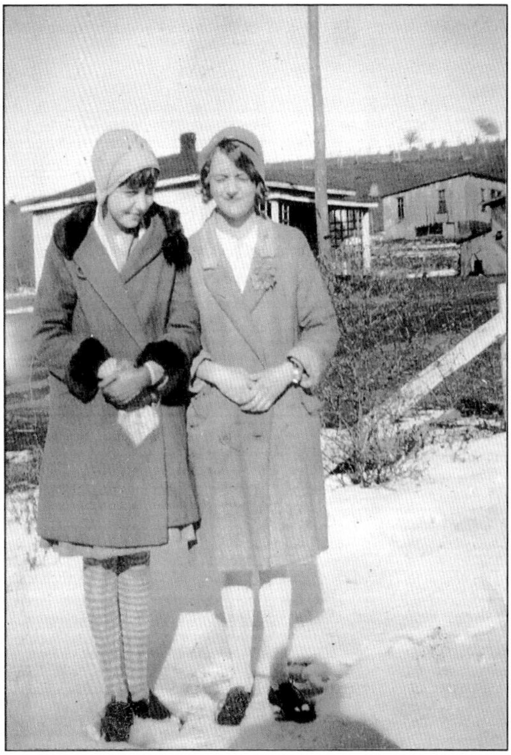

SISTERS ENJOYING A WALK, 1928. Ella Sue Vannoy Colvard (left) and Annie Vannoy Gray (right) are dressed in the latest style.

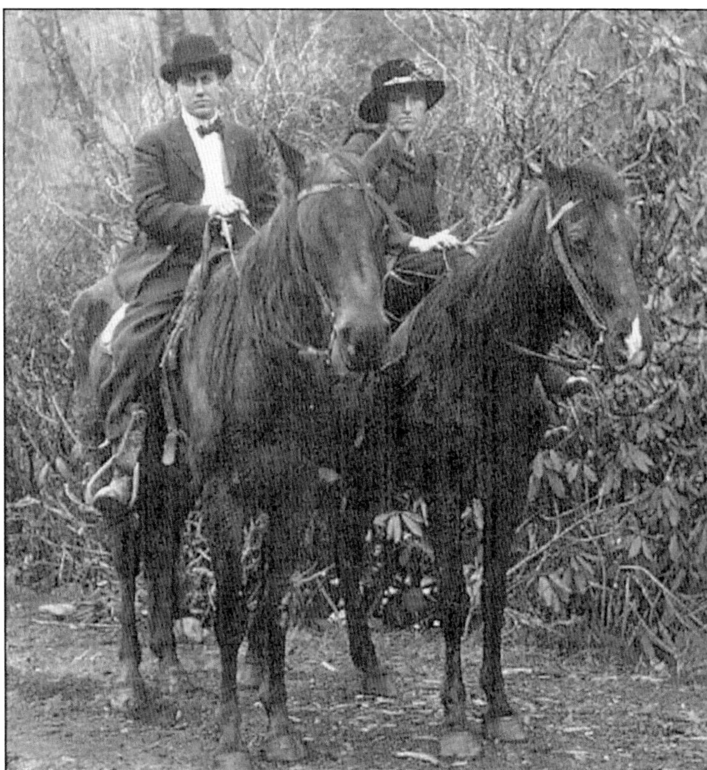

NETTIE MILLER AND CHARLIE ROOP. This couple is out for an afternoon ride on Little Horse Creek.

Boys with Their Pet Cow. Carl F. Colvard treats his son, Frank, and cousin, Jack Whittington, to a ride on a cow. Giddy-up!

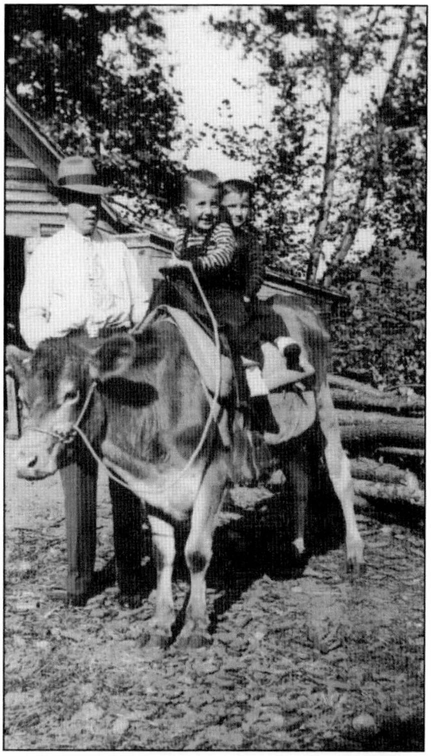

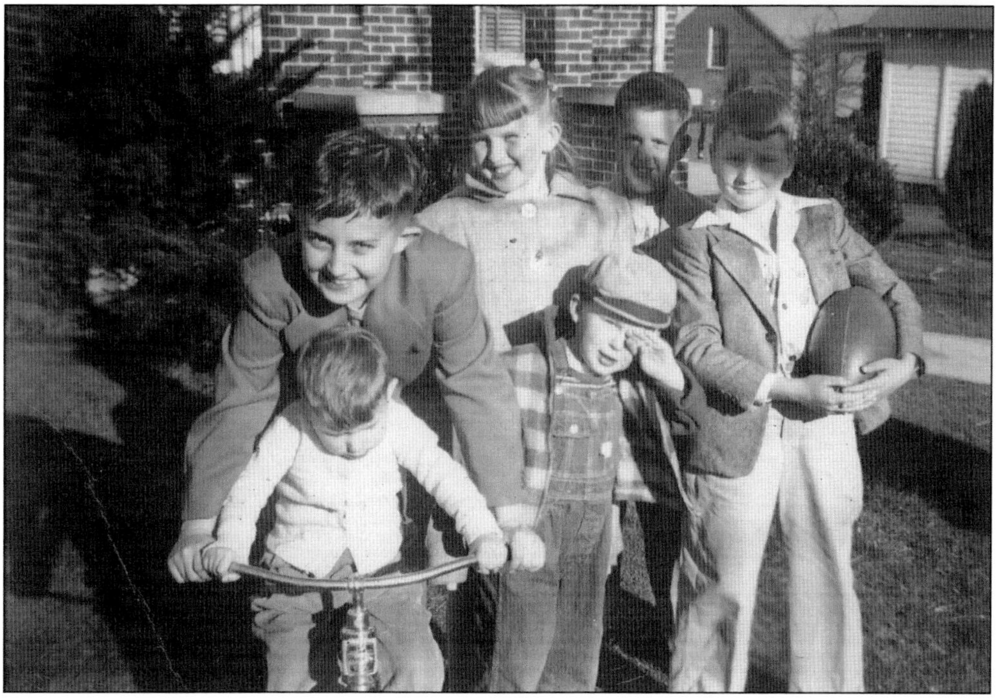

Kids at Birthday Party in West Jefferson. Shown here, from left to right, are the following: (front row) David Blackburn and Stephen Shoemaker; (second row) Frank Colvard, Ann Shoemaker, Bill McEwen, and Buddy Blackburn.

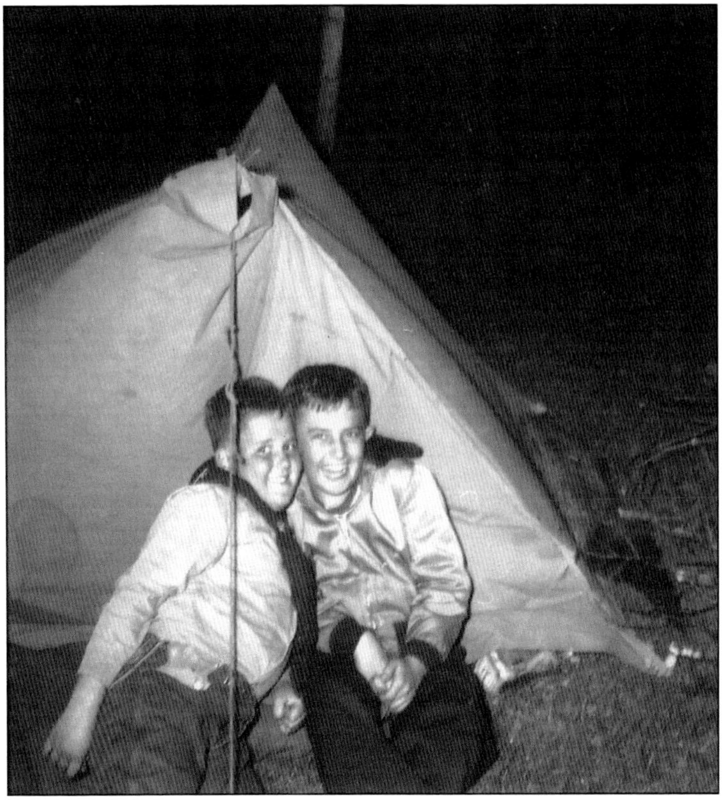

Two Boy Scouts, Buddy Blackburn and Frank Colvard. The boys were on a West Jefferson Troop scouting camporee in 1940.

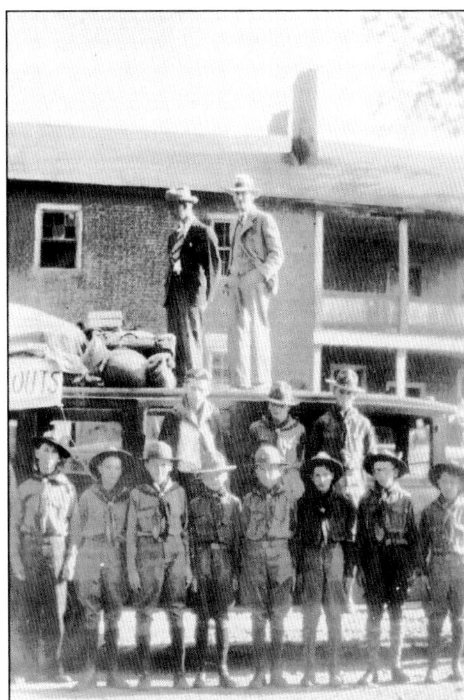

Jefferson Boy Scout Troop Prepares for Trip. Troop #48 is off to Washington, D.C. in 1929. Joseph Cox Worth and Gwyn B. Price are loading the luggage on top of the bus.

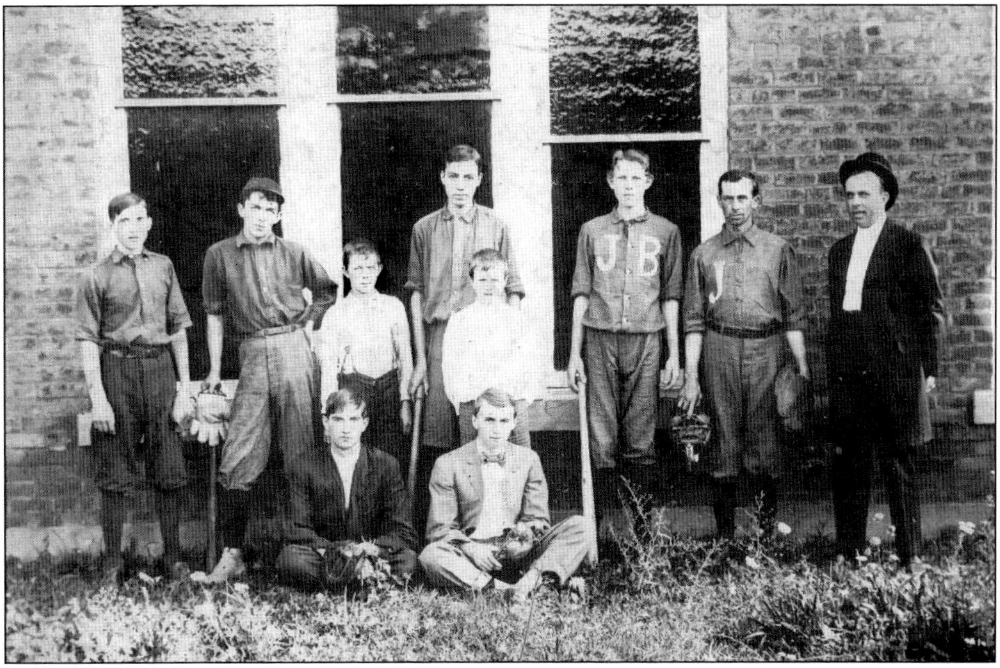

JEFFERSON CRACKERS BASEBALL TEAM. Pictured here, from left to right, are the following: (sitting) Jim Weaver and Bower Colvard; (standing) Oscar Elliott, Roger Barr, unidentified, Roy Badger, unidentified, Wirt Neal, Ed Koontz, and Donald Todd, manager.

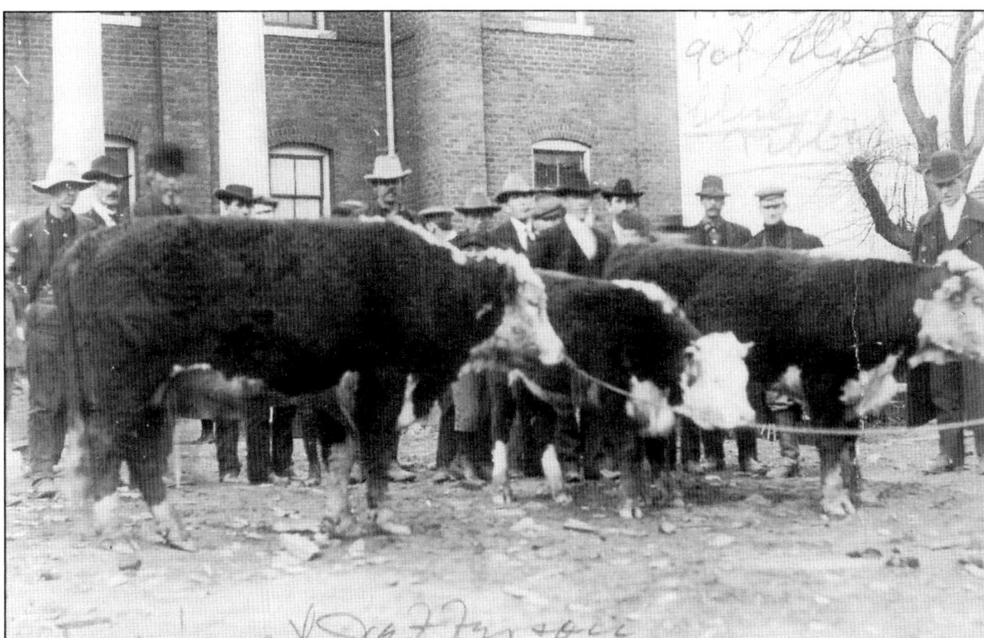

ASHE COUNTY FAIR. The courthouse lawn was used for the cattle exhibition.

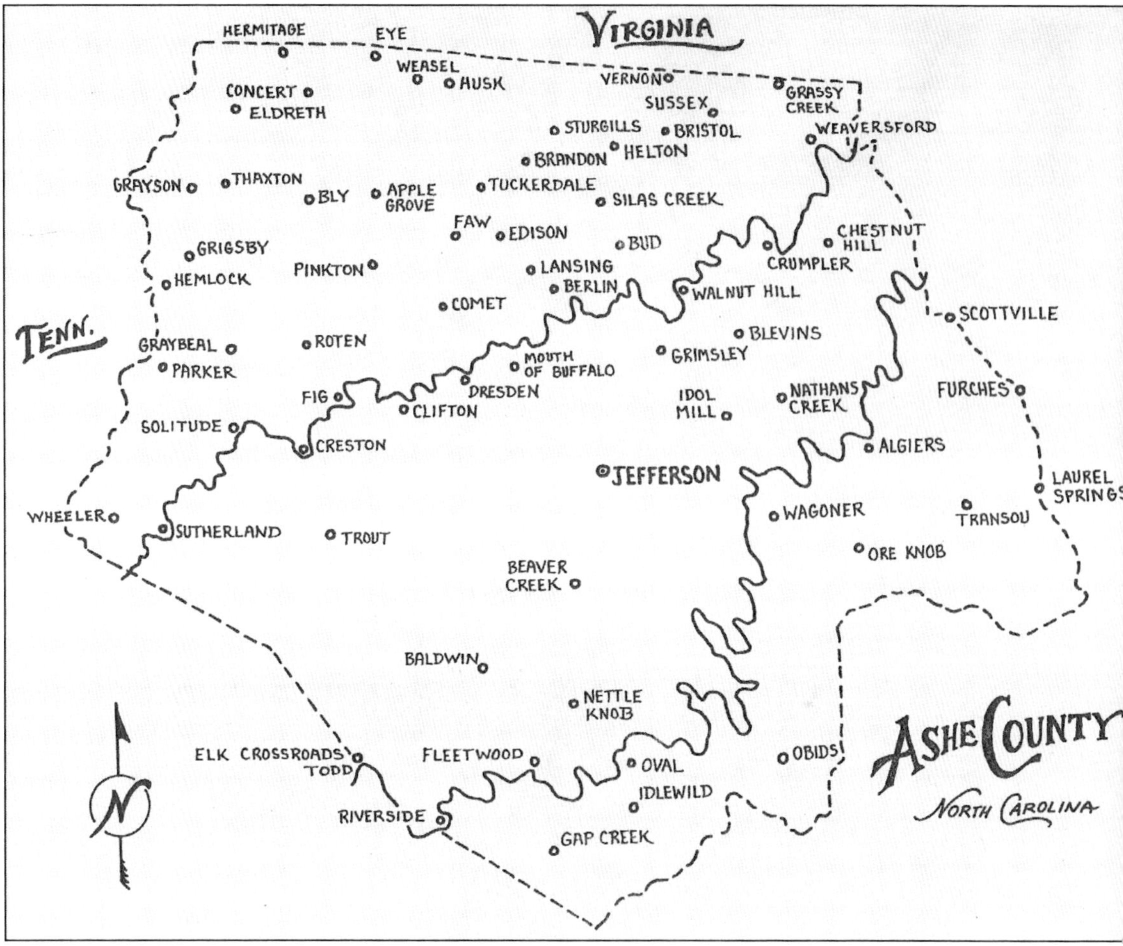

MAP OF ASHE COUNTY POST OFFICE SITES (C. 1900).